Diane Warner's

Big Book
of Parties

Creative Party Planning
For Every Occasion

By
Diane Warner

New Page
BOOKS

A DIVISION OF THE CAREER PRESS, INC.
FRANKLIN LAKES, NJ

DIANE WARNER'S BIG BOOK OF PARTIES
Cover design by Lu Rossman
Typesetting by Eileen Munson
Printed in the U.S.A. by Book-mart Press

To order this title, please call toll-free 1-800-CAREER-1 (NJ and Canada: 201-848-0310) to order using VISA or MasterCard, or for further information on books from Career Press.

The Career Press, Inc., 3 Tice Rd., P.O. Box 687, Franklin Lakes, NJ 07417

Library of Congress Cataloging-in-Publication Data

Warner, Diane.
    Diane Warner's big book of parties : creative party planning for every occasion / by Diane Warner.
        p.   cm.
    Includes index.
    ISBN 1-56414-398-8 (pbk.)
    1. Entertaining.   2. Cookery.   I. Title.   II. Title: Big book of parties.
    TX731.W35   1999
    642'4—dc21   99-26863
                                                                          CIP

To my children, Lynn and Darren.

Thank you for your love and encouragement

through the years.

Mom

I have so many people to thank, including my longtime, faithful California friends; my creative friends from my new hometown of Tucson, Arizona; those who answered my questionnaires; and those who responded to my Internet newsgroup inquiries.

My sincere thanks also go to my daughter, Lynn; my daughter-in-law, Lisa; and my sister, Linda, all of whom contributed helpful research for this book and continually "pumped me up" with their love, support, and enthusiasm.

A special thanks to quintessential hostess Mary Christensen of Sun City, Arizona, who allowed me to use her creative, one-of-a-kind ideas.

I would also like to thank my editor, Betsy Sheldon, for her support and helpful suggestions.

Thank you all for contributing to the success of this book.

CONTENTS

Entertaining
From the Heart

I have written this book in the hopes that it will become your "party ency-clopedia," a practical reference book for planning any party you're likely to encounter—from birthdays to anniversaries, farewell parties to family reunions, and seasonal parties to teen parties. Novelty parties—such as a Mardi Gras (see Chapter 15), a Karaoke Party (see Chapter 96), or a Tacky Party (see Chapter 93)—are covered, as well. In fact, more than 150 theme parties are described in this book.

In addition to learning how to plan theme parties, you'll be refreshed on the basics of planning any party in Part 1. You'll learn all about etiquette, party style, venues, invitations, decorations, games, activities, entertainment, and the all-important "party progression," the key to preventing party boredom.

Also included are seven chapters filled with recipes telling you how to make the foods suggested for each of the parties.

Although this book is bulging with the mechanics of hosting a successful party—and I'm sure that's why you purchased it—I hope to inspire you to remember the most important element of all: having a heart for your guests. You'll find that even when the mechanics break down and the party doesn't flow the way you had hoped, it will still be a successful party if you demon-strate love and care for each guest.

Bottom line:

> There's nothing more important than
> entertaining from your heart.

Part 1
Basics of Party Planning

"Entertaining others cultivates and nurtures friendships."

Although you probably plan to use a party theme described later in this book, you will still need to know the basics of planning a party. Here you will find tips on the party essentials, such as etiquette, style, venues, guest lists, invitations, decorations, games, activities, entertainment, and party progression.

So, let's get started. And remember, if you have a heart for your guests, you can't fail.

1

PARTY ETIQUETTE

The first lesson we face in "Party Planning 101" concerns party etiquette, a topic unfamiliar to many hosts and hostesses. Etiquette comes into play when composing your guest list; relating to your guests during the party; serving food and drink; and handling problems that may arise. There are also basic rules of etiquette when hosting a children's party.

Here are answers to the most frequently asked questions concerning party etiquette:

✧ **What should I consider when making out my guest list?**

✦ Don't invite more guests than you can comfortably accommodate.

✦ Keep the "friendship factor" in mind. The best word of advice? Be sensitive to people's feelings. Try not to exclude anyone who would be hurt if not invited, even if it means adjusting your space or planning a less expensive menu. For example, if two or three couples usually pal around together and are always invited to the same parties, don't exclude one of them if you can help it.

✦ Keep the personalities and interests of your potential guests in mind to create a harmonious mix. Give some thought to their compatibility.

✦ Try for a balance of male and female guests, especially for a formal sit-down dinner party.

✦ It is said that the ideal number of guests for a formal dinner party is no more than six to eight, the perfect number for gathering comfortably around most dining room tables.

✦ When composing your guest list for a wedding shower, it is proper etiquette to invite only those who will also be invited to the wedding.

✦ Be as specific as possible when telling guests how to dress. If you have invited guests from other states, keep in mind that what is appropriate for a certain type of party in one part of the country may not be in another. Here are some helpful definitions regarding party attire.

1. "Black tie" usually means dinner jackets for men and long or short evening dresses for women.
2. "White tie" indicates white ties and tails for men and long dresses for women.
3. "Informal attire" *technically* means that the men should wear suits and the women should wear suits or dresses. This is often confused with "casual," however, which means dressing in appropriate, comfortable attire for the occasion, such as jeans and Western shirts for a barbecue, or shorts and tennis shoes for an old-fashioned picnic.

In any case, be specific about what is expected, or suggest the guests call you so there are no misunderstandings. There is nothing more embarrassing than arriving in a nice dress when what the hostess really meant by "informal attire" was jeans and a T-shirt.

✧ What are my duties as host?

- ✦ Introduce the guests to each other as they arrive.
- ✦ Chat with each individual guest for at least a few minutes during the party.
- ✦ Guests tend to cluster in fixed groups during a party; try to break up the cliques by introducing a member of one group to a member of another.
- ✦ "Hover" over your party, keeping an eye on it as it develops. Remove empty glasses, refresh appetizer trays, and refill empty bowls of snacks.

✧ How should a sit-down meal be served?

- ✦ The guest of honor is always seated on the host's right and is served first.
- ✦ Once the guest of honor has been served, service continues around the table in a counterclockwise direction until the host is the last to be served.
- ✦ Food should be served on the guest's left and cleared from the guest's right.
- ✦ As soon as the host picks up his or her fork, the guests may begin eating. However, if there are more than eight people being served at one table, the guests may begin eating as soon as four or five guests have been served.
- ✦ Remove all dinner plates, salad plates, butter plates, salt and pepper shakers, and condiment dishes *before* dessert is served.
- ✦ If the meal is *very* formal, you may want to furnish finger bowls (shallow bowls filled with water and a twist of lemon). These should be brought to the table on individual dessert plates covered with white doilies.
- ✦ A dessert plate is presented with the dessert fork on the left of the plate and the spoon on the right.

✧ How do I get the guests to stop mingling and be seated for dinner?

✦ Usually, when guests notice that you have filled the water glasses and lighted the candles, they will begin drifting toward the dining room table. If not, simply say, "Dinner is ready. Won't you come and be seated?"

✧ How long should I delay the meal if a guest is late?

✦ Don't delay the meal for more than 15 or 20 minutes. To do so would be rude to guests who arrived on time. When your tardy guest finally arrives, smile and say something such as, "We were worried that something happened to you. I'm so glad you arrived safely. Please sit down; we knew you would want us to go ahead."

✧ How do I keep my guests from smoking in the house?

✦ Casually mention, "Our smoking room is on the patio," and be sure to have ashtrays and comfortable seating provided there.

✦ Invite your friends who smoke to an outdoor party during the spring or summer months.

✦ Another ploy is to set "Thank you for not smoking" plaques around the house, which I've always found to be a little offensive. Personally, I've never had any problem once I casually mentioned our outdoor "smoking room."

✧ What if guests offer to help with the cleanup?

✦ It's common for the guests (usually the women) to offer to help clean up the kitchen after a meal. If it's a very informal get-together of close friends, you might allow them to scrape the plates and help load the dishwasher, depending on the precedent set on previous occasions.

✦ If the dinner is at all formal, it is unacceptable to let guests help with cleanup. If it is a formal sit-down dinner and your budget permits, you could hire professional help to clear the table and clean up the kitchen. Otherwise, bring the plates to the kitchen, set them in the sink, turn off the lights, and rejoin your guests in the living room. To do otherwise will defeat the purpose of the dinner—inviting guests for a chance to relax, enjoy a leisurely meal, and engage in pleasant conversation.

✧ What should I do when some guests won't go home?

✦ First, consider it a compliment. Lingering guests are often a sign that you've hosted such an enjoyable party that they hate to give up the fun and go home.

✦ Start putting things away, including the alcoholic beverages.

✦ Start "busying" yourself by bringing dirty glasses and dishes to the kitchen.

✦ Glance discreetly at your watch from time to time.

✦ If guests still don't take the hint, ask, "Would anyone like a cup of coffee for the road?"

✦ Or tell guests, "Now that the party's over, I'm suddenly famished—would you like to join us at the all-night diner for a quick snack before we turn in?" (This will almost *always* elicit a declination and people will take the hint and go home.)

❖ **What should I do if a guest has had too much to drink?**

✦ Offer to call a taxi or drive the guest home yourself.

✦ If convenient, drive the guest home in your car and have someone else follow with the guest's car, which can then be left at the guest's home.

❖ **What are the rules for a child's birthday party?**

✦ Usually, the younger the child, the fewer number of guests, although 12 guests is considered to be a comfortable maximum for most children's parties.

✦ An unspoken rule of etiquette is to invite a child to your child's party if your child was invited to that child's party.

✦ If you're planning a party for a baby or toddler, always invite a parent or guardian of the child as well. It helps to have a few extra adults around to keep things running smoothly.

✦ It's usually advisable to invite children who are close friends with each other. This can get a little out of hand, I admit, but it's important not to exclude one or two children who expect to be invited. For example, if most of the children in your child's preschool class—or most of your child's neighborhood friends—are being invited to the party, you should invite *all* the children. I know this makes for a large party, but the last thing you want is hurt feelings.

✦ If you do end up with a huge crowd of children, plan the "biggest bang for the buck." For example, a party in a park with hot dogs, chips, fruit punch, and a birthday cake, plus a few balloons and competitive games, may be an affordable alternative to that pricey theme party you had in mind. It's better to tone down the party than have hurt feelings.

Tip – Before planning your party menu, ask whether your guests have any food allergies or dietary restrictions.

2

PARTY STYLE

Did you know that every party has its own style? A party's style depends on several elements: the size of the guest list; the theme of the party; the formality of the occasion; the party's ambiance; and, most of all, your host or hostess profile—that is, your personality and your comfort zone when it comes to entertaining. The questions that follow will help you determine your party style.

Does entertaining come naturally for you?

Not everyone is a natural hostess—that rare and wonderful person blessed with the gift of hospitality, who can throw a party together with very little effort. Some are willing to host a party, but only if they have a lot of help. Then there are others who avoid entertaining at all costs. According to a survey I did, here are the top six reasons why.

1. I'm too busy to entertain.
2. I don't have the energy.
3. I can't afford it.
4. My home isn't nice enough.
5. I lack confidence.
6. I don't have a "party personality."

If you've ever used one of these excuses, let me offer some encouragement:

✦ We're all busy. Between work, carpools, cleaning house, grocery shopping, weeding the garden, and all the other kinds of running around we do, it's a wonder any of us has time to plan a party. If you're a super-stressed, super-busy person, here is my advice: Keep your guest list small; plan something casual; and purchase ready-to-serve eats.

✦ To conserve energy and cut down on stress, allow as much time as possible to get ready for the party. For example, if you work Monday through Friday, plan the party for Saturday night and give yourself all day to clean, decorate, and prepare the food. Or, if your budget permits, you can hire a cleaning service to clean your house for you while you're doing other things. You can also hire the service for post-party cleanup! And don't feel guilty about it—you deserve a break!

✦ A party doesn't have to be expensive to be successful. Remember what I said in the Introduction about being a host with a heart? If you really care about your guests, your sincerity will come across, and it won't matter if you're serving hot dogs or lobster. And when it comes to decorations, there are dozens of easy, affordable ideas in Chapter 5.

✦ What is a "party personality," anyway? The ability to tell jokes and engage in clever repartee? Not at all! As a matter of fact, you don't even *need* a "party personality." All you need is to be yourself—don't try to be someone you're not. If you take care to introduce your guests to each other and show love and care for them as individuals, you'll be the ideal party host. So just relax, be yourself, and enjoy your guests.

Do you like to entertain formally or informally?

When it comes to formality, each of us has a natural, personal style of entertaining—a style that feels comfortable. You may enjoy hosting a structured formal sit-down dinner party, where everything is choreographed and things seem to stay under control. Or you may prefer an informal get-together in which you can "wing it" as you go along.

The important thing to remember is this: Never force a style that feels uncomfortable to you. If you do, your guests will sense it and there will be a "stiffness" to the party. If you choose a style that comes naturally for you, however, you will feel comfortable and relaxed, and so will your guests.

Do you prefer to entertain a small group or a large crowd?

Every hostess has a "pain threshold" when it comes to her guest list. It's important for you to respect yours. In other words, don't expand your guest list unless you feel comfortable doing so—not everyone can handle more than a dozen guests at a time.

Do you enjoy planning a party around a theme?

The big trend in parties these days is to plan around a theme. As you read along you'll notice that the bulk of this book is devoted to party themes and how to incorporate a theme into the invitations, the decorations, the menu, the entertainment, and so on.

Choose a theme that sounds like fun to you, because if you're excited about it, you'll not only enjoy incorporating it into your party plans, but your guests will get caught up in the spirit of the theme, as well.

If you would feel more comfortable planning a party without a specific theme, that's fine, too. I have a feeling, however, that you'll become more enthused about theme parties as you read through the remaining chapters.

3

Party Venues

The most popular party venue is your own home or patio, as is true for most of the parties included in this book.

There are other venues that may be preferable, however, for a number of reasons: You may need a larger place; a location more suitable to your theme; or one where the food can be furnished and served by the site's staff.

For example, a Big "D" Barbecue (Chapter 78) might be more fun if it took place on a ranch or in an old barn. And wouldn't it be nice if a Hawaiian Luau (see Chapter 77) could be on the water?

Here are popular party venues for you to consider:

- ✦ Country club.
- ✦ Church hall.
- ✦ Restaurant.
- ✦ Winery.
- ✦ Paddleboat.
- ✦ Private banquet hall.
- ✦ Public park.
- ✦ Senior center.
- ✦ University or college facilities.
- ✦ Community clubhouse.
- ✦ Public or private garden.
- ✦ State or national park.
- ✦ Country estate.
- ✦ Private mansion.

- ✦ Houseboat.
- ✦ Club meeting room.
- ✦ Yacht.
- ✦ Office meeting room.
- ✦ Hotel banquet room.
- ✦ Beach.
- ✦ Marina.
- ✦ Museum.
- ✦ Historical Society facilities.
- ✦ Zoo.
- ✦ Art gallery.
- ✦ Bed & breakfast.
- ✦ Elks' Lodge.

Check with your local parks and recreation office or chamber of commerce for available public and private facilities, as well as your local historical society, which may offer the most charming sites of all.

Before you book a site, here are some important questions to ask:

+ How much is the rental fee?
+ What is the required deposit?
+ What are the fees for other services (custodial, parking, coat attendant, etc.)?
+ What is available for my use (tables, chairs, utensils, coffeepots, linens, dishes, etc.)?
+ Are there any restrictions (smoking, alcohol, loud music, bringing in food, drinks, or a caterer)?
+ Are there parking facilities?

4

PARTY
INVITATIONS

A typical party invitation is a fill-in-the blanks, store-bought card, and this is what usually comes to mind when planning a party. These invitations are perfectly acceptable; however, depending on the party's theme and degree of formality, you may opt for another type of invitation. The most popular trend, in fact, is to create novelty invitations that reflect the party's theme. Novelty invitations are included in the theme party chapters found later in this book.

Meanwhile, this chapter will familiarize you with the basics, including suggested wording for various types of formal and informal parties.

Invitations 101

✧ Before addressing the invitations, verify all mailing addresses. You can do this by simply calling the phone number you currently have for a guest, by sending an e-mail asking for address verification, or—if you get a notice that a number has been disconnected—using a "people search" engine on the Internet to find a new address.

✧ Use the prettiest or most festive postage stamps available.

✧ If you are mailing or hand-delivering invitations, be sure each guest receives one. Don't invite some guests verbally and others with a written invitation.

✧ Unless the invitation says "no gifts please," gifts are expected.

✧ In addition, these 10 things should always be included in an invitation:
  1. Name of the honored guest.
  2. Name(s) of the host(s).
  3. Location of the party (with directions and map, if necessary).
  4. Date of the party.
  5. Time of the party.

6. Party's theme, if applicable, and dress code—for example, casual (such as jeans and a T-shirt), formal (such as black-tie), or costume required. Of course, if the affair is normally assumed to be either formal or casual (for example, a wedding reception or a barbecue), you need only mention the required attire if something out of the ordinary is planned (such as a wedding reception barbecue!).
7. What type of food will be served (lunch, supper, cake, etc.)?
8. Request for an RSVP (it's a good idea to include a deadline).
9. Your telephone number. (It's also okay to include your e-mail address on an informal invitation.)
10. Suggested gift ideas, if applicable.

Invitations to informal parties

If you're having an informal party, there are several acceptable ways to invite guests. One way is to do it over the phone, but if you choose to do this, always follow up with something in writing. If you don't, some guests may not remember the correct date, time, or—worse yet—the party! Here are some other ways to invite people to an informal party:

+ In person.
+ Via e-mail or fax.
+ Using fill-in-the-blanks, store-bought invitations.
+ Using invitations you created on your computer.
+ On postcards.
+ By handwriting invitations on note cards.

See pages 23-24 for sample informal invitations. Also see page 26 for a sample reminder card.

Invitations to formal parties

Formal affairs—such as engagement parties, wedding rehearsal dinners, wedding receptions, wedding anniversaries, bar or bat mitzvahs, sweet 16 parties, and formal lunch or dinner parties—usually require formal invitations. The following types of invitations are appropriate for a formal party.

+ Invitations handwritten on fine-quality note paper.
+ Elegant note cards with the information written in calligraphy.
+ Engraved invitations.
+ Invitations that were laser-printed, but only on high-quality card stock with a satin finish.

Be sure to mail invitations to formal parties at least three weeks in advance, and enclose a response card.

See page 24-25 for sample formal invitations. Also see page 26 for a sample response card.

Invitations to theme parties

Novelty invitations are the way to go if your party has a theme. The invitation to your party sets the tone for what's to come; if the invitation is unique and creative, the guests will sense that the party will be, too. By "novelty" invitation, I mean one that reflects the theme of the party, such as an invitation with a lei attached for a Hawaiian Luau (see Chapter 77) or with a black armband enclosed for an Over-the-Hill Party (see Chapter 45). You will find invitation suggestions for each type of theme party within each theme party chapter.

Tip – Hand-deliver or mail your homemade, theme-oriented novelty invitations. Or to really get into the spirit of things, have a theme-oriented character hand-deliver the invitations!

Invitations to children's parties

You've learned a lot about invitations so far, but not all of it will work for children's parties. Here's some specific advice and ideas for children's parties:

✦ Invitations may be extended by telephone. However, if your child is at an age in which he or she places the calls, be sure to follow up with the parents to be sure there are no misunderstandings.

✦ It's usually not a good idea to have your child hand out invitations at school. Not only can invitations become lost, but there can be hurt feelings for any children who are not invited.

✦ Buy a coloring book, and have your child color one page per guest. Remove the page from the coloring book, print the invitation across the top of the page, and mail.

✦ Buy a book of paper dolls. Write the invitation on back of each paper doll and mail.

✦ Use your child's handprint, made with colorful finger paint, to decorate the front of the invitation.

✦ Write out the invitation on postcards, using crayons or felt-tip markers. Cut each postcard into a jigsaw puzzle, and send the pieces inside an envelope (or send it whole).

✦ Print the invitation on strips of paper approximately four inches by two inches. Roll the strips into scrolls, and insert them into balloons. Mail the balloons (not inflated, in envelopes) with instructions to blow the balloon up and pop it to find a surprise.

✦ Wrap a sturdy piece of cardboard to resemble a present. Write the invitation on a small card, and attach it to the gift's ribbon.

✦ Mail a store-bought invitation in an envelope stuffed with confetti. The confetti will spill out when the invitation is opened (hopefully making a *positive* impression).

✦ Create a customized party invitation using a computer program designed for making greeting cards, invitations, calendars, and so on.

Sample Informal Party Invitation 1

We're Planning a Bon Voyage Party, and You're Invited!

For: Our favorite couple, Jason and Ashley
When: Friday, July 11
Time: 6 p.m.
Where: Jack and Lisa's patio
              1010 Jameson Drive, # 714
Bring: Your swimsuits and your appetites

P.S. Bring something fun for their cruise to Acapulco!

RSVP: 669-9953 or bcrane@tlg.com by July 4

Sample Informal Party Invitation 2

You are invited for cocktails
on Saturday, March 16,
at 7 p.m.
at the home of Bill and Candi Barrows
311 North Bell Drive

RSVP (regrets only): 555-0101 or klt575@aol.com

Sample Informal Party Invitation 3 (for anniversary celebration hosted by couple's children)

Dear Bill and Terri,

Will you join us for dinner at Hazel's Dinner House on Friday, October 10, at 6 p.m. to help us celebrate Mom and Dad's 30th anniversary?
Hope to see you there.

Bill and Cathy
and
Greg and Rebecca

Sample Formal Party Invitation 1

You are invited to attend a formal bridal tea
in honor of
Miss Elizabeth Anne Crowley,
hosted by the Misses Amber Grayville and Susan Jacobs
Saturday, May 17 at two o'clock
1712 Arbor Circle

Please RSVP by May 10:   *Bridal registry:*

818-7792   *Carlisle Gifts & Treasures*

Note: Don't be afraid to include a deadline for your RSVP, especially in the case of a formal affair, or when you need to give a head count to a caterer by a certain date.

Sample Formal Party Invitation 2

Mr. and Mrs. William Carlisle

request the pleasure

of your company

at dinner

on Saturday, the fifth of September

at eight o'clock

335 North Windsor Drive

Marin City

RSVP by August 29: 555-1110

Sample Formal Party Invitation 3 (for anniversary celebration hosted by couple's children)

In honor of the

twenty-fifth anniversary of

Mr. and Mrs. James Chesterfield,

Mr. and Mrs. William Chesterfield

request the pleasure of your company

on Saturday, the sixth of August,

at seven o'clock

100 Garland Drive

RSVP: 555-2009

Note: The fourth line of the invitation may also state "Their daughters" or "Their sons and daughters" in place of names.

Sample response card for a formal party invitation

Mr. and Mrs. Gregory Simpson

Accept _____

Regret _____

Sample reminder card for informal party

To remind you
Saturday, March 16
7 p.m.
at Bill and Candi's

Invitation for Formal or Informal Party (for anniversary open house hosted by couple or couple's family, friends, or community group)

Open House

to celebrate the fiftieth wedding anniversary

of

Mr. and Mrs. John Axelson

Sunday, March 17

2 to 4 p.m.

Grace Presbyterian Fellowship Hall

10 Berryville Avenue

5

PARTY AMBIANCE

Creating a scintillating party ambiance is very much like designing the set for a theatrical production—you need to use props and backdrops to set the mood. But you don't need to spend a lot of money to accomplish this, as you will see in this chapter. Also included in this chapter are easy, theme-related ways to create favors, name tags, place cards, napkin rings, and centerpieces.

Let's begin by discussing some ambiance enhancers that will give you the biggest bang for the buck!

Biggest decorating bangs for the buck

✧ **Flowers**. Order from your retail or supermarket florist, or make your own floral arrangements using fresh-cut or silk flowers. If you're serving a sit-down dinner, be sure the centerpieces are low enough for guests to see each other across the table (as a general rule, keep them under 11 inches high).

✧ **Balloons**. Balloons have to be the absolute *biggest* bang of all! They are colorful, versatile, and festive. Helium-filled balloon bouquets can be used as centerpieces, attached to chair backs or napkin rings, or tied to your mailbox where they'll cheerfully announce, "The party is here!" A dozen or more may be hung from a chandelier over the table, with their colorful, curled ribbons hanging down and overflowing from the table to the floor.

You can save money by buying your balloons in bulk from a party supply catalog or store and renting your own helium tank.

✧ **Banners**. You can purchase banners from a party supply store, or you can create your own on your computer using a computer program that creates cards, invitations, banners, calendars, and so on.

✧ **Candles**. Surround a group of votive candles or floating candles with fresh or silk flowers inside hurricane lamps. Or cluster a group of long tapered candles, mounted in elegant candlesticks of various heights.

✧ **Tiny white light strands**. Those tiny white lights, usually purchased as Christmas tree decorations, can do wonders for a setting. They create a magical ambiance, especially for an evening affair. Wind a string of lights down the center of serving tables or around silk ficus trees, or drape them over doorways and along banisters. They can also dress up your entryway.

✧ **Crepe-paper or holographic streamers.** Tastefully used, streamers are an affordable way to splash a little color around your party site. Holographic streamers are available through party supply stores or a catalog such as Anderson's Prom and Party Catalog (see Resources).

✧ **Luminarias**. Welcome your guests by lining your driveway, walkway, or entryway with luminarias. They are easy to make. Fill ordinary brown paper lunch bags with three inches of sand, and set a lighted votive candle inside each one.

Another way to welcome your guests—or to make an outdoor setting look wintry—is to line your walkway with "ice lanterns." Freeze water in 36-ounce coffee cans, loosen the blocks of ice by running warm water over the coffee cans, chip a hole into the top of each ice block, and insert votive candles.

Place cards, table decorations, and other tokens

✧ **Name tags.** Unless you're hosting an intimate gathering of close friends and family members, it's a good idea to furnish each guest with a name tag. Name tags can be purchased from a party supply store, or you can create your own. For theme parties, you can cut simple theme-related shapes out of construction paper and use them as name tags. For example:

✦ Palm trees for a Hawaiian Luau (see Chapter 77).
✦ Cowboy hats for a Little Cowboy or Cowgirl Party (see Chapter 56).
✦ Family trees for a Family Reunion (see Chapter 38).
✦ Watering cans for a Country Garden Party (see Chapter 86).

Tip
– Don't use address labels as name tags because they'll fall off halfway through the party. If you're going to use name tags with adhesive, purchase tags designed for this purpose.

✦ Don't let guests write their own names (they're rarely legible). Print their names for them with felt-tip pen.
✦ Place the tags on your guests yourself to be sure they wear them.
✦ Place the tags on guests' right shoulders so they can read them easily when they shake hands.

✧ **Table art.** What we used to call "setting the table" has evolved into something grand called "table art"—the art of decorating your dinner table in a unique, creative way, complementing the party's theme. It takes an artistic flair to combine one-of-a-kind candlesticks, figurines, unusual fabrics, or conversation pieces into a creative table display. You'll need to think of your tabletop as a canvas. You are the artist, and it's up to you to paint an appealing picture for your guests.

Essentially, table art is what you do with these items:

1. Tablecloth, place mats, and napkins.
2. Dinnerware, glassware, and flatware.
3. Place cards.
4. Centerpieces.
5. Decorative accessories.

❖ **Tablecloth, place mats, and napkins.** If it's a formal affair, use a linen tablecloth or a lace cloth laid over a solid color liner. For an informal dinner, you may use decorative place mats, a print or striped tablecloth, a paper tablecloth, or a flat twin-sized bed sheet decorated in a theme-related way. Whether formal or informal, choose a color or pattern that best serves as your "canvas" and complements your place settings, centerpiece, and decorative accessories.

Matching napkins may be placed in a variety of ways. For a formal sit-down lunch or dinner, you may want to fold them into one of the elegant designs that are popular these days. Here three such designs that are easy to do:

+ **The fan fold:** Fold the napkin in half. Starting at one end, fold the napkin back and forth into a fan shape. The napkin can be secured at one end or in the center with a napkin ring and placed at a place setting, or it can be folded in the center and placed inside a long-stemmed glass.

+ **The simple roll:** Fold the napkin in half, and simply roll it up. Tie it in the center with gold braid or ribbon attached with a silk or fresh flower.

+ **The roll with flared top:** Roll the napkin at the base, leaving the top flared out. Tie the base of the napkin with a two-inch ribbon.

For an informal buffet or a barbecue, you can wrap the napkins around sets of utensils, tie them with raffia, ribbons, or colorful bandannas, and place them in a basket. Or you can roll each napkin lengthwise (from corner to corner) and tie it in a single knot around the handles of the utensils. You can buy decorative napkin rings for either formal or informal dining.

Tips   – For informal entertaining, don't be afraid to layer tablecloths. For example, you might cover a rectangular table lengthwise with a solid-colored tablecloth, then place two square checkered or print cloths asymmetrically (or "kiddie-corner") on top of it.

  – For an informal lunch or dinner, you can set a coffee table for a meal, arranging pillows around it as seats.

❖ **Dinnerware, glassware, and flatware.** China dinnerware is usually used at a formal dinner party, and earthenware and stoneware are popular for informal occasions. High-quality plastic dinnerware is fine for casual entertaining, especially for an informal buffet or patio party.

There are many qualities of glassware, from fine lead crystal to ordinary lime glass. Lead crystal is preferable for formal dinners because of its elegance and sparkle. Set one glass for each type of beverage to be served. For example, if two varieties of wine are served, you would set a total of three glasses at each place setting: two wine glasses and one water goblet. If you will also be serving champagne or cordials, additional stemware will be required. Everyday glassware (lime glass, tumblers, or bar ware) may be used for all types of informal entertaining, from breakfast to lunches to after-dinner drinks.

Flatware may be sterling silver, silver-plated, or stainless steel. Silver flatware is expected for formal dinners, although high-quality, finely crafted stainless steel is also acceptable. Stainless steel flatware may also be used for informal entertaining. However, for very informal patio parties or barbecues, sturdy plastic flatware is a popular alternative.

✧ **Place cards.** Formal dining requires that white place cards be handwritten, preferably with black ink and a calligraphy pen. For less formal entertaining, you may take ordinary white or colored place cards and dress them up in the following ways.

✦ Write the guests' names with a silver or gold glitter pen.

✦ Glue on borders made of gold or silver braid, ruffled lace, or narrow acetate bows with tiny silk flowers.

✦ Punch a small hole through both sides of the place cards and slide a fresh or silk rosebud through the holes.

A clever trend is to attach guests' place cards to party favors. For example, if you plan to give each guest a small box of Godiva truffles, attach the place card or write the guest's name on the box itself.

Tip – You can make your own place cards by cutting three-and-a-half-inch squares of heavy paper using a mat knife. Lightly score the cards in the center, then fold them along the scored crease.

✧ **Centerpieces.** Use a low floral arrangement for your table centerpiece, or muster up your creativity and artistic talents to "paint your canvas" with a centerpiece that's unique and special. For example:

✦ Float a single flower in a crystal bowl sitting on a mirror.

✦ Arrange a low basket of fruits and flowers, such as white tulips, huge red strawberries, and clusters of Thompson seedless grapes.

✦ Embellish a low topiary or houseplant by wrapping its pot with Mylar polyester film, tying a ribbon around it, and adding eye-catching items related to your theme, such as seashells, or Precious Moments figurines.

◆ Arrange flowers in a theme-related container such as, a decorative bird cage for a Country Garden Party (see Chapter 86), a 10-gallon hat for a barbecue, or a beer stein for an Oktoberfest (see Chapter 25).

◆ Using an uneven number, group together interesting collectibles, such as candlesticks of different heights, a collection of Oriental fans, or antique dolls. The possibilities are limitless. Look around your home for treasures that can be clustered or mixed with flowers or plants to create fascinating "art" for your table.

◆ One of the most popular trends today, which can be seen in many women's magazines, is to use an arrangement of edible fruits and vegetables—such as cabbage, cherry tomatoes, Brussels sprouts, broccoli, oranges, apples, squash, and artichokes—as a centerpiece.

◆ You can also use fruits and vegetables as "candlesticks" by hollowing them out and inserting tall or votive candles. Gourds, artichokes, apples, and small pumpkins work very well.

◆ Fill terra cotta pots with Styrofoam plastic foam and cover with Easter basket grass, fake moss, pebbles, or gumdrops. Insert bright colorful lollipops (tied at their necks with ribbon) or several tall tapered candles. The pots may be wrapped with fabric or paper, painted, or left natural.

Tip – Check your local library for books featuring full-color photos of creative table art. I recommend *The Art of Tabletop Design* by Jim Kemp and *Decorating for Dining & Entertaining* by The Home Decorating Institute. Also, you'll discover wonderfully creative ideas on home decorating shows on cable TV's Home and Garden Television (HGTV).

Props

Many everyday, outdoor, or easily obtainable items can be used as props to create ambiance, especially for theme parties. Here are some examples of items that you might have on hand or can buy, rent, or borrow:

◆ Parasols or umbrellas.	◆ Tiki torches.
◆ Bird cages and bird houses.	◆ Carousel horses.
◆ White wrought-iron patio furniture.	◆ Bird baths and fountains.
◆ Trellises.	◆ Park or patio benches.
◆ Baskets.	◆ Silk or live plants and trees.
◆ A gazebo.	◆ A portable dance floor.
◆ Arches, arbors, and picket fencing.	◆ Posters.
◆ Murals.	◆ Mirror balls.
◆ Flower filled rafts for a pool.	◆ Neon sign.

The list is endless, as you'll see if you visit a party supply store or browse through a party supply catalog (see Resources). By the way, you'll find *specific* theme-related decorating ideas in the theme party chapters that follow.

6

PARTY GAMES AND ACTIVITIES

It isn't always necessary to play games at parties. For example, at a formal sit-down dinner, an enjoyable meal and pleasant conversation are all that's required. At a "get-to-know-you" party, such as a Welcome Neighbor Party (see Chapter 103) or a Block Party (see Chapter 101), a game may actually become an annoying interruption to the socializing.

However, for those parties that do require games or activities, this chapter offers a variety to choose from. As you read them over, keep several things in mind: the formality of your party, the theme of your party, and the ages of your guests. The idea is to choose games and activities that will come as close as possible to pleasing everyone.

This chapter gives you tons of games you can use for your party, organized according to four main types: icebreakers, active games, passive games, and door prize contests. We'll begin, as parties usually do, with icebreakers.

Icebreakers

✧ **Who Am I?** This is a great get-acquainted game because it forces the guests to talk to each other. Buy a supply of 3″ x 5″ index cards, and write the name of a different famous person on each one. Pin a card to each player's back. Everyone can see the names on other players' backs, but not on their own. Players have to determine whose name is pinned on their backs by asking other people questions about that person. Each player is allowed to ask only three yes or no questions per round, such as, "Am I living?" or "Am I a female?" or "Am I an American?"

The first player to guess the name on his or her back wins a prize. By the way, be sure to have a few extra prizes on hand, in case of a tie.

✧ **Mystery Guest Game.** Give each guest a pen or pencil, paper, and a list of five questions to ask as many guests as possible in 20 minutes. The guests should record the answers as they go along. When the 20 minutes are up, the host describes a "mystery guest," and the first person to identify that guest wins. The point of this game, of course, is to help the guests get acquainted with each other. You can come up with your own list of questions, but here are some examples:

+ What is your hobby?
+ What is your occupation?
+ How many children do you have?
+ How many brothers and sisters do you have?
+ Where are you from originally?
+ Where did you go to school?

✧ **The Memory Game.** Have everyone sit in a circle, and begin by saying your name and hobby—for example, "My name is Ginny, and my hobby is gardening." The next person must repeat that information and add his or her own: "Her name is Ginny, and her hobby is gardening. My name is Jim, and my hobby is classic cars." The third person then adds his or her name and hobby to the list: "Her name is Ginny, and her hobby is gardening. His name is Jim, and his hobby is classic cars. My name is Gail, and my hobby is making teddy bears." And so on.

Of course, it gets tougher and tougher to remember all of the information the further around the circle you go, which makes the game a lot of fun. The last person who can recite everyone's name and hobby wins.

Active games

✧ **Charades.** Charades is probably the most popular party game in America today. Divide the guests into two teams—evenly divided or males against females, older generation against younger generation, and so on. Each team comes up with the titles of six to eight books, movies, television shows, or songs and writes them on pieces of paper, which are folded up and placed in a basket. One person from a team draws a piece of paper from the opposing team's basket, looks at the title without showing it to anyone else, and gives his or her team nonverbal clues as to what the title is. A timer is set, and this person has three minutes to silently act out the title, using hands, body, and facial expressions to communicate the title to his or her team. If the team guesses the title before time is up, the team gets 10 points. If time runs out before the team has guessed the title, the opposing team gets five points. The teams take turns acting out and guessing each other's titles. After each team has had six to eight turns, the team with the most points wins. In another version of this game, players draw the clues instead of acting them out, as in the Pictionary board game.

Tip — Not everyone is comfortable acting out in front of a group. It's a good idea to have fewer turns than team members so that certain team members can decline graciously, without feeling pressured.

✧ **The Newlywed/Oldywed Game.** We all know how the Newlywed Game is played. It works for "Oldyweds," as well. Choose four couples to compete. Ask the men to leave the room, then ask the women about four or five questions (some ideas follow). Write down their responses. Invite the men back into the room, and ask the same questions. The object is for the men to respond with the same answers as their partners. Then the game is reversed, and the women leave the room as the men are asked questions, and so on. The couple with the most matching answers wins. Here are some typical questions:

✦ Who is his favorite professional sports hero?
✦ Who is her favorite male movie star?
✦ When was your last fight?
✦ When was the last time she burned the dinner?
✦ What is the most embarrassing thing that ever happened to him?
✦ What is her most obnoxious habit?
✦ What turns him off about a woman?

✧ **Masquerade Race.** This is another fun men vs. women game. Fill two large shopping bags with clothes ahead of time, one with men's clothes—pants, a belt, a long-sleeved shirt, a tie, a hat, and gloves—and the other with women's clothes—a large dress or housecoat, a belt, jewelry, a scarf, a hat, socks, and slippers.

The men volunteer someone to be "it," and the women do the same. When they are given a signal, the man and woman have to turn their backs to the guests and get dressed, over their own clothes, as fast as they can, the man donning the woman's clothes and the woman the man's. The first one completely finished wins (all zippers must be zipped, all buttons buttoned, the tie correctly tied, and so on).

✧ **The Liar Game.** Fill a basket with old or peculiar-looking cooking utensils and construction tools, things that the average person may not recognize. Let each guest select an item and describe it with great eloquence—its name and purpose and a "true story" about how and when he or she used it. (Guests who recognize a certain tool or utensil will be telling the truth, but those who don't have a clue will need to fabricate their stories.) Each guest is given a piece of paper and pen or pencil to record opinions on who might be lying and who is telling the truth.

Finally, after everyone has had a turn, the host awards a prize to the guest who had the most correct answers and to the one who told the most creative story.

✧ **The Communication Game.** You'll need three or four pairs of contestants to play this game. The rest of the guests can be entertained as they watch two people desperately try to communicate with each other! One pair of contestants will compete at a time. The pair sits with their backs to each other, each person holding a tray on his or her lap. One person's tray holds 15 or 20 objects that have been arranged in a certain way. The other person's tray contains the same objects—but piled in a heap in the middle of the tray. You can use any small objects for this game, just as long as you have two of everything. Examples include buttons, empty spools, chopsticks, pencils, cans of soup, giant paper clips, crayons of various colors, small paintbrushes, forks, pieces of cord or string, children's blocks, and golf balls or tees.

Once you have two of everything, the fun is in arranging the items in a complicated way—for example, circling the string under one item and over another, or balancing a chopstick on top of the can of soup. Of course, if you plan to have four pairs play this game, you will need to have four trays arranged ahead of time and hidden away until game time. The person with the prearranged objects has to describe the arrangement in such a way that his or her partner can duplicate it exactly on his or her own tray. When they feel they have satisfied this requirement, the pair turns around and faces the guests, at which time no one cares who actually won, because it was so much fun to watch!

This game is not as easy as it would seem! Try the game out beforehand with a partner so you'll know how it works.

✧ **The Dictionary Game.** To play this game, you will need a pad of paper and a pen for each player, and a dictionary. Here's how the game is played:

1. One player is chosen to be the "leader."

2. The leader selects a word from the dictionary, one that the other players should be unfamiliar with, and announces it. (If anyone knows the meaning of the word, another word must be selected.)

3. The leader writes the dictionary definition of the word on a piece of paper, without showing anyone, while each player writes down a fictional (but believable) definition of the word on a piece of paper.

4. Everyone gives the pieces of paper to the leader. The leader reads aloud each definition, including the dictionary definition, while maintaining a straight face.

5. Each player announces which definition he or she believes to be true.

Each player who chooses the correct definition receives one point. Each player whose false definition is chosen by another player receives one point. The leader receives five points if no one chooses the correct dictionary definition. A new leader is chosen and the steps are repeated, until everybody has a turn. The player with the most points wins.

Passive games

✧ **Clothespin Game.** Purchase a supply of colorful plastic clothespins. Pin one clothespin on each guest's clothing, and let the game begin. Set a timer for 20 minutes. During that 20-minute period no one is allowed to say the word *no*. The idea of the game is to ask the guests questions about themselves, baiting them to answer no. Any guest who does must give his or her clothespin to the person who tricked him or her into saying the forbidden word. When the timer rings, the guest with the most clothespins wins.

By the way, a variation of this game, especially popular at bridal showers, is played throughout the party. The guests are told their clothespins will be taken away by anyone who catches them crossing their legs. The guest who has caught the most women crossing their legs during the party wins.

✧ **Handwriting Analysis.** Add a special "RSVP" to your invitations requesting handwriting samples from the guests to be returned to you at least two weeks in advance of the party. This gives a professional handwriting expert time to study the samples and complete an analysis of each guest's personality traits. These traits are posted on a master list under coded names. This list is then used by the guests to try to determine which guest matches which code name on the master list. The detailed handwriting analyses become party favors that are given to the guests as gifts.

✧ **The Observation Game.** Arrange 15 or 20 items on a tray, such as a pocket knife, a pencil, a fork, and so forth. Then ask a friend or your co-host to walk slowly around the room, displaying the tray for all the guests to see.

Everyone is given paper and a pencil, and as soon as your friend has left the room with the tray, the guests will be asked to write down as many things as they can remember about *your friend* (color of hair and eyes, what she was wearing, etc.). The guests will moan and cry "foul," of course, but they'll finally settle down and start recording things they remember about your friend. The guest who has recorded the most accurate description wins a prize.

✧ **Identification Game.** This is another humorous men vs. women contest. String a couple of sheets on a clothesline across the room. Have the men stand behind the sheets exposing their bare legs and feet, from the knees down. Then have each woman try to identify her partner's legs, at which time she stands in front of the sheet at that spot. Then, the sheets are removed, and prizes go to those women who were right. (If this game is played by couples who have been together for a while, you'll be surprised at how many women can't identify their partners' legs and feet!)

There are several fun variations to this game. For example, you can cut holes in the sheets and have the men try to identify the women's eyes, or have the women try to choose which noses belong to their partners. (This is my favorite because there's nothing quite so funny as a row of noses poking through the holes in the sheet!)

✧ **Baby Picture Identification Game.** For this game, you will need:
  + A baby picture from each guest. + Paper and a pencil for each guest.
  + A bulletin board or cork board. + Stickpins or thumbtacks.

When you send out the party invitations, request a baby picture from each person. After all the guests have arrived and supplied you with their baby photos, give each photo a number and pin it on the bulletin board. The guests are given paper and pencils and 10 minutes to guess the identity of each photo. The person who correctly identifies the most baby photos wins.

Door prize contests

Guests love the idea of door prizes, which may be things you've purchased and wrapped ahead of time, or part of your decorations, such as centerpieces, potted plants or floral arrangements. Here are a few of the most popular ways to determine who wins a door prize:

✦ Number the backs of the name tags before they are given to the guests as they arrive, beginning with the number "1." Then put corresponding numbers on pieces of paper, wad them up, and place them in a basket. Near the end of the party, ask the guest of honor to draw a wad of paper out of the basket. The winning number receives the prize.

✦ Insert three wads of paper (with predetermined numbers) inside three balloons before they are blown up with helium gas. Arrange the balloons in a bouquet as part of the decorations. Then, near the end of the party, ask the guest of honor to select one of the balloons and burst it by sitting on it (no hands allowed!). The wad of paper is then unfolded and the number read. The person with the corresponding number on the back of his or her name tag wins a door prize. Repeat this same procedure for the second and third balloons.

✦ If the party is a sit-down dinner, randomly place stickers under the seats of two or three dining room chairs. After dessert has been served, ask the guests to look under their chairs to see who has the stickers. Those who do win prizes.

✦ Let the guests guess how many chocolate kisses, candy hearts, or roasted almonds there are in a large, clear glass jar. The guest who comes closest to the correct answer wins the jar full of goodies.

Tips   – In addition to active and passive games, you may want to consider playing board games, as long as you're sure your guests like to play them. I, for example, hate playing the Monopoly real estate trading board game—I always land on the properties that have a zillion hotels!

– If you're looking for specific engagement party games, see Chapter 32. For wedding shower games, see Chapter 34. For lots of helpful details on planning engagement parties and wedding showers, you may want to pick up a copy of my book *Complete Book of Wedding Showers.*

– If you're looking for baby shower games, see Chapter 31. You can also find great information on baby showers in my book *Complete Book of Baby Showers.*

7

Party Games and Activities For Children

Unlike adults' parties, all children's parties require some games or activities to keep the children occupied and provide some fun. The children's activities described in this chapter are organized according to three types: active games and activities, passive games and activities, and opening of the gifts.

Active games and activities

- **Kazoo Marching Band:** Provide kazoos for the children to play as they parade around the house, the yard, or—if you dare—around the block. Let the adults play other "instruments," such as oatmeal box drums, sandpaper cymbals, or rhythm sticks (see Chapter 97). Choose a melody the children already know, such as "Twinkle, Twinkle, Little Star" or "Mary Had a Little Lamb" (not that anyone will actually recognize the melody!).

- **Pin the Tail on the Donkey**: We all know how this game is played. You can purchase the game from a store, or create your own by drawing a donkey (or any other animal, such as a cow, a cat, or a pig) on a large piece of butcher paper.

- **Musical Clothes Bag:** A few weeks before the party, begin assembling a trash bag full of silly clothes, boots, scarves, coats, hats, clown noses, novelty nightshirts, ski goggles, etc. Arrange the children in a circle around the trash bag. Hand an apple to one of the children, and have music begin to play. As the music plays, the children must pass the apple around the circle as fast as they can. When the music stops, the child caught holding the apple must go to the trash bag, close his or her eyes, pull something out, and put it on. Start the music again, and let the game continue until the trash bag is empty.

- **Penny Drop:** Provide each child with 10 pennies. Have the child stand straight and try to drop the pennies, one by one, into a container sitting on the floor at the child's feet. Use an unbreakable container with a fairly narrow opening, such as a decorated soup can, a plastic glass, or a one-pound coffee can.

✦ **Flashlight Tag:** This is a version of hide-and-seek that needs to be played in the dark. The children run and hide, and the person who's "it" looks for them with a flashlight. Each child who is "tagged" by the flashlight's beam is out. The game continues until the last child is found; that child becomes "it" for the next round.

✦ **Simon Says:** Everyone knows how to play Simon Says. The gimmick, of course, is that you unexpectedly throw in commands that are *not* prefaced by "Simon says" (such as, "Touch your toes"), and any child who does what you say is out of the game. Keep throwing these into your commands until there is just one child left—the winner!

✦ **Shoe Basket:** Ask the children to remove their shoes and dump them into a large laundry basket. When you say, "Go," all of the children run to the basket to find their shoes and put them on. The first child to tie the laces, or buckle the straps, on *both* shoes is the winner. (For children under age five, it isn't necessary to lace or buckle the shoes.)

✦ **Mummy Wrap:** Divide the group into two teams. One member of each team volunteers to be the mummy. Furnish each team with a large roll of toilet paper and a roll of transparent tape. When you say, "Go," team members begin to wrap their mummies in toilet paper (avoiding the face, of course). If a piece of toilet paper breaks off, they must tape it back on. The first team to use up the roll of toilet paper wins.

✦ **Untie the Knots:** Choose one child to be "it." That child leaves the room while the remaining children join hands in a circle and tie themselves in "knots" by ducking under, stepping over, and winding around each other without letting go of each other's hands. The child who is "it" is called back and must untie the knot without undoing the clasped hands.

✦ **Mystery Socks:** Fill a dozen or so socks with a variety of items that have identifiable shapes, such as a clothespin, a fork, a yo-yo, etc. Provide each child with a piece of paper and a pencil, then arrange the children in a circle. Ask the children to identify the items by feeling them through the socks and to write down what they think they are. When each child has had a turn, empty the socks onto the floor. The child with the most correct answers wins.

✦ **Children's Sing-Along:** Younger children enjoy singing traditional pre-school and primary-age songs, such as "Inky Dinky Spider," "The Farmer in the Dell," "Ring Around the Rosie," "If You're Happy and You Know It," and "Mary Had a Little Lamb." If you aren't already familiar with these songs, you can pick up a sing-along tape from a bookstore, music store, or teachers' supply catalog. You can also find these kinds of songs on an audiocassette called *Sing Along Birthday Songs* (see Resources).

❖ **Ping Pong Table Tennis Ball Hunt:** Upon arrival, give each guest a Ping Pong table tennis ball with his or her name on it. Ask him or her to hide the ball very well anywhere in the house, the yard, a certain room, etc. When the last guest has arrived and hidden his or her ball, send all the children on a Ping Pong table tennis ball hunt. The winner is the one whose ball is hidden the best—the last ball to be found.

❖ **Spoon Race:** Divide the group into even-numbered teams, and arrange the teams into lines. Furnish each player with a teaspoon and each team with one item to be passed from spoon to spoon, such as a cotton ball, a Ping Pong table tennis ball, an olive, a grape, or a piece of popped popcorn. The team leader, who is at the head of the line, passes the object from his or her spoon to the spoon of the next team member in line, and so on down the line (no hands allowed). Every time the object is dropped, the team must start over. The first team to pass the object from beginning to end without dropping it wins. Some variations on this game include:

❖ **Raw Egg Race:** The game is played outdoors, with a raw egg as the object on the spoon.

❖ **Tennis Ball Race:** Players pass a tennis ball using only their elbows.

❖ **Balloon Race**: Players pass a balloon using only their knees.

❖ **Straw and Ball Race**: Players compete to be the first to get a Ping Pong table tennis ball across the room or lawn by blowing on it through a drinking straw. A variation on this is the Lemon Race, in which players roll a lemon across the floor or lawn using the eraser end of a pencil.

❖ **Obstacle Course Relay Race:** Enlist the help of your spouse or a friend to design an obstacle course in your backyard. The course should have a starting point and a finish line, with a dozen or so obstacles in between. Obstacles can include:

- ✦ Old tires to hop in or out of.
- ✦ A long plastic tube to squiggle through.
- ✦ A wading pool to walk through after taking off socks and shoes (the obstacle includes putting them back on).
- ✦ A rope to jump rope with while hopping on one foot.
- ✦ A large trash bag, stuffed with crushed newspapers, to jump over.
- ✦ A croquet ball to knock through a hoop.
- ✦ Monkey bars to swing across.
- ✦ A Frisbee flying disc to balance on head while running a certain distance.
- ✦ A narrow plank, about a foot off the ground, to walk on.

Divide the players into two or three teams. One team at a time sends a player through the course. As soon as the player has finished, he or she tags the next team member, who then traverses the course. Continue in this way until all team members have participated. Record the time it takes for each team to run the course. The team with the shortest time wins.

✧ **Kiddy Limbo:** Two adults stand at the ends of a six-foot dowel or broomstick and hold it three feet off the ground. As festive limbo music plays, the children lean backward and pass under the stick one by one. If they touch the stick with any part of their body or the ground with their hands, they are disqualified. After all the children have made it under the stick, the stick is lowered and the children give it another try. The stick continues to be lowered until only one child is able to make it through without falling or touching the stick or the ground.

✧ **Musical Statues:** Assemble the children in a circle. Whenever the music plays, the children are to dance around the circle, freezing in place whenever the music stops. When the music stops, anyone who moves is out of the game—even blinking or smiling counts—and the music starts again. (Believe me, it won't take long!) Continue until only one child is left and is declared the winner.

✧ **Create a "Box City":** How does the saying go—"Children would rather play with the box"? Well, in this case it certainly is true. Before the party, collect a huge assortment of large cardboard boxes (preferably from your local appliance store). Set them in a row in your party room or on your patio, creating a miniature street. Provide the children with felt-tip markers and an assortment of crayons, and let them design a city, with one box as the grocery store, another as the barber shop, another as the gas station, some as houses, and so on. Or depending on your party's theme, they can turn the boxes into spaceships, pirate ships, prehistoric caves, or doll houses.

Passive games and activities

✧ **Decorated Mural:** Tape a long piece of butcher paper horizontally along a wall, and assign each guest a section to decorate. Be sure each child signs or initials his or her section so it can be cut out and brought home as a souvenir. If your party has a theme, such as a Mother Goose Party (see Chapter 49), ask the guests to draw appropriate characters. Or you can have the children sit at a table and decorate a white plastic tablecloth.

✧ **Coloring Books and Crayons:** Give the guests their own coloring books and small boxes of crayons as they arrive for the party. Provide a table where they can sit down and color quietly as the rest of the guests arrive.

✧ **Small Craft Project:** Provide materials for a small craft project, such as stringing bead necklaces or making marshmallow snowmen. (Visit a teacher's supply store or crafts store for ideas.)

✧ **Try to Remember:** Place several items on a tray, such as a can of dog food, a hairbrush, a spoon, an action figure, etc. The older the children, the more items on the tray. Ask the children to look at the items and try to remember them. Then remove the tray. Have the children name the items from memory.

✧ **Face Painting:** Children love to have their faces painted. Hire a professional to paint clown faces, or purchase face paints and do it yourself. Older children can paint each other's faces.

✧ **Play Dough:** This is a great end-of-party activity, something to entertain the children as parents are arriving to pick them up. Give each child a plastic bag of homemade colored dough. Seat the children around a table that has been covered with a plastic disposable tablecloth. The children can amuse themselves by forming their dough into various shapes. To make enough dough for eight children, combine 2 cups white flour, 1 cup salt, 4 tablespoons vegetable oil, and one drop food coloring. Add water, one drop at a time, until the dough is workable. (You can adapt this recipe for a greater number of children.)

✧ **String-a-Necklace Contest:** Provide bowls of miniature marshmallows, Cheerios breakfast cereal, Life Savers candy, popcorn, miniature pretzels, pitted olives, gumdrops, licorice, or any other foods that can be threaded onto a string. Give each child a long piece of string, prethreaded onto a large, blunt needle. Tell the children to begin threading their necklaces when you say, "Go." Set a timer for three minutes. When the timer rings, the child with the most items on his or her string wins. Provide first, second, and third prizes. Of course, the children may keep their necklaces as party favors.

✧ **Story Time:** There is nothing like a good story to fill five or ten minutes of party time for the younger set. The best stories are those with big, bright pictures, with plenty of action or mystery, or with a little "acting" required on your part. Practice reading or telling the story several times before the day of the party, giving thought to what props you might use.

✧ **The Whisper Game:** Arrange the children in a circle. Begin the game by whispering a sentence into the ear of the first child in the circle, such as, "The little boy went to the store to buy a green yo-yo for his Grandpa." The first person whispers the sentence to the next person, and so forth, until finally the last person repeats it out loud. The fun of the game is that the final version of the sentence won't mean anything close to the original. For example, "We went to the beach this summer, and I found a big seashell" could become "We went to a bridge this summer with a pig named Michelle." Once the children get the hang of the game, they can make up their own sentences to whisper to each other.

✧ **Door Prize Contest:** Give one blown-up balloon to each child. Each balloon has a number inside that corresponds to a gift displayed on a table. The child sits on his or her balloon until it pops, then takes the number to the table and finds the corresponding gift, which becomes his or her door prize or party favor. This is a good idea for birthday parties; young children sometimes feel sad because they don't have a gift to open.

Opening of gifts

The opening of gifts sounds like a pretty innocent activity, doesn't it? But it can sometimes turn ugly. One common problem is that the child—especially a young child—may have built up such high expectations regarding his or her gifts that he or she may be disappointed. Or he or she may receive duplicates or triplicates of the same gift. This can be a huge letdown for the child, and tears or even a temper tantrum might result. And even if there aren't any tears or temper tantrums as the gifts are opened, the child might be pretty candid (as children often are) about any negative opinions of the gifts, causing hurt feelings for the children who brought the gifts.

Another problem can be the reluctance of a guest to part with the gift he or she has brought to the party. In fact, a little coaxing might be necessary to get the child to give it up.

A solution to the first problem is to make gift-opening the last activity of the party. That way, if the birthday girl or boy is less-than-enthused about the gifts, there will be less time to show it. Days before the party, the child also should be coached on how to act courteously when it's time to open gifts at the party.

The second problem has an easier solution. In order to ease the pain of relinquishing a gift, load the child up with lots of small gifts of his or her own to take home—prizes, a party bag containing favors, small games and toys, and candy, and a party hat.

Tip – Here are some other games you can use (and where to find them):
- Nursery Rhyme Game (see Chapter 49).
- Wild Animal Obstacle Challenge (see Chapter 52).
- Mr. Pumpkin Contest (see Chapter 57).
- Water Balloon Contest (see Chapter 59).
- Snowman Contest (see Chapter 61).
- Scavenger Hunt (see Chapter 67).

8

PARTY ENTERTAINMENT

Every party requires some type of entertainment; it can range from simple background music during a dinner party, to something on a grander scale, such as a choreographed production of "This Is Your Life." Or, you may decide to hire novelty entertainment, such as mariachi singers or a stand-up comic.

This chapter offers dozens of ideas, including:

✦ Musical entertainment.

✦ A "This Is Your Life" skit about the guest of honor.

✦ A roast.

✦ Karaoke.

✦ Specialty entertainment.

Musical entertainment

◇ **D.J. or live band.** If your party theme lends itself to dancing, such as a party with an ethnic theme, a barbecue with a country-western theme, or a formal engagement dinner, you may want to hire a D.J. or a live band with a singer. To locate the best band or D.J. for the money, ask around—word of mouth is always the best reference. Otherwise, check your yellow pages under "Disc Jockeys" and "Music, Live or Pre-recorded." If you're lucky, you'll find a good D.J. in the $250 to $300 range.

◇ **Jukebox.** Guests get a kick out of an old-fashioned jukebox, not only because of the novelty of it but because they can select their own music. This is a great idea for any informal party. To rent a jukebox, check your yellow pages' listings for "disc jockeys," "entertainment," or "party rentals."

◇ **Instrumentalists or vocalists.** If you're hosting a formal party, you may decide to hire professional musicians to perform during the meal service. The light harmonies of a stringed trio, a harpist, or a pianist can do wonders for your party's ambiance. If you really want to impress your guests as they enjoy their after-dinner coffee, arrange for a soloist or instrumentalist to present a mini-concert.

If your party is going to include dancing and you'd like instrumentalists to play the music, you can hire a three-piece combo (usually string, piano, or drum), a group (usually six to eight members), or a full-size dance orchestra.

Ethnic parties call for special music, as well. For example, you may want to hire a mariachi for your Mexican Fiesta (see Chapters 19 and 85) or strolling violinists for your Italian Pasta Party (see Chapters 85 and 87).

◇ **Christmas caroling or a sing-along.** Certain parties, such as Christmas or ethnic parties, lend themselves to group singing. If you include caroling or a sing-along as part of your entertainment, be sure to furnish song sheets for each of the guests. (I'm always amazed at how few Christmas carols we know by heart, especially when it comes to the second and third verses!)

◇ **Background music.** If nothing else, be sure to provide soft background music. It should be loud enough to add to the party's ambiance, but not so loud that the guests have difficulty carrying on a conversation. It's a good idea to create a party tape ahead of time. Purchase a high-quality cassette tape and record songs from tapes and CDs on it, putting the selections you want in the order you want them to play. Whether the tape will be used as background music or as a dance tape, it will give you confidence to know you have a tape filled with exactly what you want your guests to hear (with no musical "duds" to endure along the way).

"This Is Your Life"

Your party's entertainment could be a skit based on the old television show *This Is Your Life.* In this show, a guest of honor is surprised by dear friends and family members who appear unexpectedly to tell the story of the person's life. For this skit, your cast should include, a master of ceremonies, the guest of honor, and mystery guests who help tell the story of the person's life.

For your set, you'll need:

✦ A special chair for the guest of honor.

✦ A large scrapbook whose front cover reads "This Is Your Life, [name of guest of honor]."

And here's a beginning script for the show:

Master of ceremonies: *(approaching the guest of honor)*
  Are you having a nice time at your party?

Guest of honor:
  Yes.

Master of ceremonies:
  Well, it's wonderful to be honored this way by your friends and family, but we have an even bigger surprise for you, [name of guest of honor]— this is your life! *(The master of ceremonies holds up the book to show the guest*

of honor. Someone escorts the honored guest to a "chair of honor." Someone else rushes over to present the guest of honor with a bouquet of flowers.)

Master of ceremonies:

It all began in [city and state where the guest was born].

Off-stage mystery guest (from another room):

I remember it well—I almost didn't make it to the hospital in time. (Out comes the guest's mother, of course, who hugs her child and continues with any humorous or interesting facts relating to her son or daughter's birth.)

One by one, other relatives begin telling humorous stories "off stage" about things the guest did growing up and then appearing to the surprised guest. For example, an aunt or uncle tells a story about what the guest of honor liked to eat or how she found a kitten and brought it home. Or a sister tells what the guest of honor was like as a teenager—how she always got into her sister's lipstick or borrowed her clothes. Her best friend talks about the time they got lost in a snowstorm because she was too stubborn to stop and ask for directions. Her high school drama teacher talks about the time she played the lead in the senior play. The guest's grandmother, or someone who traveled a long distance to surprise her, tells how proud she was of her on the day she graduated from high school, college, and so on.

The mystery guests' stories should be told in chronological order. For example, someone first talks about how sweet or ornery the guest of honor was as a toddler, the next person talks about the winning science project she made in third grade, and the next talks about how she led her team to the state softball championship in junior high. The last guest is the honored guest's significant other, who has been hiding in a back room. Of course, his appearance is the best surprise of all, bringing her story to an end.

Obviously, you can have a lot of fun with this, but it will take some preparation. Start by calling the honored guest's mother, who can fill you in on her child's story in chronological order and suggest various people from her child's past who might be willing to participate.

If you can pull this off—and it's *actually* a surprise—the party will be a guaranteed success!

"Amateur Night"

This is another name for a talent show that is put on by your guests. It can be the evening's entertainment or your party's theme (see Chapter 97).

A roast

At a roast, guests take turns making jokes and telling embarrassing little stories about the guest of honor, but only in fun—never revealing anything too personal or humiliating.

For example, the honored guest's best friend might tell about the time she unknowingly stepped in a "doggie gift" on her way to speak at a women's luncheon and how the stench permeated the room throughout her speech. Or Dad might tell about the time he taught his son to drive...and all the klutzy driving maneuvers that ensued.

A successful roast depends on how well you've done your research and how prepared the guests are to tell their (harmless) stories.

A roast also makes a good theme for a bachelor party (see Chapter 33).

Karaoke

Rent a karaoke machine, and you'll have all the entertainment you can handle! Usually, with just a little encouragement, one or two guests who have used one before will be glad to demonstrate. The next thing you know, they're really enjoying themselves, encouraging the rest of your guests to give it a try.

In most areas, you will be able to find karaoke machine rentals by contacting the companies listed under "disc jockeys" in the yellow pages.

Specialty entertainment

If you're planning a theme party, consider these entertainment ideas:
+ Polynesian dancers and performers (such as knife jugglers).
+ Folk dancers (great for ethnic parties).
+ A cosmetologist to do makeovers.
+ Synchronized swimmers (for a pool-side party).
+ A caricaturist. Everyone gets a kick out of seeing what he or she looks like in the eyes of a caricaturist!
+ Horse-and-carriage rides.
+ Hay wagon or sleigh rides.
+ Hot-air balloon rides.
+ Hula lessons.
+ A mime.
+ A barber shop quartet. They love to entertain and keep their form of music alive. You can locate one through your chamber of commerce.
+ A magician.
+ A juggler.
+ A clown.
+ A balloon artist.
+ A stand-up comic.
+ A photographer, who can take instant photos that can be passed around and placed in an album for the guest of honor to keep as a memento.
+ A videographer, who can film the decorations before the guests arrive, then capture the games, activities, gift opening, and other party happenings. In advance of the party, you can ask your guests to prepare "a little something" to say about the honored guest on tape. The tape can then be given to the guest of honor as a gift.

9

PARTY PROGRESSION

Most of us don't know much about "party progression," but we should. It's vitally important to any party's success. If we say a party has "progression," we mean that it doesn't take place in a single spot but progresses from one venue to another, throughout the party site, even if that site is just your home or yard.

Progression adds interest to the party, along with a sense of anticipation and a fresh tingle of excitement as the personality of the party changes with the progression. Tease the senses with each change of venue. Here's an example of how this works:

1. As soon as your guests arrive, you usher them to the room or venue where appetizers and cocktails are being served. For example, appetizers may be served in a well-lit, "stand-up" venue, where soft music is a backdrop to the chatter. This venue may be decorated very simply with forced bulbs blooming in interesting containers.

2. Then, when it's time for the main meal, invite your guests to the next venue—the dining room, family room, or patio. This venue may have subdued lighting, soft candlelight, a fascinating centerpiece, and inviting place settings, creating an atmosphere conducive to quiet conversation.

3. When the main meal is concluded, adjourn to yet another venue for dessert, coffee, and after-dinner drinks. These may be served on the patio, where the guests can experience the tranquilizing ambiance created by flaming tiki torches and a stunning sunset.

Does that give you the idea? A successful party is like a theatrical production. It needs to be choreographed from beginning to end, or it will stagnate and the guests will conjure up all kinds of reasons why they need to leave early.

10

DELEGATING YOUR TASKS

Don't be afraid to ask for a little help if you need it. You'll find that, not only are others happy to help out, but will often ask if they can do so.

A host usually needs help when:

+ Hosting a cocktail party of 20 or more guests (you'll need one or two bartenders).

+ Hosting a lunch or dinner buffet for 25 or more guests (you'll need one bartender and one kitchen helper).

+ Hosting any menu where certain foods need constant attention (need at least one helper).

+ Hosting a buffet where meat is to be carved as guests are served (you'll need one carver).

+ Hosting a birthday party for a baby or young child (invite one parent per guest). This is quite common and acceptable. The parents are glad to help and they enjoy the party, too.

+ Hosting a party for an older child (you will need one adult per six to eight guests). This will help reduce your stress level considerably!

+ Hosting an adult party with more than 12 guests (ask a friend or two to help you with the party plans). Here are a few of the responsibilities that can be delegated to others:

+ Compiling the guest list, including addresses and telephone numbers.

+ Addressing invitations.

+ Making decorations, name tags, place cards, and favors.

+ Cooking or baking some of the food.

+ Decorating.

+ Arranging the gifts.

+ Recording the gifts as they are opened (the name of the donor and what was given).

✦ Passing the gifts around the room for all the guests to see, being sure the cards stay with their corresponding gifts.

✦ Conducting the games, if any.

✦ Serving the food and drink.

Do you need to hire a caterer?

If you want to splurge and pamper yourself, why not hire a caterer to pre-pare and serve the menu? Although most hosts can handle a small dinner party on their own, some prefer to leave it to a caterer so they can relax and enjoy visiting with their guests.

Ask friends for references, then interview several of them before making your selection.

When engaging the services of a caterer, here are some things you should get in writing, either by contract or in a letter agreement:

✦ Per-person or total menu cost, including beverages.

✦ Name and telephone number of contact person.

✦ Equipment to be furnished by caterer.

✦ Equipment you will furnish.

✦ Description of services included in cost (cleanup, serving of predinner or after-dinner drinks, dessert, etc.).

✦ Whether tax and gratuities are included in the fees.

✦ Deposit required and terms of final payment (many caterers only accept cash or check).

✦ The servers' attire.

✦ Exact time of arrival and how many hours of service are included in cost.

Do you need to hire a professional party consultant?

A professional party consultant plans the entire party for you, including theme, menu, decorations, and so forth. If you're planning a large scale event, one of these professionals can be very helpful. The best way to find one of these professionals is by word-of-mouth. Ask around. Who do you know who hosts large get-togethers and may have hired professional help?

Tip – When hiring help, whether it's via word of mouth or through an agency, always ask for references!

PART 2
Seasonal Celebrations

"A party can bond friends together."

If you're looking for an excuse to throw a party, every month of the year offers a new one—with holidays such as New Year's Day, Memorial Day, the Fourth of July, or Christmas Eve. This section is filled with traditional, tried-and-true seasonal party ideas, mixed with imaginative and creative new ways to entertain.

Have fun as you plan your holiday party!

11

New Year's Eve

New Year's Eve is a nostalgic, emotionally charged night of the year. It's a night of reflection mixed with optimism and joyful anticipation of the year ahead. Most people like to spend it with close friends, with whom they already have a special bond. Others prefer to host a noisy, glittering party with a mixed group of guests.

Invitation ideas

✧ Photocopy the page for the month of December from your calendar. Fill in the December 31 box with the place and time of the party and other party information. Roll the sheet into a scroll, tie with a ribbon, and hand-deliver or mail.

✧ Create a fill-in sheet for listing New Year's resolutions, with the party invitation printed across the top. This can be computer-generated or designed by hand and duplicated on a photocopy machine. In the invitation, ask the guests to fill out the sheets and bring them to the party. Roll the sheets into scrolls, tie with ribbons, and hand-deliver.

✧ Send a list of common New Year's resolutions whose final resolution tells the guests, in large type, to go to your party and gives all the information.

Attire

✧ Attire will depend on the formality of the evening. A formal dinner dance will require evening wear, while an informal party will require more casual dress.

✧ At a "black-and-white" party, something that has become popular recently, the guests dress up in black tuxedos and black or white evening gowns.

✧ New Year's Eve costume parties are also trendy in certain communities around the country.

Ambiance

✧ Remove ornaments and all Christmas decorations from your Christmas tree and transform it into a "New Year's Tree" by adding glass icicles, bright party streamers, noisemakers, and a decorated party hat for the top of the tree.

✧ Decorate with balloons and streamers, and don't forget the hats, horns, and plenty of confetti!

✧ If your celebration is an intimate dinner party, turn the lights down low and light the candles—it will add a magical quality to the evening.

✧ For an eye-catching table centerpiece, fill a silver bucket with ice and champagne bottles arranged to look like flowers blooming in a pot.

✧ Provide one party horn and one paper blowout for each guest (available through party supply stores or catalogs—see Resources). By "paper blowout," I mean the party toy that looks like a party horn, but shoots out a colorful paper tube when blown.

Amusements and activities

✧ Ask the guests to count their blessings from the year past and to read their New Year's resolutions.

✧ Make "joyful noise" at midnight, using any festive, harmless means you see fit—horns, pots and pans, or fireworks (laws permitting). Sing "Auld Lang Syne." Provide kazoos for those who can't remember the words!

✧ Before the party, blow up balloons filled with confetti. At the stroke of midnight, burst them and let the confetti fly!

✧ How about inviting the guests at your home to move the party over to a hotel or resort club for dancing, entertainment, and a traditional midnight celebration? (Call ahead to find out the cover charge and whether tickets need to be purchased in advance. Reserve rooms ahead of time so everyone can crash when they want without needing to drive home.)

Edibles

✧ Depending on the formality of the evening, serve snacks and appetizers (see Chapter 107), a late-night supper (see Chapter 108), an international menu (see Chapter 110), or a formal menu (see Chapter 109).

✧ Progressive dinner parties are popular on New Year's Eve, especially if the homes are within walking distance, or a short driving distance, from one another. The party at one of the homes can extend past midnight, culminating with a royal New Year's morning breakfast buffet.

✧ Toast the strike of midnight with champagne or any other beverage of your choice (for example, nonalcoholic drinks such as sparkling cider or icy cold cream soda).

12

NEW YEAR'S DAY

New Year's Day is definitely a laid-back, hang-loose kind of day, especially after the night before! This is a day for all the armchair quarterbacks to enjoy great snacks, irresistible finger foods, and an easy brunch or lunch buffet.

This is also a day of hope as everyone looks forward to the year ahead, sure to be filled with happiness, success, good health, and financial prosperity. In fact, a New Year's Day party is a no-fail event, because your guests are guaranteed to be the most upbeat, ecstatic crowd you could ever hope to entertain!

Invitation ideas

✧ Use one of the informal invitation suggestions in Chapter 4, or if you plan to watch the bowl games on TV, cut football-shaped invitations out of brown construction paper, add black laces, and print the invitation on the back.

Attire

✧ Encourage your guests to dress as casually as they would like, wearing football jerseys, sports-oriented T-shirts, or sweatshirts.

Ambiance

✧ In honor of the Rose Bowl, decorate the room with vases of silk or fresh roses, in addition to garlands of silk roses and greenery draped over doorways, backs of chairs, and over the top and sides of the television set.

✧ Get a hold of as many football posters as you can; tack them up all around the room.

✧ Decorate your home's entryway, TV room, and a buffet table with as much football memorabilia as you can find, including pads, uniforms, helmets, footballs, etc.

Amusements and activities

✧ Watch the parades and bowl games on TV.

✧ Have a couple of footballs on hand for a game or two of flag football.

✧ Plan a halftime show with lip-sync or karaoke contests, a swing-dancing contest, or a skit or two.

Edibles

✧ New Year's Day is an "eat finger foods all day" type of day. Create a buffet of popcorn, pretzels, cheeses, crackers, chips, dips, egg rolls, chicken wings, pizza strips, plus other snacks from Chapter 107 or lunch menus from Chapter 108. You can place snacks in rotating serving trays that have a container for dip in their centers. Place the trays within arm's reach for the guests.

13

CHINESE NEW YEAR

Chinese New Year begins on the first day of the first moon, between January 21 and February 19, and lasts 14 days. Although each night has a theme—such as cleaning house or the lighting of lanterns—it's appropriate to host an all-purpose, one-night Chinese New Year's party any day during this time period.

Invitation ideas

✧ Handprint or computer-generate the invitations on small pieces of parchment paper, approximately two inches square. Roll tight and tuck into fortune cookies. Hand-deliver these fortune cookie invitations, or pack carefully and mail in small boxes.

✧ Handprint or computer-generate each invitation onto parchment paper, approximately three inches by eight inches, wrap around a pair of chopsticks, tie with a gold ribbon, and mail in a padded envelope.

✧ Use a ribbon to attach each invitation to the base of a small folding Oriental fan. Mail in a padded envelope.

Attire

✧ When you send out your invitations, request that your guests wear Oriental attire to the party, such as Mandarin-style shirts, dresses with standup collars, or any close-fitting, sheath-style dresses. Females with long hair can roll it into a bun, secured with chopsticks.

Ambiance

✧ Decorate with red—it's the preferred color for Chinese New Year decorations because it conveys good wishes for the new year, as well as harmony, beauty, and happiness.

✧ See if your local travel agent can spare a few travel posters or brochures about China.

✧ Visit your favorite import store, such as Cost Plus or Pier I, to purchase Chinese paper lanterns, kites, masks, dragons, fans, or chopsticks, and anything decorative made out of bamboo.

✧ Purchase take-out cartons from a Chinese restaurant or a restaurant supply store. Spray-paint the cartons red, and fill them with live or silk plants. Embellish with pairs of gold-sprayed chopsticks.

✧ Create displays of borrowed Oriental tea sets.

✧ To make party favors, tie the base of small Oriental fans with gold ribbon. Place them in the center of each place setting.

Amusements and activities

✧ Require your guests to eat with chopsticks.

✧ Borrow a few sets of Chinese checkers to set around the room.

✧ Shoot off a few fireworks (laws permitting).

✧ Wave Chinese wands in figure-8 formations with your guests. Make wands by attaching two-foot lengths of narrow red ribbon or crepe paper strips to the ends of chopsticks.

✧ Make fake Chinese New Year firecrackers for children at the party by inserting a small toy into an empty toilet paper tube, wrapping with red paper, leaving three inches extra at each end, twisting the ends of the paper, and tying with bright red ribbons.

✧ Furnish the guests with fortune cookies; ask them to read their fortunes out loud.

Edibles

✧ A Chinese buffet (see recipes in Chapter 110).

✧ Rice wine.

✧ A bowl of oranges—a traditional sign of good luck.

✧ Of course, fortune cookies are a must!

14

VALENTINE'S DAY

Valentine's Day, February 14, is a day to express love to your sweetheart. The holiday originated from a love letter written by St. Valentine to his beloved.

Invitation ideas

✧ Purchase a box of children's valentines to use as party invitations. Attach one valentine to each invitation, or print the invitation on the back of each valentine.

Attire

✧ Encourage everyone to wear red or pink.

✧ Pin red carnations on the guests as they arrive.

Ambiance

✧ Decorate with large red, white, and pink hearts cut from construction paper and embellished with red ribbons and white paper lace.

✧ Invert a colander, and insert red heart-shaped lollipops into the holes. Tie each lollipop at its neck with a red ribbon.

✧ Set small red heart-shaped boxes of chocolates in the center of each place setting as party favors.

✧ Sprinkle the table with metallic heart-shaped confetti, available from a party supply store or catalog (see Resources).

✧ Place clusters of heart-shaped balloons around the room or on the serving table, or tie groups of three to the backs of chairs.

✧ Add red, white, and pink crepe-paper streamers to the lamppost in the front yard, to the entryway, or to doorways.

❖ Add a backdrop to your ambiance with a mural; you'll find several with Valentine's themes available through Anderson's Prom and Party Catalog (see Resources).

❖ Turn off *all* the electric lights, and give the room a romantic glow with strings of tiny white lights and dozens of pink and white candles.

Amusements and activities

❖ Ask several couples to tell how they met and fell in love. Ask any newly engaged or newly married couples the same questions, along with questions about the juicy details of the marriage proposal! (Who proposed? Where? What was the immediate response? How long before they were married?)

❖ Divide into two teams. See how many songs with the word *heart* in them each team can sing.

❖ See how many legitimate words the guests can make out of the words *Valentine's Day* in five minutes. (Set a timer.)

❖ Have the guests guess how many candy hearts are in a certain container. The winner gets to keep the candy hearts.

❖ Play the Newlywed/Oldywed Game (see Chapter 6).

❖ Convert your patio or floor into the dance floor of a romantic "nightclub" for after-dinner dancing. Clear away the furniture, string up tiny white lights and a few helium balloons, and play some dreamy recorded music, such as Roberta Flack's "The First Time Ever I Saw Your Face" or Tony Bennett's "My Funny Valentine."

Edibles

❖ Provide an elegant, romantic, candlelit sit-down dinner or...

❖ Have an informal supper buffet with as many red foods as possible—red gelatin salads, tomato sauce and spaghetti, fresh red strawberries, red fruit punch, and so forth.

❖ Serve decorated heart-shaped cookies or a heart-shaped cake.

15

Mardi Gras

Mardi Gras, also known as "Fat Tuesday," is usually celebrated on the day before Ash Wednesday, which begins the Christian season of fasting and repentance called Lent. It is one of the liveliest and most colorful festivals celebrated in our country. Mardi Gras is known for its riotous parades, jazz and Dixieland music, masquerade balls, pageants, floats, and street festivals.

Invitation ideas

✧ Attach the invitations to metallic masks, which you can send through the mail in small boxes obtained from the post office. Ask your guests to wear these or any other masks of their choice to the party, along with a costume. It's just not Mardi Gras without some kind of costume! (Metallic masks are available for less than $1 each from Anderson's Prom and Party Catalog. See Resources.)

Attire

✧ Everyone should wear costumes and masks, of course—lavish or bizarre.

✧ Females can wear lots and lots of gaudy jewelry, obtainable from a local flea market or thrift store.

✧ Provide guests with traditional Mardi Gras beads, which can be obtained through a party supply store or catalog (see Resources).

Ambiance

✧ Think loud, bright, and colorful! There are no rules when it comes to Mardi Gras. Decorate with balloons, crepe-paper streamers, garish masks, and Mardi Gras posters, if you can find them.

✧ Display a mural that has a Mardi Gras theme, such as one of several available from Anderson's Prom and Party Catalog (see Resources).

✧ Set up a display of jazz instruments, such as a trumpet, trombones, tambourines, drums, etc. As an alternative, you can display photos of such instruments.

✧ Sprinkle your table with metallic confetti in the shape of tiny masks, obtained from a party supply store or catalog (see Resources).

Amusements and activities

✧ Depending on how tolerant your neighbors are, a Mardi Gras parade may be in order with jazz or Dixieland music played from a boom box. Give prizes for best costumes. If you don't think your neighbors will appreciate your Mardi Gras parade, you can at least parade around your home and yard.

✧ Provide plenty of noisemakers!

✧ Turn the lights down low and dance a while to a prerecorded tape of jazz and Dixieland music. (Rent a dance floor if necessary.)

✧ Videotape the evening's activities, and watch the tape with your guests at the end of the party.

Edibles

✧ Serve a Cajun menu, including jambalaya, shrimp in Creole sauce, rice, and pecan pie.

✧ End with a Mardi Gras cake, a white, pastry-like cake glazed with icing and colored sugar, with a plastic baby figurine baked inconspicuously within the cake. It is considered a portent of good luck if you find the baby in your slice of the cake. Check your local bakery or the baked goods section of a large supermarket for these cakes.

Tips – The fact that the guests arrive in costume will provide a lot of fun and entertainment in and of itself.

– Remember that a Mardi Gras party should be *loud* and *joyous*!

16

St. Patrick's Day

March 17 is St. Patrick's Day, a day that honors St. Patrick, the patron saint who brought Christianity to Ireland in the fifth century. It has become a festive holiday for the modern-day Irish in America, with Irish pubs packed from noon on, everyone wearing a touch of green, parades—complete with bagpipers—taking place all about, and everyone having a great time.

Here are ideas for an at-home St. Patrick's Day party:

Invitation ideas

✧ Cut eight-inch shamrocks (three-leaf clovers) out of heavy green paper. Print the invitation on the back, or attach the shamrocks to computer-generated invitations. Mail along with a request that guests wear something green and a decorated St. Patrick's Day hat.

Ambiance

✧ Greet your guests at the door with a life-sized leprechaun, available through Advanced Graphics (see Resources).

✧ Talk your travel agent into giving you a few Ireland travel brochures or posters to decorate with.

✧ Haul in the biggest rock you can carry and set it on a bed of crushed green tissue. Label it "Blarney Stone," and encourage your guests to kiss it.

✧ Think "green and white" for this party—for everything from balloons to crepe-paper streamers.

✧ Make "pots o' gold" party favors. Fill nut cups with gold-foil covered chocolate coins, and cover the nut cups with gold foil.

✧ Decorate with shillelaghs, shamrocks, clay pipes, and rubber snakes (St. Patrick is said to have chased all the snakes out of Ireland).

Amusements and activities

✧ Of course, your party doesn't have to be just for people with true Irish heritage. But if you find yourself with a room full of Irish folk, you're bound to have a lot of fun. For one thing, they love to sing. See if you can get them interested in singing along to Irish favorites, including "Oh, Danny Boy" and "When Irish Eyes Are Smiling."

✧ Give prizes for the most creative, most beautiful, and funniest decorated St. Patrick's Day hats.

✧ See if you can talk a few guests into doing an Irish jig.

✧ Hold a limerick-writing contest. A limerick is composed of five lines. Lines one, two, and five rhyme, and lines three and four, which are shorter, also rhyme. A limerick has a certain rhythm to it, and once you get the hang of it, it's easy to create one of your own. Make copies of the example below to give to your guests. Then, turn your guests loose, and see who can compose the best limerick.

> A tow-truck driver named Joe
> Found business wherever he'd go,
> 'til the girl of his dreams
> Walked by in tight jeans—
> Now she has *him* firmly in tow.

Edibles

✧ Serve an Irish buffet (see Chapter 110) and plenty of Irish beer.

✧ Serve Irish Appleberry Crunch (see Chapter 111) and Irish Coffee (see Chapter 112).

17

Easter Day

Easter, a Christian holiday celebrating the resurrection of Christ, falls on a Sunday in early Spring, depending on the vernal equinox, so you need to check your calendar to see what day you should plan your celebration. It is said that more Christians attend church on Easter Sunday than on any other day of the year. When the church service is over, families usually share a lavish Easter meal at a restaurant or in someone's home, followed by traditional Easter Day activities.

Ambiance

✦ Decorate your table with pink, yellow, and blue balloons, as well as with plastic eggs filled with candy or marshmallow bunnies.

✦ Cluster interesting objects together in an artistic arrangement. For example, arrange a small white wicker basket filled with decorated Easter eggs alongside a white ceramic bunny and a single daffodil in a white bud vase.

✦ To make Easter egg favors, hard-boil one egg per guest. Decorate the eggs with Easter egg dye, writing the guests' names near the tops of the eggs. Display the eggs in soft-boiled egg cups, tiny baskets filled with Easter basket grass, or homemade egg cups made from egg cartons (cut out each section and spray with gold paint). Place one egg cup or basket at each place setting.

✦ Set tiny decorated Easter baskets filled with candy at each place setting as party favors.

✦ Create a table centerpiece by filling a large Easter basket with plastic grass and stuffed bunnies.

✦ Set blooming tulips and daffodils on the buffet table and elsewhere around the room.

Amusements and activities

✧ If weather permits, play yard games, such as lawn croquet, horseshoes, badminton, or volleyball.

✧ An Easter egg hunt is a *must* for children, who revel in the thought that the Easter bunny hid the eggs. Hide decorated hard-boiled eggs, wrapped candies, or marshmallow bunnies around the yard. Give each child a basket, and send the children on the hunt. You can provide a candy prize for the child who finds the most eggs.

✧ Have an egg decorating contest for the children. Provide hard-boiled eggs, Easter egg dye, crayons, paper lace, construction paper, felt pieces, glue, and so forth.

✧ Have a traditional egg roll for the children. Poke holes in the ends of raw eggs and blow out the contents of each egg, leaving a light, delicate shell. Reinforce the ends of each egg with colored tape or notebook paper hole reinforcements. Establish starting and finishing lines about 45 feet apart. Ask the children to get down on their hands and knees at the starting line and blow their eggs to the finish line. The first child to blow his egg over the finish line without breaking it is declared the winner. As an alternate activity, have the children roll their eggs with their noses.

✧ Play Pin the Tail on the Rabbit (a variation of Pin the Tail on the Donkey).

✧ Have an Easter bonnet decorating contest for the children. Purchase a supply of plain white paper painters' hats, along with silk flowers, ribbons, and craft supplies for decorations.

Edibles

✧ Serve a traditional Easter lunch: ham, yams, vegetables, rolls, fruit salad (with colored mini-marshmallows), and cherry pie for dessert.

Tips – Videotape the day's activities, and show the tape at the end of the day.

– Encourage the older generation to relate stories of their childhood Easter celebrations (be sure to capture these treasured stories on videotape).

– After the small children have finished their Easter egg hunt, hide plastic eggs filled with coins for the older children. Even though they no longer believe in the Easter bunny, they will still enjoy the hunt.

18

MAY DAY

May Day, which always falls on May 1, has been celebrated in the past with a traditional spring festival that includes dancing around a Maypole, crowning a May queen, gathering fresh flowers, pageantry, theatrical performances, dart contests, hoop-rolling, archery, parades, and other games. The ideas in this chapter could also be used for a "First Day of Spring" party.

Traditionally, a May Day party should take place outdoors, preferably in the woods or beside a stream. However, you'll probably host your party on your patio, in your backyard, or in case of bad weather, inside your home.

Invitation ideas

✧ Tie nosegays of silk flowers at the stems with pastel-colored satin acetate ribbons. Attach to the invitations, and hand-deliver.

Attire

✧ Springy pastel colored attire.

Ambiance

✧ Because May Day is a "welcome spring" celebration, you can borrow decorating ideas from Chapter 17. Decorations may include bouquets of fresh tulips and daffodils, decorated bird houses, and bedding plants wrapped with pink Mylar polyester film and tied with pink and white checked ribbons.

✧ Transform ordinary umbrellas into colorful May Day decorations. Cover the spokes with ribbons, wrap ribbon or crepe paper strips around the handles, glue on buttons, beads, bows, silk flowers, rickrack, braiding, and anything else you can round up from your sewing box.

Amusements and activities

✧ Decorate a Maypole (any tall pole) by wreathing it with long, bright paper streamers and silk or fresh flowers. Encourage your guests to take hold of the streamers, intertwining them as they dance around the Maypole.

✧ Honor a special guest as the May queen (provide a crown and scepter).

✧ Another traditional activity on May Day is to hang a paper cone-shaped basket filled with fresh flowers over someone's front doorknob, ring the bell, and run. The cone-shaped baskets are easy to make by rolling 8 ½" x 11" sheets of pastel construction paper into horns of plenty, stapling together, and adding handles made from one-inch strips of paper. Fill with a white paper lace doily and fresh or silk flowers. The fun of this old-fashioned idea is to grace the doorknob of someone very special.

✧ You can ask your guests to bring decorated "May baskets" to the party and give prizes for the prettiest, most creative, etc. Then, after the judging, you and your guests can deliver them to the doors of friends' and neighbors' homes, or to the elderly in convalescent homes.

✧ If weather permits, have fun outdoors flying kites, tossing a Frisbee flying disc, or playing volleyball or lawn croquet.

✧ Have dart and archery contests.

✧ Historically, May Day guests have danced an old-world dance called the "Morris dance," but in today's world, American square dances have become popular choices. You may want to rent a dance floor and hire a square dance caller or instructor.

✧ In lieu of theatrical productions, the traditional May Day entertainment, play charades (see Chapter 6). Better yet, see if any or your guests will agree to put on a skit.

Edibles

✧ Serve a light luncheon menu (see Chapter 108) or the menu suggested for Easter Day in Chapter 17.

19

CINCO DE MAYO

Cinco de Mayo means "the fifth of May." It is a national holiday in Mexico that commemorates the victory of the Mexican army over a French invasion on May 5, 1862. It is celebrated with parades, dancing, feasts, and speeches.

Invitation ideas

✧ Attach the invitation to the stem of a large, colorful paper flower, which you may create yourself or obtain from a craft, floral arrangement supply, or imports store.

Attire

✧ Traditional dress for this national holiday consists of white shirts and pants for males and white skirts and blouses for females, embellished with colorful jewelry, shawls, serapes, and flowers worn in the hair.

Ambiance

✧ Decorate with any and every Mexican prop you can find, including:

- ✦ Large, colorful paper flowers.
- ✦ Crepe-paper streamers.
- ✦ Sombreros.
- ✦ Piñatas.
- ✦ Red, white, and green balloons.
- ✦ Mexican flags.
- ✦ Mexican travel posters.
- ✦ Candles and strings of lights.

✧ Miracle candles, those wonderful, tall candles that sit inside a painted glass. These are usually carried by Mexican grocery stores, if you can locate one in your area, or in the ethnic foods section of large grocery stores.

Amusements and activities

✦ Hire a mariachi band.

✦ If you can't afford a band, track down an album by Herb Alpert and the Tijuana Brass, or purchase one of the many great mariachi tapes and CDs on the market.

✦ Dance the Macarena and the Mexican Hat Dance.

✦ Have a Cinco de Mayo parade. Furnish children (and adults if they're up for it!) with rhythm sticks, bells, tambourines, maracas, drums, and rhythm blocks made of rough sandpaper secured to pieces of wood.

✦ Have guests take turns trying to break open piñatas filled with candy, using a stick (this is especially fun for children).

✦ Take instant photos of guests wearing giant sombreros, and give the photos to the guests as party favors. (Sombreros are available from party supply stores or catalogs—see Resources.)

Edibles

✦ Create a Mexican buffet with as many traditional Mexican dishes as you can (see Chapter 110 for menus and recipes).

✦ Be prepared to serve margaritas by the pitcher, along with plenty of Mexican beer.

Tip – If you live close to the Mexican border, pick up the decorations you need at affordable prices. Otherwise, visit your local import store for ideas.

20

MOTHER'S DAY

Mother's Day falls on the second Sunday in May. It's a day to honor our mothers with a lovely meal, flowers, gifts, a mushy, sentimental card, and other expressions of our love.

Ambiance

✧ As a starter, why not order Mom a large, extravagant corsage, especially if you plan to take her to church or out for a Mother's Day brunch? If you're providing a brunch or luncheon in your home, you can offer her a corsage or a bouquet of flowers, depending on what you think she would prefer.

✧ Decorate with flowers, or create a display of framed photos of Mom and her kids at various stages growing up. Add candles and weave a little lace and ribbon around the photos, and you have a lovely nostalgic centerpiece.

Amusements and activities

In addition to the opening of gifts, you may want to add one of these activities to your Mother's Day celebration:

✧ A nostalgic video show, consisting of old photos, home movies, and video-tapes that have been spliced together on a single videotape. Gather up all the heart-tugging photos you can find of Mom with you when you were a baby, or Mom with her arms around your brother when his team won the regional basketball finals, or Mom holding her new granddaughter in the hospital right after she was born. Moms are sentimental creatures, so you're guaranteed to bring a tear to her eye as she views this tape. Of course, the tape will be given to her as a gift to take home and enjoy repeatedly.

✧ Give your mom a "certificate of honor" or a "special achievement" award. These can be hand-printed on parchment paper or created on your computer by using one of the many publishing programs available.

✧ Another poignant activity is to have each child read a poem he or she has composed in advance or talk about a favorite memory the child has of the mother being honored.

Edibles

✧ If you decide to cook, note that mothers seem to appreciate elegant luncheons and Victorian tea parties. See Chapter 109 for menu ideas.

Tips – There is nothing that pleases Mom more than being surrounded by her children, not only on Mother's Day but on any day of the year. So, whether you plan a casual picnic or take her to the Four Seasons restaurant for its spectacular buffet, the fact that you've given up your Sunday to spend time with her and shower her with love is what really counts.

– A note to Dads: If your children are young and you're trying to plan a party for Mom on their behalf, what she'll appreciate most are a few cards or gifts the children have made themselves. You may also want to buy her a corsage for the big day—this will mean a lot, especially if you're all going to church together, followed by a visit to her favorite sit-down restaurant (McDonald's doesn't count!).

– This is a day for hugs!

21

MEMORIAL DAY

Memorial Day is celebrated on the last Monday in May. It honors all members of the armed forces killed during a war. It is a day of pride and solemn reflection. It is also a day that announces the beginning of summer, a time for our activities to migrate outdoors.

Invitation ideas

✧ Handprint or computer-generate the invitation. Attach a tiny American flag to the invitation, tying it to one corner with a narrow red ribbon. (You can obtain these flags through a party supply store or catalog. See Resources.)

Attire

✧ Casual, of course!

Ambiance

✧ Go for a red, white, and blue theme—American flags flown at half-mast and red, white, and blue crepe-paper streamers, balloons, tablecloths, and plastic tableware.

✧ Create a centerpiece of red paper poppies in a white bowl with blue ribbons.

Amusements and activities

✧ Play old-fashioned picnic games, such as flag football, Frisbee flying disc contests, softball, tug-of-war, raw egg toss, three-legged races, horseshoes, volleyball, etc.

✧ Play recorded music of patriotic songs.

Edibles

✧ Memorial Day is synonymous with picnics and barbecues. Plan a potluck picnic lunch (ask for "patriotic" foods, such as red watermelon, red gelatin salad, red strawberries, etc.) or a traditional barbecue.

✧ Have plenty of refreshing drinks on hand—soda, lemonade, iced tea, ice-cold beer, etc.

22

FATHER'S DAY

Father's Day was made a permanent U.S. holiday in 1972. It falls on the third Sunday in June. It's a day to honor our fathers by giving them gifts and mushy, sentimental cards. Another way to honor Dad is to prepare his favorite meal.

Ambiance

✧ Use a "hunting lodge" theme to decorate the dining room—use a deep, rich burgundy or hunter green tablecloth and napkins, and wood or pewter serving bowls and accessories.

✧ Create a table centerpiece with an arrangement of Dad's mementos.

Amusements and activities

✧ Present Dad with thoughtful gifts and cards, along with a few humorous gifts, such as tacky or goofy ties (try your local thrift shop).

✧ Each child can decorate a solid-colored baseball cap for Dad, using felt-tip markers to create pictures of Dad's favorite hobby and writing Dad's nickname across the bill.

✧ Dad will appreciate a nostalgic video show as much as Mom does on Mother's Day (see Chapter 20).

✧ Have each child relate a favorite memory of Dad from his or her childhood. Put all these memories into writing and bind them as a gift for Dad. I heard of one family whose children made lists called "20 Things I Learned From My Father." These lists were read aloud, including one from a grown child who wasn't able to attend.

Edibles

✧ Serve your Dad's favorite meal (if you're not sure what that is, ask him.)

✧ Make or order a cake that depicts Dad's favorite sport (fly-fishing or golf, for example).

Tips – Whatever you decide to do for Dad, he'll appreciate it, just as long as he has your undivided attention for one day of the year. The fact that you've given up your Sunday to spend it with him is what really counts.

– Moms: If your children are young, have them make homemade gifts or cards for Dad—they will mean more than anything store-bought will.

– Be sure Dad gets lots of hugs—even grown sons can break down and hug their Dad once a year!

23

FOURTH OF JULY

The Fourth of July holiday celebrates the signing of the Declaration of Independence on July 4, 1776. It is the granddaddy of all patriotic holidays and calls for a granddaddy of a celebration—the loudest, happiest, most colorful party of the summer!

Invitation ideas

✧ Attach your invitations to palm-sized American flags. Ask your guests to wear patriotically decorated hats.

Ambiance

✧ Greet your guests with a six-foot-tall stuffed Uncle Sam, available through Sally Distributors for about $6 (see Resources).

✧ Go crazy with red, white, and blue—in everything from the balloons to the checkered tablecloth to the crepe-paper streamers to American flags.

✧ If you want to wall off certain sections of your yard, do it by stringing red, white, or blue quilts or colorful sheets from tree to tree using clothespins.

✧ Half of a watermelon with small American flags inserted into it makes a fun centerpiece. (You can obtain these flags through a party supply store or catalog. See Resources.)

✧ Another centerpiece idea: Place four-inch pots of blooming red geraniums inside white paper lunch sacks, and roll down the top of each sack to create a "collar." Tie a two-inch wide blue ribbon "necktie" around each collar.

Amusements and activities

✧ Hold a parade to show off the guests' decorated hats. Have them march to a recorded John Philip Souza march. Give awards for the most patriotic, the most creative, etc.

- ✧ If laws permit, shoot off a few fireworks after dark, or light sparklers. Provide children with harmless "fireworks"-blown-up balloons for them to sit on until they pop.

- ✧ Travel en masse to view a local fireworks show.

- ✧ Have the guests take turns cranking an old-fashioned ice-cream maker.

- ✧ Hold a karaoke contest (see Chapter 96).

Edibles

- ✧ Have an old-fashioned Fourth of July picnic, with fried chicken, barbecued hot dogs and hamburgers, corn-on-the-cob, watermelon, baked beans, potato and macaroni salads, homemade berry pies, etc.

- ✧ Be sure to have coolers or tubs filled with ice, canned sodas, and plenty of beer.

- ✧ For dessert, serve ice cream and a cake decorated with American flags and sparklers. Turn off all the lights, and light the sparklers before serving.

24

LABOR DAY

Labor Day, the first Monday in September, is a legal holiday established as a tribute to working people. It is a day for parades, picnics, barbecues, and much-deserved, relaxing time away from the office. It also marks the end of the summer season, a chance for one last fling before cool weather sets in.

Invitation ideas

✧ Attach the invitation to a help-wanted page from your newspaper

Ambiance

✧ Decorate with red, white, and blue flags, banners, and posters

✧ Create a table centerpiece from workers' tools (a plumber's helper, wrenches, hammers, saws, paint brushes, etc.).

Amusements and activities

✧ Prior to the party, attend a Labor Day parade, a sports event, or visit the zoo together.

✧ Play softball, volleyball, horseshoes, or flag football.

Edibles

✧ Serve the menu for a Good Old-Fashioned Picnic (see Chapter 79), but instead of paper plates, provide lunch buckets and brown bags.

25

OKTOBERFEST

Oktoberfest is a traditional German festival that began October 17, 1810 to celebrate the wedding of King Ludwig I of Bavaria. It's a joyful, spirited celebration with seemingly endless polka dancing, loud singing, sausage eating, and beer consumption—a very lively party!

Invitation ideas

✧ Attach the invitations to German travel brochures, preferably showing an Oktoberfest scene.

✧ Wrap the invitations around cans of German beer and hand-deliver.

Attire

✧ Males may wear lederhosen (short leather pants) with suspenders, low-cut leather hiking boots, peasant shirts, and Tirolean hats.

✧ Females may wear white Tirolean peasant blouses with full skirts and embroidered vests, or traditional dimdl dresses.

Ambiance

✧ Hang German flags.

✧ Display German and Bavarian travel posters.

✧ Incorporate the colors of the German flag: black, red, and gold.

✧ Arrange flowers in German beer steins.

✧ Decorate the table with cuckoo clocks and Hummel figurines.

Amusements

✧ Have lively polka music greet your guests as they arrive.

◇ Dance the polka. Rent a dance floor if necessary.

◇ Hire Bavarian folk dancers to entertain.

◇ If you can't find any dancers, ask someone to play polkas on an accordion.

◇ Play soccer.

Edibles

◇ See Chapter 110 for a German menu and recipes.

TIP – Raid the imported foods department at your local supermarket or deli for German food delicacies.

26

Halloween

Halloween is the evening of October 31. The word *Halloween* is actually a shortened version of the holiday's original name, "Allhallows Eve"; it is the eve of All Saints' Day, or "Allhallows." It has evolved from an annual church festival to a day of merrymaking, masquerading, fascination with all things spooky, and celebrating autumn.

Invitation ideas

✧ Send each guest a mask with an invitation attached. Ask your guests to wear costumes and/or masks to the party.

✧ Cut pieces of black poster board into bat shapes. Write the invitation on a sheet of paper, paste it on the back of the bat, and mail. Be sure to ask the guests to arrive in costume.

Attire

✧ Costumes or masks.

✧ Greet your guests at the door wearing a Halloween costume or the scariest rubber mask you can find. Or wrap yourself up from head to toe with gauze bandages or strips of old white sheets and answer the door as "the mummy."

Ambiance

✧ String tiny white light strands across your front porch, or from tree to tree, in a "spider web" design. Add big black spiders (available at party supply stores, or make your own from black felt).

✧ Decorate your entryway with sack pumpkins—orange and black trash bags stuffed with leaves or crushed newspapers, obtainable from a party supply store or the seasonal section of a supermarket or variety store. Hang ghosts from tree limbs and a black and white paper skeleton on the front door.

✧ Cut six-foot strips of black and orange crepe paper. Hang them all around the room—from a fishing line secured along the edge where the walls meet the ceiling. This will cover the walls with fluttering strips of color.

✧ Arrange cattails, milkweed, and dried pods, along with any weeds you can find, in a wicker basket. Add gourds, small pumpkins, and squashes around the base of the basket.

✧ Suspend black bats cut from construction paper from the ceiling.

✧ Decorate the room with sprayed cobwebs, orange and black balloons, crepe-paper streamers, and scary pumpkins.

✧ Darken the room except for black-and-orange candles or jack-o-lanterns.

✧ Cover the top of your serving table with a ghost with a head, arms, and a puffy body—made out of a white sheet filled with crushed tissue paper. Place serving dishes on the flat parts of the ghost.

Amusements and activities

✧ Hold a pumpkin-decorating contest. Provide one large pumpkin and 30 plastic toothpicks per guest, plus plenty of materials for creating different parts of the pumpkin's face. For example, for the ears, provide fallen leaves, mushrooms, pipe cleaners, and radishes; for the eyes: mushrooms, radishes, apple slices, and whole cranberries; for the eyebrows or a mustache and beard: licorice strips, orange rind, and steel wool; for the lips: apple peels, pipe cleaners, and red pepper rings; for the teeth: mini-marshmallows, candy corn, and colored pushpins; for the nose: small pears, carrots, Brussels sprouts, cucumbers, a cork, and celery; and for the hair: lettuce leaves, yarn, and green beans.

Other items that might be fun to use as "accessories" for the pumpkin include straw hats, corncob pipes, silk flowers, hair wigs, mop heads, bandannas, scarves, jewelry, and eyeglasses made out of pipe-cleaner. Amazingly, every pumpkin will have its own personality *and* will add to your festive Halloween decor!

✧ Videotape all the festivities and show the tape at the end of the party.

✧ Go on a Halloween hay ride—it's fun, frightening, and gives the guests a chance to show off their costumes! Hay rides are usually held at large garden centers or farm stands.

Edibles

✧ Hollow out small pumpkins to use as serving bowls for snacks and appetizers, such as Party Gorp and Snack Mix (see Chapter 107) or chips and dips and Halloween candies.

✧ If you include a light supper, refer to the suggested menus in Chapter 108.

✧ Serve caramel apples for dessert. You'll need:

1 small apple per guest

2 pounds caramels for every 10 apples

4 tablespoons water

1 cup chopped peanuts

1 wooden skewer per apple

Place apples in foil cupcake liners. Remove the apple stems, and insert skewers. Melt caramel with water in microwave until smooth and creamy. Dip the apples in the caramel mixture, roll in chopped peanuts, return to the cupcake liners, and refrigerate until ready to serve.

✧ Make "witches' brew." Combine pineapple juice and scoops of orange sherbet. Pour in ginger ale and watch it bubble and foam. Instead of adding ice, float a fake hand in the mixture. Freeze a plastic glove filled with water and secured at the wrist with a rubber band. When ready to use, dip briefly in warm water, slide the hand out, and add it to the witches' brew.

Tip – For something a little different, plan a Halloween party around one of the other themes in this book. For example: Polynesian Halloween Luau (see Chapter 77), Halloween Karaoke Party (see Chapter 96), Halloween Progressive Dinner (see Chapter 84), Halloween Block Party (see Chapter 101), Halloween Wine-Tasting Party (see Chapter 81), etc.

– For costume ideas, see *The Halloween Costume Book* by Katharine Thornton and *The Halloween Book* by Jack Macguire (see Resources).

Special tips for children's Halloween parties

Sometimes it's safer—and a lot more fun—to have an at-home Halloween party for the children than to have them go trick-or-treating around the neighborhood. It can be a lively, fun, scary, or exciting party that actually results in more take-home "tricks and treats" than going door-to-door.

Ambiance

✧ At each place setting, as a party favor, place a ghost made out of a large round lollipop wrapped in white tissue. Tie at the neck with a black ribbon, and draw large ghostly eyes on the tissue with black marker.

Amusements and activities

✧ Hold a costume parade. Have the children parade around the house, yard, or neighborhood, showing off their costumes. Give prizes for scariest, most creative, cutest, etc.

✧ Let the children bob for apples. Fill a large tub with water and small apples. Give each child one chance to grab an apple in his or her teeth (no hands allowed). This is messy (which is probably why the children love them), so cover the floor with plastic beforehand.

✧ Play the Mr. Pumpkin Musical Chairs game (see Chapter 57).

✧ Have an apple-biting contest. Suspend apples from the ceiling with strings. Ask the children to place their hands behind their backs and at a given signal begin to bite their apples. The object is to bite the apple down as close to the core as possible. The difficulty, of course, is to keep the apple from swinging around when taking bites. The child who has chewed his or her apple closest to the core at the end of three minutes wins.

✧ Hold the Mr. Pumpkin Contest described in Chapter 57.

✧ Play Old Dead Joe's Cave—a deliciously scary activity for the older kids. Set up a darkened room ahead of time, and place "Old Dead Joe's body parts" in bowls around the room. Here's how to make the body parts:

✦ **Guts:** Fill a large bowl with wet, slimy noodles.

✦ **Eyes:** Put two large grapes in a small, shallow bowl of water.

✦ **Teeth:** Fill a metal pot or bowl with small rocks or candy corn.

✦ **Hair:** Set a wig on a wig stand.

✦ **Tongue:** Place a piece of raw liver in a shallow bowl of warm water.

✦ **Bones:** Use old steak bones or any kind of bones.

✦ **Ears:** Use two large leaves of an artichoke with the sharp tips cut off.

✦ **Nose:** Use a raw potato carved into the shape of a nose.

✦ **Blood:** Fill a crock pot with warm tomato juice.

Blindfold the children who are brave enough to enter the "cave." Holding a flashlight, lead them one at a time from bowl to scary bowl, telling them which body part is there and asking them to dip their hands into it. The rest of the children sit quietly and listen intently to the screams and squeals of the children being led through the cave. Have a towel ready to wrap around each child's hands after he or she has dipped them into the fake blood. As you exit, keep up the act, saying, "Hurry, Jimmy, let's wash the blood off in the sink," "Don't let the blood drip on the floor," etc.

✧ Go trick-or-treating at a shopping mall that is providing Halloween entertainment for children or to a local church or school providing festivities.

✧ Tell ghost stories. Turn the lights off and have the storyteller hold a flashlight under his or her chin as he tells the stories. (See *Best Ghost Stories* and *The Collected Ghost Stories of Mrs. J. H. Riddell* in Resources.)

✧ Videotape the festivities and show the tape at the end of the party. The children will especially love the part about "Old Dead Joe."

Edibles

✧ Hot dogs, chili, potato chips, soda, Halloween candies, and Old Dead Joe's favorite Cupcake Spiders (see Chapter 113).

✧ Old Dead Joe's favorite Worm Cake, made by topping a chocolate sheet cake with crumbled Oreo cookies and inserting gummy worms so they look as if they're crawling out of the cake.

27

Thanksgiving or Harvest Dinner

Thanksgiving Day is an annual holiday observed on the fourth Thursday of November as a day of giving thanks and feasting. It commemorates the Pilgrims' celebration of the good harvest of 1621. It's a family holiday—a time to gather together at a table lavishly spread with traditional harvest foods.

Invitation ideas

✧ Invitations to Thanksgiving dinner are usually extended in person or over the telephone. As a twist, write the invitations on thank-you cards, enclosing "I'm thankful for..." sheets for the guests to fill out and bring to the dinner.

Ambiance

✧ Set the table with your finest china, crystal, silver, and linen.

✧ Create a centerpiece by filling a horn-of-plenty basket (cornucopia) to overflowing—with nuts, apples, gourds, Indian corn, fall leaves, and silk or fresh mums.

✧ Frame your centerpiece with a pair of off-white candles set in silver or crystal candle holders.

✧ Incorporate harvest colors into your decor: browns, golds, reds, yellows, and oranges.

✧ Decorate the room with baskets of fruit, a glass or porcelain turkey, and Thanksgiving decorations your children may have made at home or at school.

Amusements and activities

❖ Steer the conversation toward happy memories of Thanksgivings of the past and blessings of the present. Thanksgiving dinner should be a prolonged feast conducive to warm, fuzzy feelings of love and family.

❖ Ask guests to read their "I'm thankful for…" sheets around the table. Ask a family member to videotape each guest reading from his or her list.

❖ Ask a man to dress up as a Pilgrim or a woman as an Indian maiden and to read a Thanksgiving story to the children. (Ask the children's section librarian at your local library for story suggestions.)

❖ After dinner, watch football games, play a few board games, and end the day with a walk around the block in the crisp, early evening air.

Edibles

❖ Serve a traditional Thanksgiving dinner, with the following foods:

✦ Turkey.

✦ Dressing.

✦ Mashed white potatoes.

✦ Gravy.

✦ Creamed onions.

✦ Cranberry sauce and relishes.

✦ Baked yam casserole (sliced yams alternating with layers of drained crushed pineapple, brown sugar dotted with butter, and walnut slices, topped with a layer of mini-marshmallows and baked at 350 degrees for one hour).

✦ Molded gelatin salad and/or Waldorf salad (chopped celery, apples, and walnuts, topped with a dressing of mayonnaise mixed with enough pineapple juice to give it a creamy texture).

✦ Cloverleaf or crescent rolls.

✦ Pecan pie.

✦ Pumpkin pie.

28

HANUKKAH

Hanukkah is a celebration of the Jewish victory over the Syrians more than 2,000 years ago when the Maccabees recaptured Jerusalem. When the Jewish people returned to rededicate their Temple, they discovered a miracle: A single cruse of oil, sufficient only for one day, still burned after eight days. Because of this miracle, Hanukkah has become known as the "Festival of Lights" and is celebrated for eight days during December.

Although this celebration is happy and joyous, it also has solemn significance to the Jewish people as they rededicate themselves to the ideals of the Maccabees: religious freedom and political liberty under God.

The "hanukkiah," a menorah or candelabra that holds eight Hanukkah candles, is the central symbol of the celebration. The lighted candles are traditionally placed in the windows of Jewish homes, proclaiming the miracle to every passerby. On the first night of Hanukkah a single candle is lit, and an additional candle is lit each night that follows. The eight candles represent: faith, freedom, courage, love, charity, integrity, knowledge, and peace.

Invitation ideas

✧ Handcrafted invitations are very special. Make them in the shape of a dreidel (a top with four sides, on each of which is a Hebrew letter), a menorah, or any Jewish symbol.

Ambiance

✧ In addition to the display of the menorah, Jewish homes are decorated with Hanukkah motifs.

✧ The color scheme is white, silver, and blue.

Activities

✧ Prayers and blessings are said each night as a candle is lit.

✧ Children and adults exchange gifts. Parents and grandparents often distribute Hanukkah gelt, real coins or gold-foil wrapped chocolate coins, to the younger children. Parents present special gifts to their children each night of Hanukkah, usually saving the best gifts until the last night.

✧ Hanukkah games are played, including a traditional game played with a dreidel, a spinning top.

✧ Hanukkah songs are sung, including two favorites: "My Dreidel" and "Hanukkah O Hanukkah."

✧ Adults play card games or table games while the children are involved with games and activities of their own.

✧ The older generation tells stories and presents riddles to the children.

Edibles

✧ Traditional Jewish foods are served, including a special delicacy—potato latkes.

Tip – Visit your public library to find books to help you with your planning. Look for *The Book of Religious Holidays and Celebrations* by Marguerite Ickis, which contains the words and music for many Hanukkah songs, including the songs mentioned previously.

29

CHRISTMAS

Christmas day always falls on December 25. It's a warm, fuzzy holiday celebrating Christ's birth—a time of loving, sharing, and lots of hugs and kisses, especially when you're caught under mistletoe!

Invitation ideas

✧ Use a black felt-tip marker to print the invitation on a bright red Christmas ornament, which you should hand-deliver or mail in a carefully packed box. Or attach any Christmas ornament to a hand-printed or computer-generated invitation.

✧ Attach a candy cane to a store-bought, fill-in-the-blanks party invitation.

Attire

✧ Encourage your guests to wear bright red and green clothing.

Ambiance

If it's at your home, a Christmas party is one of the easiest parties to host because you can take advantage of any decorations you already have on display in your yard and house. Nevertheless, here are some additional decorating tips:

✦ Decorate your home with traditional Christmas symbols: evergreen garlands draped over the mantel and doorways, an abundance of lighted red candles, a nativity scene, evergreen or pine cone wreaths, a Yule log embellished with holly and mistletoe, a large lighted Christmas candle displayed in a front window, and, of course, a lighted Christmas tree.

✦ Be sure to hang plenty of mistletoe from ceilings and doorways.

✦ Cover your serving tables with bright red or green felt.

✦ Fill the house with fragrance by simmering cinnamon sticks in a potpourri pot.

✦ Decorate the entryway, bathrooms, and a few tables with containers of poinsettias or forced bulbs, such as amaryllis, hyacinth, and narcissus, wrapped with red Mylar polyester film and tied with gold ribbons.

✦ If you are serving a buffet meal, skirt and swag your table with table linens or solid-colored sheets. By "skirting," I mean draping the linen so that it touches the floor on the sides and one end of the table. By "swagging," I mean draping a second layer of fabric over the table and gathering it up every few feet with ribbons, evergreenery, or Christmas decorations.

✦ Create a table centerpiece by filling a wicker basket with pyracantha berries and six or eight white candles of various heights, or arrange giftwrapped boxes around sprays of evergreen boughs dotted with tiny white Christmas tree lights.

✦ Wrap Christmas napkins around the silverware and tie with gold metallic ribbon.

✦ If you have table favors, wrap them as Christmas gifts and set one in the center of each place setting.

Activities

✧ If your celebration is a family party that takes place on Christmas Eve, you can light the candles on the Advent wreath, a circle of greenery around which four candles—usually three pink and one purple—are equally spaced. (Traditionally, each pink candle is lighted on each of the first three Sundays before Christmas and the purple candle is lighted on the last Sunday before Christmas.)

✧ Another family tradition is to attend a Christmas Eve or Christmas morning church service together, followed by opening gifts. (Of course, the small children believe their gifts are from Santa Claus.)

✧ The guests can caravan together to see holiday lights, returning for Christmas wassail (see Chapter 112) and dessert. Send the children to the den to watch holiday videos and enjoy their own snack bar while the adults visit. (Hint: Children love their own supply of maraschino cherries and fancy cocktail umbrellas.)

✧ Go caroling en masse around your neighborhood.

✧ Have an open house, with neighbors coming and going throughout the evening.

✧ Ask your guests to bring wrapped Christmas ornaments, with no gift tags. Stack them together, and let each guest select a gift from the pile. Ask the guests to open the gifts, one at a time. After a guest has opened a gift, give him or her the option of keeping the gift, selecting another from the pile, or "robbing" another guest of his gift. Each guest has three "steals" until the last gift has been opened. This idea works with white elephant and other types of gifts as well; limit the dollar amount to $5 or $10 per gift.

Edibles

✧ A traditional sit-down Christmas dinner usually consists of:
  ✦ Baked ham, roast beef, or turkey.
  ✦ Dressing (with turkey).
  ✦ Mashed white potatoes or baked yams
  ✦ Gravy.
  ✦ Cranberry sauce and relishes.
  ✦ Creamed onions.
  ✦ Molded red gelatin salad and/or Waldorf salad (chopped celery, apples, and walnuts, topped with a dressing of mayonnaise mixed with enough pineapple juice to give it a creamy texture).
  ✦ Cloverleaf or crescent rolls.
  ✦ Lemon meringue pie.
  ✦ A variety of Christmas cookies.
  ✦ Homemade fudge.
  ✦ Pecan pie.
  ✦ Pumpkin pie.
  ✦ A fine wine for toasting.

✧ A lighter Christmas buffet may consist of:
  ✦ Smoked fish, including trout and salmon.
  ✦ Miniature loaves of cranberry or nut bread.
  ✦ Cheeses and crackers.
  ✦ Apple pie.
  ✦ Christmas cookies.
  ✦ A fine wine for toasting.

✧ A potluck buffet is a popular option, as well as a Christmas progressive dinner with dessert and holiday coffees served at the last house.

Tips – How about planning a tailgate party in the parking lot of a mall after a hectic day of Christmas shopping? (See Chapter 82.)

– You can host a Christmas party *after* Christmas, during the lull between Christmas Day and New Year's Day.

30

KWANZAA

Kwanzaa is a seven-day African-American tradition observed from December 26 through January 1. It celebrates and reaffirms traditional African-American values and principles. Created by Dr. Maulana Karenga in 1966, the holiday is based on traditional harvest festivals practiced in Africa. In fact, the word *kwanzaa* is Swahili for "first fruits of the harvest." African-Americans have many reasons for celebrating the holiday, including their desire to achieve the following goals:

1. To bring African-American families and communities together to celebrate the fruits of their labors.
2. To pay tribute to ancestors.
3. To give thanks.
4. To evaluate their contributions to family and community.
5. To set goals for the upcoming year.

There are seven important symbols of Kwanzaa:

1. **Mkeka** *(m–kay–cah)*: A straw mat, representing the foundation on which all else rests. All other Kwanzaa symbols are placed upon it.
2. **Kinara** *(kee–nah–rah)*: A candleholder that holds seven candles. It represents the original stalk or ancestry from which African-Americans sprung.
3. **Mishumaa saba** *(mee–shoo–maah sah–bah)*: Seven candles representing the seven principles—three red, three green, one black.
4. **Muhindi** *(moo–heen–dee)*: Corn symbolizing the offspring and the challenges and hopes children bring. One ear of corn is placed on the mat for each child in the household.
5. **Mazao** *(mah–zah–oh)*: Fruits, nuts, and vegetables representing the rewards of collective labor (fruits of the harvest).

6. **Kikombe cha umoja** *(kee–coam–bay chah–oo–moe–jah)*: The unity cup used to pour the libation in honor of ancestors.

7. **Zawadi** *(sah–wah–dee)*: Meaningful gifts that may be exchanged on each of the seven days or saved and presented on the last day of Kwanzaa. Preferably, these gifts are handcrafted and have an educational or functional purpose, encouraging growth and self-development during the coming year.

Invitation ideas

✧ Handcraft the invitations using construction paper in the traditional Kwanzaa colors: black, green, and red. Trim with raffia or ribbons in the same colors.

Attire

✧ Encourage family and friends to wear garments made from traditional African kente cloth.

Ambiance

✧ Purchase a bolt of African fabric (preferably in Kwanzaa colors), and use it to decorate your room and table.

✧ Because the first day of Kwanzaa is the day following Christmas and most African-American families celebrate both, decorate your tree with African products such as cowrie shell stars, carved gourds, or straw fans.

✧ Display the mkeka, the straw mat mentioned above. Place the other Kwanzaa symbols upon it.

✧ Display bowls filled with kernels of corn, symbolizing the community's children.

✧ Display quilts that have been made and passed down from generation to generation.

✧ Borrow or purchase African artwork (visit your local import store), and display it around the room.

✧ Display the kinara (see above).

✧ Fill baskets and bowls with the abundance of the harvest: fruits, nuts, and vegetables, with the emphasis on the Kwanzaa colors.

Tip — Paint nuts red and green and tie red bows to green apples.

Amusements and activities

✧ Provide a background of traditional African music.

✧ Share meaningful songs, stories, poems, or dances that recall the traditions and accomplishments of African-Americans.

✧ Ask family members to bring pieces of fabric for a commemorative quilt that can be created for the following year's Kwanzaa celebration. Ask them to explain why the pieces are significant and who wore the clothes or used the items they came from.

✧ Ask a child to light that day's candle on the kinara.

✧ Videotape the family members and guests as they tell about their accomplishments of the past year and their goals for the year to come.

Edibles

✧ Many adults choose the option of fasting until the traditional Kwanzaa feast is served, which consists only of fresh fruits, nuts, vegetables, and juices.

✧ The kikombe cha umoja (unity cup) is a communal cup used to serve the juice; pass it from guest to guest.

Tip   – I recommend these books to help you plan your Kwanzaa celebration: *Kwanzaa* by David A. Anderson, *Let's Celebrate Kwanzaa* by Helen David Thompson, *Kwanzaa* by Deborah M. Newton, and *Kwanzaa: Everything You Wanted to Know But Didn't Know Where to Ask* by Cedric McClester. See Resources for more information.

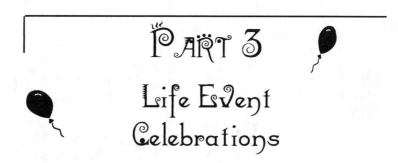

Part 3

Life Event Celebrations

"Let the celebration reflect your love and care for the guest of honor."

In each person's life, certain milestones should be celebrated, including birthdays, weddings, births, and wedding anniversaries.

These celebrations should be joyous retreats from the often monotonous, everyday workaday world. So why not commemorate each milestone in an especially memorable way? You can do this by personalizing a party in such a way that the honored guest will feel loved and appreciated.

Customizing a life event celebration is easier than you may think, as you will discover in the chapters that follow.

31

WELCOME BABY PARTIES

A Welcome Baby Party is a celebration of the fruit of a couple's love—a baby. It might take place following the baby's christening or baptism, or on the day Mommy and baby arrive home from the hospital. It may also be in the form of a baby shower scheduled a month or so before the baby is due.

There's a definite trend toward co-ed baby showers that are more festive and party-oriented and less like the traditional shower (a low-key gathering centered around the opening of gifts by the expectant mother). The nice thing about any modern-day baby shower is that there are no strict rules to follow, and it may be hosted by anyone—friend, relative, or co-worker.

I've included a few tips for gift displays, invitations, and baby shower games. Then, I describe unique ideas for specific party themes, followed by activities. The themes are divided into two types: "Mommy parties" (traditionally female parties) and co-ed parties.

Invitation ideas

✧ To make baby-diaper shaped invitations, cut triangular pieces from stationery, construction paper, or fabric. Fold into a trifold diaper, fastening with a safety pin or diaper pin.

✧ Write your party information on narrow tags that can be attached to chocolate or bubble gum cigars. Tie the cigars with pink, blue, or yellow ribbons.

✧ Send actual or toy baby bottles with an invitation tucked inside or filled with gumdrops with the invitation tied to the bottlenecks.

✧ Use baby talk to record the invitation, worded as if from the unborn baby, saying something such as this: "Hewwo. My name is William John Carlson, Junior. I haven't been born yet, but Mr. and Mrs. Hansen are giving me a party on July 23rd at 7 p.m. My mommy and daddy—their names are Ginny and Bill—are so excited—my daddy even bought a box of cigars...."

Anyway, if you can come to my party, you're supposed to let Ginny know—call her—555-2344. I wuv you." Wrap the cassette tape with blue tissue paper, tie it with ribbon, and mail it in a padded envelope.

✧ Make your own hospital bracelets. Cut white poster board into strips. Print the party invitation on both sides of each strip, cover with contact paper, and form into a bracelet by stapling or taping ends together.

✧ Plastic baby bibs can be used as invitations by writing the information across the front with permanent marker. Fold and enclose in envelopes.

Ambiance

Use the gifts the guests bring as a decorating tool. Don't just set them on a table in the corner of the room—it's much nicer to display them in a special way, creating a focal point for arriving guests. Here are a few ideas:

✦ Place the gifts under an enormous golf umbrella covered with satin fabric and ribbons.

✦ Arrange the gifts in a decorated plastic or wicker laundry basket.

✦ Pile gifts in a toy chest, which may double as a hostess gift.

✦ Arrange the gifts in a decorated child's red wagon.

Mommy parties

✧ **Family Heirloom Shower**

This is a party attended by the female family members: mothers, aunts, great-aunts, grandmothers, great-grandmothers, and so forth—and the theme of the party is passing down family heirlooms or antiques in honor of the new baby.

✦ Items often passed down from generation to generation are:

- Christening dress.
- Silver baby spoon.
- Music box.
- Silver tooth-fairy box.
- Handknit or crocheted blanket.
- Silver hairbrush.
- Silver haircut box.
- Silver or porcelain picture frames.

✦ Use a family tree motif for your decorations. Cut trees out of construction paper or poster board for invitations and name tags, and decorate a silk ficus tree with photos of each family member and a miniature cradle ornament with the name of the expected baby on it.

✦ Transfer old family photos and home movies onto a videotape that can be shown as entertainment.

✧ **Teddy Bear Shower**

This, of course, is a shower with a teddy bear theme. Here are some ideas for this type of party:

✦ Attach miniature teddy bears to the invitations, name tags, or place cards.

+ Round up all the teddy bears you can find and use as decorations.
+ Diaper the teddy bears, using big diaper pins.
+ Decorate the cake with tiny stuffed teddy bears.

Tip – If you can't come up with enough teddy bears to carry out your theme, use any stuffed animal theme that will work.

Choo-Choo Train Party

Here are some tips for a train-theme party:
+ Cut construction paper or poster board into caboose shapes to use as invitations, name tags, or place cards.
+ An electric train can serve as the table centerpiece, or it can run on tracks that have been creatively placed around the platters of food on a buffet table.
+ Using yarn, connect boxes of animal crackers together to form trains, and set them at each place setting as party favors

Tip – Wear an engineer's cap and use a wooden train whistle as you conduct the games.

Time-of-Day Shower

For this shower, ask each guest to bring a gift to be used a certain time of day.
+ Examples of gifts appropriate for different times of the day include:
  ◆ Bath time (9 a.m.): a bath thermometer.
  ◆ Lunchtime (noon): a tipper cup.
  ◆ Nap time (2 p.m.): sleepers.
  ◆ Play time (4 p.m.): stuffed animals.
+ A grandfather clock can serve as the main party decoration. Decorate it with ribbons and baby-related items.
+ Attach toy wrist watches to the invitations

Mother Goose Shower

Guests for this shower arrive prepared to recite a nursery rhyme or sing a lullaby of their choice, which is recorded onto an audiocassette or video-tape for the baby.
+ Decorate the table with Mother Goose characters—stuffed animals or Mother Goose decorations available from a party supply store.
+ Encourage the guests to bring their own musical accompaniment if they would like. Also, let them know that original compositions will receive special recognition (give prizes to those who come prepared with something they have composed themselves). You'll need to round up a good-quality tape recorder, a microphone, and blank tapes.

✧ Stork Shower

A great idea for the hostess who is too busy to create anything, this shower has a theme for which decorations are readily available at party supply stores—storks!

+ Purchase stork invitations, name tags, and table decorations, including large stork posters.
+ Rent a stork for your front yard from a florist or party supply store. After everyone has arrived, bring the stork inside to "watch over" the gifts.

✧ Pamper Mommy Party

This is a special party designed to honor and pamper the Mommy-to-be

+ Make her feel beautiful with a free makeover, compliments of your favorite cosmetics representative; a fresh new hairstyle, compliments of a professional hairstylist; and to-die-for nails, compliments of a professional manicurist.
+ The gifts at this party are for Mommy: a lacy, feminine nightie, a satin robe and slippers, a cover-up, bubble bath, lotions, and perfume. Another great gift idea is a "hospital basket," a basket filled with comforting items for Mommy's hospital stay—books, magazines, gossip tabloids, candy, etc.

✧ Fill-the-Freezer Shower

This is a good party to hold for the mother who's expecting her second or third child, because she probably has the basics and what she really needs is some relief during the first two or three weeks after the baby is born. So, what could be better than to furnish her with frozen homemade casseroles, desserts, breads, etc.?

In addition to the frozen dishes, the guests furnish corresponding recipe cards that are placed in a recipe box to be given to the expectant mother.

✧ Gift Certificate Shower

This is another great idea when the mother is expecting her second or third child: Guests bring gift certificates redeemable for things they will do for the mom, such as:

+ One free evening of babysitting.
+ One complete dinner, delivered to her door.
+ Free membership in a "pie-of-the-month club" (one home-baked pie delivered each month for a year).
+ Three free hours of running errands.
+ One free month of chauffeuring duties (for any older children who need rides to or from school, soccer practice, etc.).
+ A group gift for the couple's "first night on the town" after the baby is born, which can include certificates for one free evening of babysitting, a corsage or boutonniere from a local florist, dinner for two at a nice restaurant, and movie, concert, or theater tickets.

Co-ed parties

✧ **Daddy Come Lately Party**

The gals have a traditional baby shower in one part of the house while the expectant father and the women's spouses or boyfriends play volleyball or horseshoes in the back yard, or watch Monday night football, baseball, or a video in another room. The men join the women for the most important element of the party: food! After the refreshments, present Daddy with a humorous gift basket that contains:

✦ Large pacifier for him.

✦ Over-the-counter caffeine pills for staying awake.

✦ Plastic disposable gloves, a surgical mask, and nose plugs (to use when changing diapers).

✦ His own personal baby bottle (a large animal-feeding bottle purchased from a veterinarian or pet supply store).

✦ Alarm clock for the 2 a.m. feeding.

✦ A humorous coffee mug, T-shirt, or sweatshirt.

✧ **Everyone's Expecting**

This is a tongue-in-cheek type of party where all the guests, including the men, arrive looking pregnant. The message of the party is: "We sympathize with you because we're all going through the same thing." Keep the idea a secret—it should be a surprise to the expectant mother.

Tip   – Suggest that the guests wear big shirts or borrowed maternity clothes over their puffy-pillow tummies. Give awards for their get-ups, such as funniest, most creative, most lifelike, etc.

✧ **A "Room for Baby" Work Party**

This party takes place at the couple's home. Guests wear their "work grubbies," and everyone pitches in to help paint, wallpaper, or decorate the baby's room. The guests' gifts are elbow grease and any supplies they contribute to the cause. Have pizza delivered at "quitting time."

✧ **Seeing Double!**

This shower is for a couple expecting twins.

✦ Put decorations and other party-related items in pairs—two baby dolls or teddy bears as a table centerpiece, twin babies on the invitations, name tags, and place cards, etc.

✦ Gifts are displayed under two umbrellas tied together with ribbons.

✦ Write babies' names on two helium balloons and tie them together.

✦ Mommy's corsage is embellished with two pairs of booties, two rattles, or two miniature baby bottles.

Amusements and activities

✧ **Baby Diapering Contest**

For this game, you will need:
- ✦ One baby doll or teddy bear.
- ✦ Two diaper pins.
- ✦ One cloth diaper.
- ✦ A watch with a second hand.

The guests take turns diapering the doll or bear. For fairness, you can require experienced diaper-changing women to wear mittens while the men do not. The person with the fastest time wins. Contestants are disqualified if the diaper falls off when the doll or bear is held up and wiggled in the air.

Another variation of this game is to have the contestant wear a blindfold while diapering the doll or bear.

✧ **Mystery Baby Food Game**

For this game, you will need:
- ✦ 10 jars of baby food.
- ✦ One plastic spoon per guest.
- ✦ Paper and pencil for each guest.

Cover the labels of 10 jars of baby food. Number them 1 to 10. Furnish each guest with paper, a pencil, and a small plastic spoon. Pass the jars around the room, one at a time. The guests must identify the food by sight, smell, and taste. (Each guest is instructed to dip the tip of the spoon into the food.) The guest with the most correct answers wins.

Tip – To make this game challenging, add a few of the new gourmet baby food mixtures, such as apples and chicken and pear and wild blueberry.

✧ **Baby Bottle Race**

For this game, you will need one juice-filled baby bottle per contestant. This is a hilarious game for a co-ed party. "Volunteer" the men to be contestants in this race. The first man to empty his bottle of juice wins. The humor, of course, is that the men are required to "suck their bottles dry" through ordinary baby bottle nipples.

Tip – No cheating allowed! Clever contestants have been known to "accidentally" bite the ends off the nipples.

✧ **The Word Race Game**

For this game, you will need:
- ✦ One sheet of paper per guest.
- ✦ A timer.
- ✦ One pen or pencil per guest.

See who can make the most words from any of the following words: *diaper pins*, the couple's first names, the name of the hospital where the baby will be born, *pacifier*, *baby formula*, *motherhood*.

Set a timer for 10 minutes. The guest with the most words wins.

✧ **The Baby Name Game**

For this game, you will need:

✦ One pen or pencil per guest.　　✦ A timer.

✦ A copy of the following list per guest.

Set the timer for 10 minutes. The guest who matches the most names with their correct meanings wins a prize.

_____ Erin	1. graceful
_____ Trevor	2. gift of the Lord
_____ Darren	3. honey bee
_____ Casey	4. pretty
_____ Matthew	5. peace
_____ Linda	6. prudent
_____ Ann	7. brave
_____ Jason	8. groundskeeper
_____ Garth	9. great
_____ Melissa	10. healer

(Answers: 5. Erin: peace, 6. Trevor: prudent, 9. Darren: great, 7. Casey: brave, 2. Matthew: gift of the Lord, 4. Linda: pretty, 1. Ann: graceful, 10. Jason: healer, 8. Garth: groundskeeper, 3. Melissa: honey bee)

✧ **Baby Word Scramble**

For this game, you will need:

✦ One pen or pencil per guest.　　✦ A timer.

✦ A copy of the following list per quest.

Here is a list of scrambled words having to do with "babies." See who can unscramble the most words in three minutes.

1. YBBA TLOBET _____

2. SARIPED _____

3. IRCB _____

4. TLYEATE _____

5. LRDAEC _____

6. RLUMFAO _____

7. IGRNKCO HRCIA _____

8. KLEBTNA _____

9. TELTAR _____

10. CRIPEIAF _____

(Answers: _baby bottle, diapers, crib, layette, cradle, formula, rocking chair, blanket, rattle, pacifier_)

32

ENGAGEMENT PARTIES

The purpose of an engagement party, of course, is to celebrate the couple's engagement, but it's also a chance for the two families to meet and get to know each other. It can be a formal or informal get-together and hosted and attended by either friends or family. Traditionally, it has been a formal party hosted by the bride's or groom's parents and attended by the couple's families.

In any case, there are two general guidelines when planning an engagement party:

+ Choose a theme appropriate for couples.
+ Discourage intimate gifts. (This is no time to shower the bride with lacy negligees or the groom with something more appropriate for a bachelor party.)

Invitation ideas

✦ For an informal party, run copies of the couple's engagement photo on a color copy machine, onto paper of a heavy stock. Then run these sheets through a copier, printing the party invitation on the back of each photo. Cut each into about 15 irregular pieces to form a jigsaw puzzle. Enclose the pieces in an envelope addressed to each guest. Of course, the guest will have to put the puzzle together in order to figure it out.

✦ For a formal party, send a formal invitation per the guidelines suggested in Chapter 4.

Formal party themes

✦ **Elegant Sit-Down Engagement Dinner**
This party is limited to members of the bride's and groom's families, many of whom have probably never met each other. The menu is usually quite elaborate and served "plate service" or "French service" (see Chapter 109).

Because the meal is so elaborate and has so many courses, it takes up most of the evening. Therefore, the party becomes a "talk party," as opposed to a "game party," and the entertainment may be limited to the bride and groom telling the story of their courtship—how they met, how he proposed, their wedding plans, and so forth.

You may decide to engage the services of professional musicians to perform during the meal service, such as a stringed trio, or if you really want to impress your guests as they enjoy their after-dinner coffee, arrange for a soloist or instrumentalist to present a mini-concert.

Tip   – Hire a limousine to transport the happy couple to your party site.

✧ **Candlelight and Roses Dessert Party**

This is an excellent choice if you would like to host a formal party, but you don't have the time or funds to plan a sit-down dinner at a restaurant. Create ambiance in your home with candles, fresh or silk roses, and lots of swirling tulle netting and delicate ribbons. Add a little more light by stringing tiny white lights along the tables, around the plants or garlands, and over doorways. This theme works best, of course, as an evening affair.

In addition to your own personal favorites, you can use the special desserts described in Chapter 111 and the dessert drinks in Chapter 112.

Because this is also a formal party, you may want to limit the entertainment to soft background music and good conversation, which is what the guests often prefer if they are trying to get to know each other.

If you like the idea of a dessert party, but you prefer one that is less formal, you can use less elaborate decorations and include any of the games or get-acquainted activities described in Chapter 6.

✧ **A Country Garden Party**

This party works best outdoors in an actual garden setting. See Chapter 87.

Informal party themes

✧ **Country-Western Barbecue**

✦ Drag out your cowboy boots, 10-gallon hats, and bandannas, and encourage your guests to get into the spirit, too.

✦ Decorate with lariats, cowboy hats, saddles, branding irons, wagon wheels, potted cactus plants, hay bales, and red-checkered tablecloths.

✦ Rent a dance floor if necessary, and provide live or taped music for a little country-western dancing after you eat. By the time your guests have done a couple of line dances, they'll be into the spirit of the party and providing their own entertainment.

✦ See the Barbecue Bash menu in Chapter 108 and more decorating ideas in Chapter 78.

✧ **Remember When? Party**

Collect memorabilia from the couple's past to use as decorations: baby pictures, little league uniforms, cheerleading pom-poms, old high school or college yearbooks, scrapbooks, pennants, awards, trophies, etc. Dress up two teddy bears (preferably the bride's and groom's own childhood bears, if they still exist). Create a veil for the bride bear out of white tulle netting and a top hat for the groom bear out of black construction paper (they don't have to be perfect—it's the thought that counts!).

If members of the couple's families who have never met attend the party, set up wedding photographs of the bride's and groom's parents, grandparents, aunts and uncles, or brothers and sisters in a corner of a table. This nostalgic corner will be a focal point throughout the party as relatives from both sides gather around to compare wedding fashions and to talk about their own engagements and wedding ceremonies.

You may even be able to add a display of wedding memorabilia, such as the grandmothers' wedding gowns, shoes, hair combs, or bridal veils. If possible, display the gowns on a dressmaker's form or a store mannequin.

Everyone will appreciate a slide or video show.

You can serve any of the informal menus in Chapter 108 or ethnic menus in Chapter 110.

Entertainment

✧ **Remember When? Slide or Video Show**

Round up photos, slides, videos, and home movies of the bride and groom from their babyhood to the present day, arrange them in chronological order, and have them converted to slides or compiled on a single videotape. My family presented one such slide show for my daughter and son-in-law's party. In the slide show, a special feature allowed one picture to gradually dissolve into the next, creating a continuous story. The slide show took place in a darkened room while a friend of ours sang "Sunrise, Sunset" and played guitar. There were many *oohs* and *aahs*, and everyone really seemed to enjoy it, including the bride and groom. (It's a good thing the room was dark, because I dribbled tears all the way through it!)

✧ See Chapter 6 for additional games and activities that are appropriate for an engagement party, such as:
  + The Newlywed Game.
  + Masquerade Race.
  + The Communication Game.
  + The Observation Game.

Tip   – Be prepared to offer engagement toasts.

33

BACHELOR PARTIES

The traditional bachelor party is considered "one last night out with the boys," complete with stale draft beer and a stripper who pops out of a cake. For many grooms, however, this idea sounds about as appealing as helping a buddy move on a hot summer day. One groom, age 26, said that he thinks a person matures a lot in the years immediately after college and is no longer the wide-eyed boy-groom of the past. He said that he's been to his share of wild bachelor parties but that the "go-go girl type of bash has gotten old." He feels there are much more interesting and mature ways to celebrate.

In fact, according to my research and that of other journalists who have interviewed today's grooms, the trend is toward more sports-oriented get-togethers, casino weekends, poker parties, and good old-fashioned roasts. Additionally, the theme is beginning to cross the gender barrier and many are planning "bachelorette" parties, as well.

So, who hosts one of these affairs? Usually the groom, the best man, or the groom's father, although it may be organized by all of the groom's buddies.

Whom should you invite to a bachelor party? All of the adult male members of the wedding party, including the groomsmen and the ushers. Lately, I've heard about several bachelor parties for which the groom's sisters were also invited.

When should you hold it? Traditionally, bachelor parties are held the night before the wedding, although holding one a week or so before the wedding has become more popular. The latter makes more sense to me, because the wedding rehearsal and the rehearsal dinner usually take place on the night before the wedding.

Here are some of the most popular ways to celebrate:

✧ **A roast**

A roast usually follows a sit-down dinner, whether it takes place in a side room of your favorite restaurant or it's a catered meal in someone's home.

The idea is to have a speaker's stand, called a "dais," located at one of the tables. The men take turns telling stories about the groom, "roasting" him by recounting the dumbest or most embarrassing things he's ever done. The key to the success of one of these parties is to be careful that you don't reveal anything too personal or humiliating. This is supposed to be a fun party, not a chance to pull skeletons out of the groom's closet!

+ Be sure to end your "roast" on a sincere, poignant note, saying what a good friend he's been to you, and so on. If you feel comfortable doing so, offer a toast to his bride.

+ If you really want the roast to be a success, try to come up with a surprise guest—one of the groom's old high school buddies, a brother or college friend who traveled a long distance, or a former teacher or professor with an embarrassing story to tell.

✧ Poker Party

An informal night of poker, or any other card game, will make a bachelor party a sure-fire success. Whether they are playing a rousing hearts tournament or a winner-take-all poker game, the men will enjoy the bonding and camaraderie.

Have plenty of food and drink on hand, plus a box of fine cigars. Load up a table with cold cuts, cheeses, breads, condiments, chips and dips, plenty of pretzels and mixed nuts, drinks, and plenty of ice. Make sure everything can be eaten with the hands so the guys won't have to juggle plates and silverware during the competition.

Tip – There's nothing like a night of male bonding to whet a man's appetite, so provide twice as much food as you think they'll eat—and it will probably be just right!

✧ Men's Night Out

Make plans to attend a "guys' movie," a boxing match, a live concert, or a performance by a favorite comedian. On the other hand, you could do what one groom did—take the guys to see the musical "Will Rogers Follies If these ideas seem a little pricey to you, you can always rent a movie or videotaped concert or watch a pay-per-view boxing match in your own family room.

✧ Sports, Sports, Sports

An active, sports-oriented get-together is one of the popular trends in bachelor parties. Play tennis, golf, volleyball, or horseshoes; go bowling; play pool or billiards; or go camping, backpacking, white-water rafting, snow- or water-skiing, or fishing. Athletic events provide a way to blow off a little steam. After all, planning a wedding has become more hectic than ever, and the physical activity is a good stress-reliever for all the guys, but especially for the groom. In fact, the more physical, the better the men seem to like it.

Provide prizes or trophies for first, second, and third place. For a golf tournament, give out prizes for "closest to the hole," "longest drive," and so forth.

Be sure to eat together after the big event, whether that means a hamburger in the clubhouse after golf or tennis, a fast-food run on the way home, or a barbecue beside the water at the end of a day of fishing or rafting.

Oh, by the way, don't forget to bring along a box of good-quality cigars—the latest trend in male bonding!

✧ **Take Me Out to the Ball Game (a.k.a. Tailgate Party)**

Buy box seat tickets and bring your gloves to a professional baseball game. Or round up tickets to watch your favorite football, basketball, or hockey team play a home game. See Chapter 82 for Tailgate Party food ideas.

Tips – One traditional element of a bachelor party is a toast by the groom to his bride. He stands, raises his glass, and says, "To my bride!" Then the men stand and join him in the toast.

– Bachelor parties need very little, if anything, in the way of decorations.

34

WEDDING SHOWERS

Wedding showers include showers given for the bride (bridal showers) or parties for the bride and groom together (co-ed).

Bridal showers

A bridal shower is usually attended by the bride's female family members and close friends, including her maid or matron of honor and bridesmaids. The party is often hosted, in fact, by one of her attendants. The purpose of the party is to "shower" the bride with affection, support, and thoughtful, loving gifts.

Here are popular bridal shower themes:

✧ **Formal Bridal Tea**

A formal bridal tea is the most elegant of all bridal showers. I'm not talking about "high tea," which is actually a hearty supper served around 6 p.m., but a proper afternoon tea.

✦ Pull out your embroidered lace tablecloths, napkins, China tea sets, and sterling silver and use them to decorate your serving table, along with old-fashioned, loosely arranged bouquets of roses and wildflowers.

✦ Arrange a display of parents' and grandparents' wedding photos.

✦ Create a table centerpiece of antique bride dolls.

✦ Give the bride-to-be a mini-corsage. Place the stems of three small flowers through the center of a white paper doily, wrap the stems with a second doily, and tie with a narrow satin acetate ribbon.

✦ Serve high-quality tea, tea sandwiches, tarts, scones, and dream puffs (see Chapter 109 for recipes).

✧ **Apron Shower**

✦ Write the invitations on the backs of aprons cut from construction paper. Enclose blank recipe cards for the women to fill out and bring to the party, and request that they bring an apron (a half-apron, a floor-length party apron, a barbecue apron, an apron with a humorous saying on it, or a sewing or gardening smock).

✦ Decorate a coat rack with ribbons and balloons. Hang a display of aprons, with cooking utensils and recipe cards protruding from their pockets.

✦ Create a "lady's maid"—actually a decorated ironing board. One arm is a toilet plunger and the other a toilet bowl brush. For the hair, attach a string mop to the back of the board and hanging its mop head over the top front. Add a colander hat, scouring pad eyes, a small sponge nose, and a nailbrush for the mouth. Tie an apron around the "waist," and tuck dishtowels and potholders into the apron's pockets. Add a little costume jewelry, and you'll definitely have a conversation piece.

✧ Gourmet Cooking Shower

✦ Use ribbon to attach the invitations to small wooden spoons or potholders, and mail in padded mailing envelopes. Be sure to add the names of the stores where the bride has registered.

✦ Decorate the room with anything cooking-related, such as chefs' hats, a cookbook display, hanging garlic braids or "bouquets" of kitchen utensils (whisks, spatulas, spoons, and ladles).

✦ Use colorful dishtowels as place mats and napkins.

✦ In addition to other games you may play, ask each guest to tell about her worst cooking disaster.

✧ Honeymoon Trousseau Shower

Women love to purchase and watch the bride open beautiful, lacy things for her honeymoon trousseau.

✦ Attach the invitations to scented potpourri bags. Include the bride's sizes along with a suggested list of trousseau gifts: lace-top stockings, negligee set, teddies, sheer satin floats, fancy shower cap, scented body splash, and so forth.

✦ Display the gifts in an open hope chest or the open drawers of an antique chest of drawers.

✦ A local lingerie store may provide merchandise to be modeled by their staff or by guests who have agreed to do so ahead of time.

✧ Linen Shower

✦ Sew miniature pillowcases, place the invitations inside, and mail. Be sure to include a list of the stores where the bride has registered for linens, along with the sizes of the couple's beds, the colors of their bedroom, baths and kitchen, and the size of their dining room table.

✦ Decorate the room by stringing an actual clothesline from one end to the other. As the bride opens her gifts, use clothespins to hang them on the clothesline, with cards attached.

✦ A nice hostess gift would be a clothes hamper.

✦ Decorate the cake with a miniature clothesline with tiny towels, pillow-cases, etc., attached with toy clothespins.

✧ **Special Times Shower**

✦ Assign a specific day, month, or time of day to each guest, requesting a suitable gift for that time. Here are some examples of times and appropriate gifts for them:

- 7 a.m.: a coffee mug and a bag of gourmet coffee beans.
- Monday morning: a basket of detergents, spot removers, etc. for laundry day.
- July afternoon: swim fins, a beach towel, a Frisbee flying disc, and suntan lotion.
- 5 p.m.: cassette tapes, CDs, or books-on-tape to play in the car on the commute home.
- September morning: bamboo garden rake for the fall leaves.

✦ Attach invitations to toy wristwatches that are set to the time of day being assigned to each guest, or attach them to pocket calendars with the month, day, or holiday circled.

✦ Request that each guest wear something appropriate as well. For example, the guest assigned to 7 a.m. might be required to wear a robe and slippers. (Encourage the guests to be as creative as possible.)

✦ Decorate with clocks and calendars, plus clever items pertaining to certain times, days, or months, such as beach towels for July or children's valentines for February.

✦ Create a centerpiece from a decorated cuckoo clock.

✦ Give a free pocket calendar from a greeting card store to each guest as a party favor.

Amusements and activities

✧ **The Mystery Spice Game**

Cover the labels on 10 jars of different spices, such as sage, ginger, chili powder, cinnamon, nutmeg, curry powder, garlic, and thyme. Number them 1 to 10. Furnish each guest with paper and a pencil. Pass the spices around the room, one at a time. The guests must identify the spices by sight and smell (they may not touch or taste them). The guest with the most correct answers wins.

✧ **The Word Scramble Game**

Here is a list of words for your guests to unscramble. They all have to do with love and marriage. See who can unscramble the most words in three minutes. (Set a timer.)

1. **M E Y C E N R O** _____

2. **O G M O R** _____

3. **D X T O U E** _____

4. **A R O E N M C** _____

5. **S R L O P A O P** _____

6. **S B I D E R S D A M I** _____

7. **A R B D I L W N O G** _____

8. **E G A T N E G N E M** _____

9. **S R G N I** _____

10. **I B R E D** _____

(Answers: *ceremony, groom, tuxedo, romance, proposal, bridesmaids, bridal gown, engagement, rings, bride*)

✧ **Bridal Shower Scavenger Hunt**

This actually takes place inside the female guests' purses. Set the timer for four minutes and see how many of these items each woman can find in her handbag. The guest with the most points wins.

20 points per item:

$100 bill	_____	Silver dollar coin	_____
Dental floss	_____	Toothbrush	_____
Dictionary	_____	Smelling salts	_____
Magnifying glass	_____	Nail polish remover	_____
Cotton swabs	_____	Alarm clock	_____
Pair of gloves	_____	Pocket knife	_____
Photo of mother	_____	Candy bar	_____
Cigar	_____	Piece of fresh fruit	_____
Cellular telephone	_____		

10 points per item:

Postage stamps	_____	Scissors	_____
Pencil with eraser	_____	Cloth handkerchief	_____
Address book	_____	Eyelash curler	_____
Mascara	_____	Face powder	_____
Pain reliever	_____	Rubber band	_____
Tweezers	_____	Nail clippers	_____
Breath mint/spray	_____	Zipper-top plastic bag	_____
Calculator	_____	Notebook	_____
Shopping list	_____		

5 points per item:

Lipstick/lip balm	_____	Hair comb	_____
Hand lotion	_____	Nail file/emery board	_____
Regular mirror	_____	Tissue	_____
Sunglasses	_____	Eyeglasses	_____
Credit card	_____	Photos of children	_____
Chewing gum	_____	Pen	_____
		TOTAL	_____

Co-ed parties

✧ **A Pound of This and a Pound of That**

For this theme, each guest brings a pound of something for the bride or groom.

✦ A pound of flour, sugar, coffee, salt, dried herbs, tea, potpourri, or bath crystals makes a good gift for the bride.

✦ Nails, toggle bolts, golf tees, pretzels, mixed nuts, popcorn, etc., are good for the groom.

✦ In addition to a pound of something, ask the guests to bring enough nonperishable food to stock the couple's pantry for their first week or two of married life.

✦ Decorate your serving table by using an old-fashioned balance scale as the foundation for your floral centerpiece.

✧ **Christmas in July**

A party with a Christmas theme can be a lot of fun in July or any other time of year. The object is to jump-start the couple's collection of Christmas decorations for their home, yard, and Christmas tree.

✦ If you're one of those organized people who saved last year's Christmas cards, you can cut them up and glue the pieces to your homemade invitations, name tags, or place cards.

✦ It's easy to decorate for one of these parties. If it's December and you've already decorated your home for Christmas, you won't need to add a thing. If the party is in July or any other month except December, you'll need to drag your Christmas boxes out of storage and display a few things, especially an artificial tree, if you have one. Tie the tree with ribbons in the bride's wedding colors and wrap it with garlands of popcorn you have strung in advance.

✦ The guests can place their gifts under the tree as they arrive. As the couple opens the gifts, any ornaments or tree trimmings can be displayed on the branches.

✦ If you don't have a tree, the gifts can be stashed in a huge white cloth "Santa's sack," or inside a cardboard box that has been wrapped with Christmas paper.

✦ Serve Christmas goodies, of course—candy canes, Christmas cookies, homemade fudge, pecan pie, fruitcake, etc.

✦ For a light Christmas buffet, serve smoked fish, miniature loaves of cranberry or nut bread, plus a variety of snacks and appetizers from Chapter 107.

✧ Basket Shower

This is one of the easiest themes to put together because baskets are so plentiful. Ask guests to bring baskets as gifts.

✦ Gift ideas include:

◆ A gourmet food basket filled with nonperishable food items;

◆ A honeymoon picnic basket filled with paper or plastic plates, cups, utensils, a red and white checkered cloth and napkins, plastic wine glasses, beef jerky, cookies, caramel corn, cheeses, candy, and wine or champagne;

◆ A beach basket filled with beach towels, sunscreen, a waterproof plastic camera, plastic sports bottles, a Frisbee flying disc, and matching sun visors;

◆ A barbecue basket filled with barbecue tools, a meat thermometer, a clever apron, tongs, skewers, and a grill brush;

◆ A gardening basket filled with gardening tools, gloves, seed packets, flower pots, and fertilizer.

◆ A game basket filled with board games plus a couple of decks of cards and score pads.

✦ Mail the invitations as scrolls tied with ribbon, placed inside miniature baskets (available from craft or party supply stores).

✦ Use baskets to decorate the room, arranging them in clusters in room corners or on serving tables.

✦ Serve food in baskets.

Tip   – Basket gifts can be pretty pricey; encourage guests to buy gifts jointly.

✧ Hard Hat Party

This is a perfect party for the couple who have already purchased or who plan to purchase their own home. The object of this shower is to furnish the couple with things for their new home, such as a hammer, screwdrivers, a measuring tape, saws, pruning shears, a lawn edger, flower seeds, gardening tools, a broom, a shovel, ladders, an electric sander, a drill, hooks, screws, nails, and any of the hundreds of other things sold in a hardware store.

✦ Attach a child's toy hammer to each invitation with a narrow ribbon, mail in padded mailing envelopes.

✦ Ask guests to wear "work grubbies" to the party, including well-worn jeans, grubby T-shirts, work boots, eye goggles, tool belts, and hard hats (or painting caps or straw gardening hats).

✦ Encourage the guests to bring their gifts "wrapped" in their original bags from the store, tied with colorful rope or string.

✦ Decorate the party site with toilet plungers spray-painted in bright colors and adorned with "thorny-thistly" weeds and tied with ribbons made from bright plastic surveyor's tape. Fill a small paint bucket with fresh flowers, and embellish it with paintbrushes, stir sticks, and paint color sample cards.

✦ Use a wheelbarrow to display the gifts (a new wheelbarrow makes a great gift from the hosts).

✧ Down and Dirty Party

Instead of wearing hard hats and work grubbies as costumes only, the guests come to this party actually prepared to *work*. Everyone pitches in to help the couple fix or spruce up their future home. Bring all the tools you'll need, whether paintbrushes, shovels, hammers, saws, or wallpapering gear.

✦ Ask guests to bring casseroles, salads, desserts, and drinks for the party that will follow the work (or you can have pizza delivered when the work is done).

✦ The guests' gifts are in the form of their elbow grease, plus any building materials they contribute to the cause, such as wallpaper, unfinished wooden shutters, or buckets of paint.

✦ As host or hostess, all you'll need to bring are a few simple decorations, plus disposable tablecloths, tableware, trash bags, and plenty of extra ice.

Amusements and activities

✧ The Word Race Game

See who can make the most words from any of the following words: *engagement*, the couple's first names, the couple's last names, *ceremony, honeymoon, wedded bliss*.

Set a timer for 10 minutes. The guest with the most words wins.

Tips — For more games and activities, see Chapter 6.

– For a co-ed party, choose a venue that means something to the couple, such as a certain restaurant or billiards parlor where they met.

– Several party themes included in this book are suitable for a wedding shower.

– Also, see my book *Complete Book of Wedding Showers* for more all-female and co-ed party themes, games, and decorations.

35

WEDDING REHEARSAL DINNERS

A wedding rehearsal dinner follows the ceremony rehearsal, usually on the evening before the wedding. It's traditionally hosted and paid for by the groom's parents, although the costs may be shared or paid entirely by the bride's parents, the couple's grandparents, members of the wedding party, or friends.

The traditional wedding rehearsal dinner is an elegant, romantic sit-down dinner with lovely table decorations, glowing candlelight, and special toasts to the bride and groom. Tradition has gone by the wayside these days, however, and the dinner may be quite an informal affair.

Informal party options

✧ A barbecue or picnic in a park (depending on the weather and time of year).

✧ Pizza or a spaghetti feed at the bride's or groom's home.

✧ A poolside party.

✧ Hot and cold potluck dishes served in a room at the rehearsal site.

✧ "Dutch treat" at a local restaurant where a private room has been reserved.

Of course, if someone wants to pay for an elegant catered dinner, that's fine, too, just so there are toasts to the bride and groom, the only required element for a rehearsal dinner.

Whom to invite

Mail written invitations to the rehearsal dinner so there are no misunderstandings, and invite (in addition to the couple and their parents):

✦ Members of the wedding party and their spouses or fiancé(e)s.

✦ The wedding coordinator and his or her spouse.

✦ Parents of any children participating in the wedding (the children them-selves, especially if very young, should be left with a babysitter during the dinner).

✦ The clergyman and his or her spouse.

✦ Special out-of-town relatives, including grandparents.

Activities

✧ The host sees that introductions are made all around. This is a wonderful opportunity for the extended families of the bride and groom to meet and get to know each other, if they haven't already.

✧ Various family members may want to tell little stories about the bride or groom when they were young.

✧ Home videos or slide shows are fun, showing the couple as they were grow-ing up.

✧ If the get-together is quite informal, you may include swimming, karaoke, mixer games, volleyball, or horseshoes—anything to loosen everyone up after the stress of planning the wedding.

✧ This is also a great time to say thank you to those present who have helped with the wedding preparations and to give gifts to the members of the wed-ding party.

✧ Toasts, the essential element of a rehearsal dinner, should proceed in this order:

1. The best man toasts the bride and groom.
2. The groom toasts his bride and her parents.
3. The bride toasts her groom and his parents.

After these traditional toasts, anyone may offer a toast. By the way, re-hearsal dinner toasts are usually more personal and humorous than those at the wedding reception.

Tips – The most important thing when planning the rehearsal dinner is to have a comfortable setting where everyone can relax and enjoy each other before the big day.

– It's possible that many of the bride's and groom's family members may not have met before the day of the rehearsal. If so, be sure everyone is introduced. If there will be assigned seating during the dinner, seat the guests beside those they don't already know. You may also want to prepare name tags ahead of time that not only show each person's name, but the relationship to the bride or groom—for example: *Edna Jameson, grandmother of the bride.*

– See my book, *Complete Book of Wedding Toasts*, for sample toasts.

36

WEDDING RECEPTIONS

A wedding reception can range from sweet and simple to grand and elaborate, depending on the wedding's theme, formality, number of guests, and the total wedding budget. The reception traditionally accounts for 30 to 50 percent of the entire cost of the wedding, so if your total wedding budget is $19,000, the average cost of a wedding today, your reception will probably cost between $5,700 and $9,500. On the other hand, if your total budget is less than $5,000, you will need to hold your reception costs at around $2,000—which *can* be done.

According to traditional wedding etiquette, a wedding reception only requires two elements: a wedding cake and toasts to the bride and groom. Everything else is optional. Nevertheless, here are the basic elements of most wedding receptions, along with the options you have for each.

Reception site

The biggest consideration when choosing your reception site is whether you are required to use the site's caterers, pastry chef, bartenders, wait staff, cleanup crew, parking valets, etc. You may want to use these for the convenience of it, or you may be looking to save money by bringing in your own food, servers, etc. The cost of the site may seem quite affordable until you realize that you are required to order from the site's wedding reception menu and pay for the services of its employees. On the other hand, the total price, once you've included the cost per person of the meal, beverages, and wedding cake, may be less than you would pay for a more expensive site that allows you to furnish your own menu or professional catering service. Just be sure to read the fine print before reserving your reception site.

In any case, the most popular reception venues include:
+ The bride's home.
+ Garden or hall associated with the ceremony site.

+ Hotel ballroom.
+ Restaurant or country club facility.
+ Catering hall.
+ State, county, or city facility.
+ Private reception facilities.

Surprisingly, some of the loveliest reception sites are owned by state, county, or city governments and cost an average of $500. For example, one of the most sought-after sites in my city is the senior entertainment center, which has a beautifully decorated dining room and a breathtaking rose garden. It can accompany more than 200 guests, for only $125.

Reception food and beverages

If you book a site that allows you to have total control, and friends and family members are willing to prepare and serve the food, you can save a lot of money on this element of your reception. If you decide to have the food professionally catered, you will need to solicit several bids and read the fine print before signing any contract. (That goes for all aspects of your wedding and reception.)

Another thing to consider if you're trying to save money on food and beverages is the time of day your reception is held. Obviously, a breakfast reception (generally from 9 to 11 a.m.) will cost less than a dinner reception (usually 7 to 9 p.m.), and if you can get by with a mid-morning or mid-afternoon menu of light finger foods and wedding cake, your costs will be the least of all. Some options include: a brunch reception (11 a.m. to 1 p.m.), a luncheon reception (noon to 2 p.m.), a tea reception (2 p.m. to 5 p.m.), and a cocktail reception (4 p.m. to 7:30 p.m.). So, before you schedule your ceremony for 7:30 p.m., decide whether you can afford to serve a dinner menu, as opposed to having a 3 p.m. ceremony that will allow for less expensive fare. See the third edition of my book, *How to Have a Big Wedding on a Small Budget*, which includes specific wedding reception menus and per-item costs.

Regardless of your menu, you will need a wedding cake and some type of beverage for the toasts, usually alcoholic or nonalcoholic champagne.

Reception theme and decorations

You can carry your ceremony theme through to your reception, or you may decide to have a special theme for your reception. If your site allows you to decorate any way you want, you might use one of the many themes in this book.

If you decide to forego a theme and decorate in a traditional way, here are some things you can do:

+ Place bouquets of helium balloons around the reception site—they are one of the most economical ways to decorate a large room.

✦ Drape, swag, and swirl tulle netting over trellises, archway, doorways, and windows. Attach tulle netting bows to the corners of the bride's table and serving tables. This is also an economical decorating trick, especially if you purchase the netting by the bolt.

✦ String small white lights over doorways, along tabletops, around silk or fresh plants and ficus trees, on the cake table, etc. They will transform an ordinary site into a magical wonderland, especially if the room can be darkened by turning off overhead lights and closing blinds. Of course, this idea works best of all for an after-dark evening reception.

✦ Dozens of tall white candles will add a romantic glow, as well.

✦ Floral arrangements for the serving table and bride's table and in a pair of stand alone white wicker baskets.

✦ You can make your own ice sculpture to use as a centerpiece for the serving table by purchasing a mold at a party or catering supply store.

✦ Rent or borrow a white lattice archway or arbor for the couple to stand under as they receive their guests or cut their wedding cake.

Visit a wedding or party rental store, where you'll find dozens of specialty props that can be rented. Here are a few examples:

✦ Antique street lamps.   ✦ Tiki torches.
✦ Tents.   ✦ Gazebos.
✦ Mirror balls.   ✦ Fountains and waterfalls.
✦ Trellises, arbors, and picket fencing.   ✦ Carousel horses.
✦ Portable bridges and gazebos.   ✦ Dance floors.
✦ White folding chairs and tables.   ✦ Tall white baskets.
✦ Silk trees and floral arrangements.

See my book *Beautiful Wedding Decorations and Gifts on a Small Budget* for specific wedding reception decorating ideas.

Reception music

Here are popular options for reception music:

✦ Take advantage of the free services of friends or family members who are talented musicians.

✦ Play music you have taped ahead of time, specially arranged to correspond with the different parts of the reception. For example, on tape number one, record background music; tape number two, romantic dance music that begins with a song for the couple's first dance; and tape number three, livelier dance music that includes ethnic favorites.

✦ Hire a pianist, stringed trio or harpist to play during the first part of the reception, followed by prerecorded dance music.

✦ Hire a D.J.

✦ Hire a dance band or small combo.

Reception extras

Extras you might want to furnish for your reception include:

+ A groom's cake.
+ A bride's throwaway garter.
+ Table skirts.
+ A bride's throwaway bouquet.
+ A cake cutter and server.
+ Favors.
+ Engraved toasting glasses for the bride and groom.
+ A guest book and pen.

Reception timetable

I'm often asked how a typical three-hour reception should progress. Here is a sample timetable of events for a wedding reception that begins at 2 p.m. and ends at 5 p.m.:

+ **2 p.m.** The bridal party stands in the receiving line as the musicians play background music.

+ **2:45 p.m.** The bridal party is seated at the bride's table where they will be served. The designated host or hostess invites the guests to line up for the buffet.

+ **3:30 p.m.** The musicians begin to play livelier dance music, and the bride and groom begin their first dance, followed by traditional pair dances (the groom with his mother, etc.), and finally by the rest of the guests.

+ **4 p.m.** The musicians stop playing as the best man offers the first toast, followed by toasts from the groom to his bride, his parents, and his new in-laws. The bride may also offer toasts to her groom, his parents, and her parents at this time, but only if she feels comfortable doing so. Guests may also offer toasts at this time.

+ **4:15 p.m.** The best man or host invites the guests to gather around the cake table for the cake-cutting ceremony. The cake is then served to the guests.

+ **4:30 p.m.** Bouquet and garter toss (optional). These days, many couples (especially older brides and grooms or couples who want a more sophisticated reception) choose not to include these activities.

+ **4:45 p.m.** The bride and groom slip away to change into their going-away outfits and say private good-byes to their parents, while the musicians continue to play and the guests continue to dance, socialize, and enjoy themselves.

+ **5:00 p.m.** The newlyweds may dash through a spray of rice, birdseed, or flower petals that are showered over them by the guests, then jump into their getaway vehicle and zoom off to their fabulous honeymoon.

As you can see, a three-hour reception goes by quickly. Unless you have a responsible person orchestrating the events, the time can get away from you. After you're off, by the way, your parents have the option of extending the dancing and partying as long as they wish, or ending the festivities by subtly discontinuing the music and thanking the guests for coming.

Indeed, a wedding reception is a big production, so you may decide to hire a professional wedding consultant to plan it for you. An experienced professional will handle all the details, including the rental of the site, the theme, decorations, food, cake, music, and reception timetable.

Tip – If children will be attending the wedding—and you probably hope there won't be too many!— plan the reception in such a way that children won't be running around the room or garden or helping themselves to the buffet table. A good suggestion is to provide a separate room for the children and several teenagers to supervise, with games, activities, and plenty "kids' food," such as corn dogs, chocolate chip cookies, potato chips, and so forth.

37

WEDDING ANNIVERSARIES

It's appropriate to celebrate every wedding anniversary, but the anniversaries usually celebrated with the most fanfare are the 5th, 10th, 20th, 25th, 40th, 50th, and 60th. Anniversaries in between are usually celebrated more informally, often by hosting a small dinner party that includes the couple's family or closest friends. Early anniversaries are often hosted by the couple. Later anniversaries, such as the 25th, 40th, or 50th, are almost always hosted by the couple's children or, if they have no children, by close friends. Here are some ideas for specific anniversaries, followed by general tips on invitations, attire, decorations, food, gifts, and so on.

1st Anniversary Party

A couple's first wedding anniversary is very special—not only because they have survived their first year of marriage—but because it brings back the romance and excitement of their wedding day.

+ Because the wedding was so recent, it is easy to decorate with wedding photos and extra invitations or favors that may have been left over from a year before.
+ Resurrect the top layer of the wedding cake from the freezer.
+ For entertainment, play the couple's wedding video, which will not only be fun for the couple to see, but for the guests who were at the wedding as well.

10th Anniversary Party

By the time a couple has been married for 10 years, they probably have children and would appreciate an adults-only party. Any of the engagement party themes in Chapter 32 would be appropriate, but a quiet, elegant sit-down dinner may also be appreciated.

25th Anniversary

A 25th anniversary is the first of the "biggies"—usually requiring a more elaborate affair than prior anniversaries.

+ Because the 25th is the silver anniversary, it is traditional to use silver as the theme, not only for decorations and table settings, but for the gifts.

+ Unlike earlier anniversaries when it's nice to have a night away from the children, the 25th usually includes the children and grandchildren, if possible.

+ Here are a few gift suggestions for a 25th anniversary party: a silver tray engraved with the couple's names and anniversary date, a silver tea or coffee service, a gift certificate for an elegant dinner in an upscale restaurant, or a surprise "honeymoon" trip provided by family and friends.

+ Create a wedding reception ambiance with your decorations by providing a wedding arch for photos of the couple, floral arrangements resembling those from their wedding day, and the couple's original wedding photos and plenty of silver balloons.

50th Anniversary

As we all know, it's rare for a couple to reach 50 years of marriage (at least to the same person!), so this special anniversary deserves the loveliest celebration possible.

+ The color scheme is usually gold and white.

+ The party may be anything from a small family dinner with toasts and tributes from children, grandchildren, and great-grandchildren to a traditional Open House Party (see Chapter 102), in which friends, neighbors, and family members come and go within a certain time frame to pay tribute to the couple.

+ Decorate as lavishly as possible, using gold as your theme—gold cherubs, gold-foil invitations, gold metallic bows, a corsage or boutonniere decorated with gold ribbon and dusted with gold glitter, etc.

+ Hire a harpist to play a golden harp.

+ Provide a wedding arch for the couple to stand under as they greet their guests and have photos taken.

+ Hire a dance band that knows the "golden oldies" from the time the couple was dating, or play tapes or CDs of "their" music.

+ Gifts are traditionally made out of gold.

+ Present the couple with a special anniversary greeting from the president of the United States. Write to: The White House, Greetings Office, Room 39, 1600 Pennsylvania Avenue NW, Washington, D.C. 20500-1600. Allow four to six weeks for delivery. A couple must be married 50 or more years to be entitled to this impressive greeting.

Invitation ideas

✧ See Chapter 4 for sample formal and informal invitations.

Attire

✧ Unless the celebration is quite informal, guests usually dress the way they would if they were attending a formal wedding.

✧ You may be surprised how many couples think it's great fun to wear their original wedding attire (assuming it fits), especially if they're going to renew their wedding vows. If the couple wears their wedding attire, members of the original wedding party can wear their bridesmaids' gowns and tuxes if they feel comfortable doing so.

Ambiance

✧ Borrow decorating ideas from Chapter 36.

✧ For a large, formal celebration, provide a table of honor. The couple sits at the center of one side of the table, flanked by their original bridesmaids and groomsmen, with their spouses or significant others.

Amusements and activities

✧ For a formal celebration, form a receiving line, in this order:

1. Host and/or hostess.
2. The honored couple (flanked by their original maid of honor and best man, if in attendance).
3. The couple's children.

✧ For an informal party, a perfect game to play is the Newlywed Game/ Oldywed Game (see Chapter 6).

✧ Videotape the activities, and show the video at the end of the party.

✧ Depending on the size and formality of the affair, you can hire a small orchestra or a pianist to provide romantic music (be sure to include the couple's favorite love song), along with popular wedding selections.

✧ A poignant moment may be the renewal of the wedding vows. The couple may repeat the actual vows they recited on their wedding day, or they may decide to recite personalized vows composed especially for the occasion. In my book *Complete Book of Wedding Vows*, you will find more than 30 versions of reaffirmation vows.

✧ Whether guests bring gifts or not, the couple's children usually jointly purchase a memorable anniversary gift for their parents. For a 25th anniversary, for example, an engraved silver tray is appropriate. For a 50th, a gold-plated tea service or anniversary cup will be a treasured gift.

✧ If guests *do* ask for gift suggestions, here are the traditional gift types for various anniversaries:

1st–	paper	10th–	tin
2nd–	cotton	15th–	crystal
3rd–	leather	20th–	china
4th–	silk	25th–	silver
5th–	wood	30th–	pearl
6th–	iron	35th–	coral or jade
7th–	copper	40th–	ruby
8th–	bronze	45th–	sapphire
9th–	pottery	50th–	gold

Edibles

✧ Two musts for any wedding anniversary celebration: a wedding cake and champagne for toasting.

✧ It's popular to try to duplicate the cake and wedding reception menu from the couple's wedding.

Tip – If you and your sibling(s) decide to host a large, expensive affair for your parents, be sure you agree ahead of time on how all the expenses will be shared. It may be that one of the children can easily contribute $300 toward the party, while another may only be able to afford $50. Also, the total expense of the party itself shouldn't be divided equally among the children if one or more must also absorb airline travel expenses in order to attend.

38

FAMILY REUNIONS

I wish more families planned reunions on a regular basis—at least every five years. They can be a lot of fun. It's amazing how many families have never gotten together for an official family reunion, planned expressly for fun, sharing, and reminiscing. (They may have met up at weddings or funerals from time to time, but that's not the same.) Here are the basic steps required to plan one of these affairs:

Basic steps for planning a family reunion

✧ Call several members of the family to see if there is an interest in having a family reunion. If so, proceed to the next step.

✧ Enlist the help of other family member by forming a committee to help with the planning.

✧ Choose a date for the reunion. Plan it around a special occasion such as an upcoming wedding, anniversary, or a holiday, such as Thanksgiving or the Fourth of July, when family members are geared up to celebrate together and out-of-towners may already be in the area for the occasion.

✧ Decide how long the reunion will last—a day? a weekend? a three-day weekend?

✧ Decide which members of your committee will take on the following roles:
  ✦ Treasurer, to collect money from each family member in advance for deposits and/or purchases.
  ✦ Hospitality chairman, to procure housing for all of the out-of-town family members.
  ✦ Clever computer person, to create and send invitations and subsequent newsletters.
  ✦ Food chairman, to enlist the services of a caterer, reserve a restaurant meeting room, or reserve a city park for a picnic.

✦ Entertainment chairman, to arrange for musical entertainment, games, and activities, including such things as attending a baseball game, a concert, or going on a hike together.

✦ Crafty party person, to plan and create decorations, name tags, place cards, favors, souvenirs, etc.

✦ Organized person, to plan and order novelty items, such as matching sun visors, comedic certificates or awards, plaques, or trophies for any contests you may have planned, or humorous T-shirts that say something such as, "I came to the Taylor Family Reunion and all I got was this stupid T-shirt."

✦ Transportation chairman, to make travel reservations, reserve limousines, vans, rental cars, etc.

✦ Photographer/videographer, to hire professionals or appoint talented family members to bring their cameras and video recording equipment, etc.

✦ Secretary, to keep track of all the decisions being made and who has agreed to do what by when.

✦ Overall coordinator and contact person, to keep track of the progress being made by each member of your committee.

Tip   – These are the basic steps. For more detailed instructions, check your library for books that tell how to plan a family reunion, such as *A Practical Guide to Planning a Family Reunion*, by Emma J. Wisdom (see Resources).

39

HOUSEWARMING PARTIES

A housewarming party may be hosted by the new owners of the home or by any friend or family member. The point of the party is to celebrate the person's or couple's good fortune in having purchased a new home, condominium, or townhouse and to "break it in" with a rousing party. Some people even plan housewarming parties for a new apartment. The party's theme may be based on the style of the home, the name of the development, or the home's address.

If the owners are hosting the party, it is considered poor etiquette for them to expect gifts, so if you're the new home owner, don't drop gift hints. When someone else is hosting the party—perhaps as a surprise—there are many appropriate housewarming gifts: a bottle of fine wine for their wine cellar, silk or live plants, address labels with their new address on them, a door knocker or nameplate, a decorated bundle of logs for their fireplace, candles, or any decorative items, especially if you're familiar with their decorating style and colors.

Invitation ideas

✧ Take a color photo of the new home. Have one copy made per invitation. Print the invitation on the back of each copy.

✧ If your party will be a surprise (see Chapter 46), be sure to say this on the invitation.

Attire

✧ Casual or in accordance with the party's theme.

Ambiance

✧ Gather brochures, maps, postcards, etc., of the city and state to use as decorations.

✧ Enlarge the map of the city, mount it on a large poster board, and attach pieces of colored yarn to the locations of interesting attractions. Connect the yarn to corresponding photos or postcards of the attractions. You can also mark places the guest(s) of honor would appreciate knowing about, such as the best Mexican restaurant in town or the store with the cheapest groceries.

Amusements and activities

✧ See the Hard Hat Party and Down-and-Dirty party themes in Chapter 33. They work well for a Housewarming Party because they furnish the new-comers with tools for their new home or help with unpacking boxes, arranging furniture, laying sod in the front yard, etc.

✧ Gather the guests in the front yard of the new home for a ribbon-cutting ceremony. String wide ribbon (or fabric cut into a four-inch wide length) across the front of the home. Use wide felt-tip pen to write the couple's names and the date across the ribbon. Have the guest(s) of honor cut the ribbon as helium balloons are released into the sky.

✧ Ask each guest to sign a guest book to be left with the newcomers. Be sure each guest's address and telephone number are included.

Edibles

✧ Serve take-home food from popular local restaurants, delis, or bakeries. That way the newcomers will be able to taste local delicacies.

✧ Or make it a potluck affair, giving several neighbors a chance to show their hospitality.

Tip — A house-blessing may be appropriate, if the guest(s)-of-honor will appreciate it. Their minister, pastor, or rabbi—or even a friend or family member—may be invited to pray a blessing over the home.

40

FAREWELL PARTIES

The reason for hosting a farewell party is usually a sad one—someone is moving away, going off to college, or perhaps leaving on a military or missionary assignment. In any case, the purpose of this party is to send the person or family off with your love and best wishes for happiness and success in their venture, whatever it may be. So, make this party as festive as possible.

Plan a party theme around the honoree's destination, or adopt one of the ideas from Part 7.

Invitation ideas

✧ Attach a printed invitation to a travel brochure for the destination of the guest(s) of honor.

✧ Print the invitations on baggage tags, which are available at luggage stores or at your local airport.

Attire

✧ Attire is casual, or ask the guests to dress in outfits appropriate to your guest of honor's destination, such as swimsuits, cover-ups, and beach shoes for Miami, or raincoats and umbrellas for Seattle, etc.

Ambiance

✧ Write or call the chamber of commerce or visitors' bureau at your honored guests' destination, and ask for brochures, maps, and information about the city. Use these as decorations. Of course, your guests will appreciate taking them with them after the party. (If you're pressed for time, pull up the city's Web site for information.)

✧ Use novelty decorations that reflect the destination, such as cowboy boots for Texas or "free speech" posters for Berkeley, California, and so forth.

Amusements and activities

✧ Encourage the guests to offer toasts, tributes, or reminiscences.

✧ Videotape these poignant or humorous farewell speeches, play them back as part of the evening's entertainment, and then give the tape to the guest of honor as a remembrance of the party.

✧ Research the destination city and state to create a trivia game. For example, if the destination city was Memphis, Tennessee, you could develop questions such as: What is Tennessee's state flower? What is the state bird? What is the population of Memphis? What are the names of adjoining states?

✧ Gifts are appropriate for one of these get-togethers. Choose gifts that relate to the guest of honor's mode of travel (such as magazines to read on the train) or the destination itself. Wrap them in small moving boxes, complete with packing paper or excelsior.

Edibles

✧ Use menu ideas from Part 11.

✧ If the party is for someone moving out of the neighborhood, plan a neighborhood progressive breakfast, lunch, or dinner (see Chapter 84).

Tip – Farewell parties are often surprise parties. See Chapter 46 for surprise party tips.

41

ACHIEVEMENT CELEBRATIONS

A special achievement should be celebrated. After all, there aren't that many important milestones in a person's life, such as graduating from college, receiving a promotion, getting a special award, or finally reaching retirement.

College graduation

✧ Choose a theme that reflects the graduate's new occupation, host an Open House Party (see Chapter 102), or help yourself to any of the party themes in Part 4 or 7.

✧ A graduation party requires a party invitation. If a guest is being invited to the graduation ceremony and a party to follow, you'll need to enclose a separate party invitation inside the invitation to the graduation ceremony. If the ceremony has already taken place, you can include the party invitation with the graduation announcement.

✧ For decorations, use streamers and balloons in the school colors, pennants, pom-poms, and a congratulatory sheet cake.

Retirement

✧ A retirement party isn't as easy to plan as you may think. First of all, you need to be sensitive to the feelings of the retiree. Is he or she thrilled to be retiring, or only tolerating it because he or she was forced into it due to poor health or company downsizing? If the latter is true, a retirement celebration needs to be as upbeat as possible with less emphasis on how wonderful it will be to sleep in and lounge around all day, and more emphasis on how great it must be to finally have the time to attend family events or pursue hobbies. In other words, accentuate the positive and downplay the negative. For the retiree who has been longing for retirement and is excited about the new chapter in his or her life, the party will be easier to plan.

✧ In addition to the clever and humorous retirement gifts available these days, suggest gifts appropriate to the retiree's hobbies, goals, upcoming trips, etc.

✧ Depending on the party's theme, you can create invitations from travel brochures, time cards from the retiree's place of business, or computer-generated invitations attached to a small object relating to the retiree's hobby or interests. For example, tie the invitation to a miniature fishing pole made from a twig, string, and a big rubber worm, put the invitation inside a tiny cookbook made from poster board and paper, or attach it to a miniature golf club or a sack of golf tees.

✧ If your guest of honor has travel plans after retirement, use travel brochures as invitations.

✧ Decorate with a year-at-a-glance calendar (available at any office supply store), with dates filled in with humorous activities, such as "1 p.m. to 3:30 p.m.—afternoon nap" or "watch boccie at the park."

✧ Borrow wooden rocking chairs from everyone you know and set them around the room for the party.

✧ Ask the guests to wear attire appropriate to the theme. For example, if the party has a "gone fishin'" theme, the guests can wear their fishing clothes and carry fishing poles. For a gardening theme, they can wear their "work grubbies" and carry rakes and hoes.

Congratulations party

A celebration is in order for any number of other achievements, as well. Here are some examples:

+ Passing the bar exam.
+ Receiving a raise and/or promotion.
+ Receiving a scholarship or academic award.
+ Receiving a sports award.
+ Receiving a master's degree or a doctorate.
+ Winning an election.
+ Being voted citizen of the year, teacher of the year, etc.

Decorate according to the award or achievement. For example, if the person won medals in the senior olympics, display the medals alongside photos taken during the competition. Sprinkle confetti and add crepe-paper streamers and colorful helium-filled balloons.

Edibles

✧ See Part 11 for menu ideas, depending on the formality of the party.

Tip   – A roast or "This Is Your Life" is appropriate entertainment for any achievement celebration (see Chapter 8).

Part 4

Birthday Parties

"A party hosted with love creates friends that last a lifetime."

A birthday party is a way to demonstrate love and honor, a celebration of a milestone in a person's life.

I've met people through the years who haven't had an actual birthday party hosted for them since they were children. That is really sad because there is no lovelier way to build a friend's self-esteem and show how much he or she is loved and appreciated than to celebrate the day that person was born.

A lively birthday party is also a way to soften the blow for those who dread growing older. The celebration can range from informal to formal, and it doesn't have to win some kind of "party of the year" award, either—the fact that you have been thoughtful enough to plan a party at all is commendable.

42

AT-HOME
PARTIES

An at-home birthday party, usually hosted by a spouse, children, or close friends, can range from a casual barbecue on the patio to an elegant sit-down dinner party to an easy-cooking Sunday brunch. It's the thought that counts!

If the honoree is reaching one of those big milestones (age 30, 40, or 50), you can host a Decade Party (see Chapter 94 for ideas) or an Over-the-Hill party (see Chapter 45).

The party's theme may also relate to the honoree's vocation or hobby. For example, if the person is a preschool teacher, ask the guests to come dressed as 4-year-olds, and decorate the room with preschool toys. If the honoree is an avid golfer, ask your guests to wear golfing attire and bring a few props, such as golf clubs, ball retrievers, score cards, balls, and so forth.

You can use other themes in this book as well, including those in Parts 7 and 8.

Invitation ideas

✧ Transfer an enlarged life-size photo of the birthday person's face onto sturdy paper plates that can be cut, tied with ribbons, and fashioned into masks. Write the invitations on the inside of the masks, and ask the guests to arrive at the party wearing their masks. (Be sure to cut holes for eyes and nose!)

Attire

✧ If special attire is required, such as a swimsuit or tennis shoes for an outdoor activity, be sure to mention this in the invitation.

Ambiance

✧ You can really go all out with at-home birthday decorations: helium balloons suspended from the chandelier or arranged in bouquets, colorful table art, personalized birthday cake, streamers, etc.

Amusements and activities

◇ For something special, hire an entertainer to liven up the party. How about a comedian or a magician?

◇ Include one or two games or activities from Chapter 6.

◇ Include "This Is Your Life" or a roast (see Chapter 8).

◇ One important element of an adult birthday party is a birthday toast. A birthday is a time to make the guest of honor feel loved and valued as a person.

◇ Other guests may also choose to toast the honored guest, read a poem, or make a little speech.

◇ Gift-opening is another important element of the party.

Edibles

◇ Birthday cake is traditional, although there's a trend toward serving the honored guest's favorite dessert, topped with candles.

Tip – Any birthday party can be planned as a surprise party, but it takes a little work to pull it off. The most important thing is for the invitation to state exactly when the guests should arrive and the time the guest of honor is going to arrive. (Nothing spoils a surprise party more than having the guests and honored guest arrive at the same time!) Be sure all guests park their cars around the block, away from the house. (See Chapter 46 for ways to surprise your honored guest.)

43

DESTINATION PARTIES

A destination party is a great idea for several reasons: It gives you a break from entertaining in your home, it doesn't require elaborate decorations, it allows you to entertain a larger crowd, and the destination provides the entertainment.

Invitation ideas

✧ A destination party is almost always a casual affair, so any of the informal invitations suggested in Chapter 4 will work.

Attire

✧ Ask the guests to wear or bring clothing appropriate to the destination's activities. For example, if you plan a hike in a park or nature reserve, followed by a barbecue on picnic grounds, suggest that the guests bring their hiking boots, sunglasses, hip packs with water bottles, etc.

Ambiance

✧ Other than a birthday cake and a few helium balloons, very little is needed in the way of decorations.

Amusements and activities

✧ Destination party locations are limitless. How about a day of white-water rafting, a clam bake on the beach, or a day on a houseboat? Check the yellow pages or call your local tourist bureau for more ideas.

Edibles

✧ Depending on your destination, you can have pizza delivered, have a barbecue in the park, or meet at an Italian restaurant after a round of miniature golf.

21st
Birthday

44

A person's 21st birthday is a milestone—finally, he or she feels like an adult and can do all those things a 20-year-old could not do (at least not legally)!

Venues

◇ Hold the party at a bowling alley, an amusement park, an elegant restaurant, or any destination the guest of honor may enjoy.

◇ Have an at-home party with one of these themes:

✦ A roast (see Chapter 8).

✦ A Hawaiian Luau around the pool (see Chapter 77).

✦ Any theme from Part 8, such as Video Scavenger Hunt (see Chapter 92), Amateur Night (see Chapter 97), or Karaoke Party (see Chapter 96).

◇ How about having the party at an actual casino? With Native American casinos, legal riverboat gambling, and other newly legalized gambling establishments springing up throughout the United States, there is probably a casino within a reasonable driving distance from your home. And isn't this the dream of many young adults who are turning age 21—to be able to gamble legally?

Invitation ideas

◇ Create fake IDs on your computer that include the guest of honor's photo and states the date of the party and that he or she is turning 21. Print the party invitations on the reverse side of these IDs.

Ambiance

◇ Party supply stores sell decorations specifically designed for 21st birthday parties. You can also include colorful streamers and congratulatory balloons.

Amusements and activities

◇ Many party themes provide their own entertainment, including the themes mentioned in this chapter. Regardless of your theme, you can incorporate karaoke, a roast, or a video scavenger hunt as entertainment.

◇ Gather up photos, slides, and videos of the guest of honor at different ages. Have them transferred onto a videotape, along with toasts from friends and relatives, including everyone present at the party, plus a few childhood classmates, junior high and high school teachers, coaches, and so forth.

◇ Ask the guests to come dressed in the types of clothing their parents wore at age 21. Give prizes for most authentic, silliest, and most dramatic.

Edibles

◇ Use any of the menus and recipes included in Part 11.

45

OVER-THE-HILL PARTIES

Birthday parties with an "over-the-hill" theme are popular for those reaching age 30, 40, 50, or 60—although I can assure you that the closer someone gets to age 60, the less likely he or she is to view ages 30 and 40 as over-the-hill!

Invitation ideas

In addition to a variety of stylized over-the-hill invitations available at any party supply store, here are a few do-it-yourself ideas:

✧ Attach black armbands, a symbol of mourning, to the invitations (ask your guests to wear them to the party).

✧ Enclose an uninflated black balloon with each invitation. If it is a surprise party (See Chapter 46), attach a note to the balloon that says, "Don't blow it."

Attire

✧ Everyone wears black.

Ambiance

✧ Provide a wheelchair, cane, or walker for the guest of honor.

✧ Decorate the room with bottles of Geritol vitamin supplements, prune juice, boxes of adult diapers, magnifying glasses, denture cleaner, ace bandages, false teeth, brochures from senior centers and convalescent care facilities, and copies of magazines for the older generation.

✧ Decorate a rocking chair with black ribbons for the guest of honor.

✧ Display an enlarged photo of the honored guest on an easel, and drape it with swags of black fabric.

Amusements and activities

✧ If ever a roast were in order, this is the time (see Chapter 8).

✧ In advance, combine old photos, slides, yearbook pictures, and videos onto one videotape, complete with humorous "eulogies" narrated in advance by the guests—for example, "I'll always remember the way Bill used to love to play golf on Saturday mornings. Of course, he's too weak and old to join us anymore…and we'll miss him…." Show the video at the party.

✧ You can also videotape the party itself. Include spontaneous interviews with the guests as well as with the guest of honor. Play back the video toward the end of the party to top off the entertainment.

✧ Play a memory game. Ask each guest to quickly recite his or her spouse's name, date of birth, wedding date, and social security number. Every guest who gets stuck is disqualified. Award prizes to those with quick recall.

✧ Play party games from the *Over-the-Hill Party Game Book* by Courtney Cooke, available at party supply stores.

✧ Play music appropriate to the guest of honor's age, perhaps tunes that were popular when he or she was a teen or young adult.

✧ See Chapter 94 for decorating ideas for Decade Parties.

✧ Open gag gifts, such as wrinkle creams, a fake container of Viagra, skin bleach for age spots, hair coloring product to cover gray hair, and rejuvenating vitamins.

Edibles

✧ Provide bibs for each guest, along with jars of strained baby food as party favors.

✧ Top a cake with black frosting and a white tombstone engraved with the honored guest's name.

Tip   – Plan an Over-the-Hill Party as a surprise (see Chapter 46).

46

SURPRISE PARTIES

A surprise party is tricky to plan. Not only do you need to figure out a way to surprise your guest of honor, but you must swear your guests to secrecy as well.

Here are 14 tips for a successful surprise party:

1. Be sure the invitation clearly states that the party is to be a surprise, explains your plan for surprising the guest of honor, and tells exactly what the guests are supposed to do to help pull this off.

2. Follow up with a telephone call to each guest, explaining *exactly* how you plan to keep the party a secret. Also, tell them when they are to arrive for the party, where they are to park so the car it won't be seen by the guest of honor ahead of time, and so forth.

3. Have the guests arrive at least 45 minutes ahead of the guest of honor (nothing spoils a surprise party more than having guests and the guest of honor arrive at the same time!).

4. Plan the party around an activity that the guest of honor does normally. For example, connive ahead of time with the members of one of the honoree's clubs (square dancing, bridge, computer, etc.) to surprise him with a party after one of their meetings. All it takes are a few refreshments and a balloon bouquet. Hopefully, the club members will be prepared with a few serious or gag gifts.

5. If the guest of honor lives with you, plan the party for a venue other than your own home—it's too difficult to keep it a secret otherwise. Also, be sure to have the RSVPs returned to a friend's home telephone number.

6. Line up someone to keep the guest of honor busy on the big day up until the time of the party.

7. Instead of having the guests arrive early, invite the guest of honor at a certain time, and have the guests arrive en masse 15 minutes later.

8. Arrange a "party walk"—one of my favorite ways to surprise the honored guest. Tell the honored guest that you want to take him or her on a special birthday walk. Arrange for guests who live in the "walking zone" to unexpectedly join you—one at a time—on the walk. Finally, when everyone has joined in, walk to a nearby party site—whether it's someone's home, a bowling alley, or a restaurant.

9. Another idea that almost always works is to invite the honoree to a restaurant for a special birthday dinner. While you're at dinner, have a friend or your co-host welcome the guests at your home. When you return to your home for birthday dessert—"Surprise!"

10. Arrange to take your spouse out to dinner for his or her birthday, but ask that he or she drive across town to pick up the baby sitter for the evening. When your spouse arrives to pick up the baby sitter, he or she is told that there was a misunderstanding—the babysitter was already dropped off at your house. When your spouse returns to pick you up, the guests have arrived, and they shout, "Surprise!"

11. Another idea is to have your guests pick up the decorations, refreshments, and so forth from a neighbor's home and bring it to the birthday person's home en masse.

12. Have guests just "happen to drop by" for breakfast on the honored guest's birthday.

13. Fill the hall closet with helium balloons ahead of time. Have the guests hide behind the sofa, in the hallway, etc. When the guest of honor arrives, ask him or her to retrieve something for you from the hall closet. As the balloons come bursting out, have the guests jump up and yell, "Surprise!"

14. After the guest of honor has arrived for a "quiet birthday dinner," have the guests ring the doorbell and sing "Happy Birthday" accompanied by a few local musicians or members of the high school band.

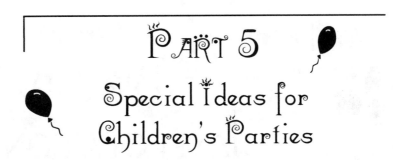

Part 5

Special Ideas for Children's Parties

"Smile—it will make the children think you have everything under control!"

This section starts off with a chapter explaining birthday expectations by age group, followed by a chapter of destination party possibilities. The remaining chapters feature theme parties categorized by age group. You'll find party games and activities in Chapter 7 and party menus in Chapter 113.

If you plan an at-home party, it may be helpful for you to know how much time to allow for each activity. Here is a loose guideline for a two-hour party:

15 minutes—Guests arrive and play with toys or games you've set out in advance, depending on the guests' ages.

15 minutes—Opening of gifts (you may want to provide small, gift-wrapped toys for each of the guests to open during this time, just so there are no hurt feelings, especially with the younger crowd).

20 minutes—Refreshments, including cake and ice cream (it doesn't take as long as you would think!).

30 minutes—Entertainment, such as a clown, a magician, the appearance of a costumed character, singing, story time, or a craft project (depending on the ages of guests).

30 minutes—Physical activities, such as games, sports, or contests.

10 minutes—Good-byes, as parents arrive to retrieve their children.

Whatever you plan, don't just go through the motions—put your heart into it. Also, if ever there were a time when your child needed extra hugs, it's his or her birthday. What a wonderful opportunity to build your child's self-esteem!

And while we're on the subject of self-esteem, you may like the idea of purchasing small gifts for any siblings—especially those who are younger and may feel left out when big brother is opening all his gifts.

47

Birthday Expectations By Age Group

As you consider the party themes in the following chapters, you'll notice they are arranged according to age level. There is no such thing as a one-size-fits-all party theme for children, so it's important to know what type of party is suitable for each age. The following is a list of expectations about birthdays and parties that children may have at various ages.

✧ **1 year old**

A baby has absolutely no expectations when it comes to celebrating his or her first birthday. The expectations come from parents, grandparents, friends, and other relatives.

✧ **2 years old**

By age 2 a child is actually able to grasp the concept of a party and is quite excited by it. Although a 2-year-old really gets into the fun of the party—with birthday hats, blowing out candles, and opening gifts—he is still a baby in many ways. Don't expect too much from this tiny guest of honor, because he will tend to tire easily and want his mommy or daddy to stay close by his side.

✧ **3 years old**

By age 3 a child has finally reached a stage where she truly understands the concept of a party. She has probably attended several and realizes that a party provides fun, gifts, and games. One problem that often arises at one of these parties, unfortunately, is squabbling among the children. However, with plenty of adult supervision, squabbling children can be tactfully separated from one another and the party can continue with little damage.

✧ **4 years old**

A 4-year-old is not only enthusiastic beyond belief but totally cooperative with the planned activities. Children in this age group usually interact well during a party and will go, go, go until they drop.

✧ **5 years old**

Oh, if only the 5-year-olds could be as amiable as the 4-year olds! But, alas, children in this age group sometimes enter a period of self-consciousness, and it might take a little more effort to coax them into participating in planned activities. Another problem with 5-year-olds is that they become very possessive of any prizes or favors they may acquire during the party and may snatch them away from one of the other guests. A solution is to provide each child with his own personalized gift bag or shopping bag to keep track of his newly acquired treasures.

✧ **6 years old**

A 6-year-old likes to get involved in the planning of his or her party and, in fact, will probably have a definite party theme in mind. Children in this age group are extremely competitive, so you'll need plenty of take-home goodies, including duplicate prizes for any games that are played.

✧ **7 years old**

A 7-year-old birthday child also wants to be involved in the planning of his party and usually works well with the adult who is making the party decisions. The party itself, however, can become a little wild—due to the exuberance of children in this age group. Be sure to have plenty of adults on hand to help control the energy level.

✧ **8 years old**

Ah, the 8-year old! You'll notice quite a change in your child from his last birthday to this one. He has become less tolerant of a lot of things—including the opposite sex, which is why a co-ed party doesn't usually work well. Also, an 8-year-old's attention span seems to revert to that of a 2-year-old, which is why you may decide to have a destination party where the children will stay entertained.

✧ **9 years old**

Although a 9-year-old may not put it exactly this way, he thinks with a "been there, done that" mentality. It takes a lot to impress a 9-year-old child! Choose a theme for his party that he's never even heard of before! Keep the party moving and add several competitive-type games, such as relays or tugs-of-war. Note of caution: Keep mixing up the teams so that no one child will feel he has caused his team to lose an event. Good luck— 9-year-olds are a challenge!

✧ **10 years old**

I love the 10-year old! He's enthusiastic, responsive to ideas, eager to help out, and appreciative of your efforts and party preparations. This will be one of the easiest parties you'll ever plan.

✧ **11 years old**

By age 11, boy-girl problems develop that can make party planning a little stressful. For example, the birthday girl may want to invite boys to her party. However, boys won't want to attend, and if they do, you may find they become insulting or obnoxious toward the girls. The birthday boy, on the other hand, wouldn't think of inviting girls to his party, and whatever you do, don't encourage it, or you may be sorry. An all-girl party has its own problems as well because 11-year-old girls tend to form cliques and rivalries. My personal advice is to plan an all-boy or all-girl party at this age, and keep the children so busy with fun activities that there is no time for friction to develop. Consider a destination where there is a high level of activity, such as a bowling alley, amusement park, or family fun center where the children can run around from one game to the other.

✦ **12 years old**

By the time a child has reached the age of 12, you'll need a less structured, more sophisticated birthday party, such as a slumber party, a skating party, a day at the ski slopes, or even pizza followed by a movie. Fortunately, by this age (what a difference a year makes!), boys and girls are getting along with each other a little better than before, and you may want to plan a co-ed party.

48

DESTINATION PARTIES FOR KIDS

A destination party can be a godsend for busy parents. There's no need for decorating the house, no need for cooking or baking, no need for making crafty party favors and knickknacks, and no cleanup! There are two ways to go about planning such a party:

1. A visit to a fun site, such as a fast-food restaurant, the zoo, a children's movie, a circus, a hands-on museum, the local fire department, an amusement park, a family fun center, or a skating rink, followed by a short party at your house with cake and gifts.

2. A special birthday party package offered by a restaurant, a movie theater (large chains, such as General Cinemas, often have party rooms you can reserve), a bowling alley, a family fun center, a miniature golf course, or an amusement or theme park.

The following are examples of actual party packages offered by two national establishments. (The costs may vary depending upon location.) When looking at these examples, you may get some ideas about the type of destination that you'd like for your child's party.

✦ **McDonald's restaurants:** A $30 option includes a sundae and orange soda for 10 children, party favors, a birthday cake, party games, a photo of the birthday child, and a group photo. A $45 option includes a meal for 10 children, party favors, a birthday cake, party games, a birthday child photo, and a group photo.

✦ **Chuck E. Cheese restaurants:** $9.99 per child (for a minimum of six and a maximum of 30) includes pizza, beverages, birthday cake, $4 in tokens per child, a decorated table, a live show with Chuck E. Cheese, and the services of a birthday hostess.

49

MOTHER GOOSE PARTY (AGES 2 TO 6)

This is a versatile theme because you can plan your party around any one or more of your child's favorite Mother Goose characters, including Humpty-Dumpty, the Three Little Pigs, Old King Cole, Little Bo Peep, etc.

Invitation ideas

✧ There are dozens of Mother Goose theme invitations available on the market, or you can create your own, depending on the characters you have chosen. For example, if you choose a Three Bears theme, you can send tiny teddy bears with invitations attached to their wrists.

Attire

✧ Greet the children at the door dressed as a Mother Goose character, such as Little Red Riding Hood.

Ambiance

✧ Move one of your silk house plants or silk trees into your party room and decorate it with tiny white lights, ribbons, and gum balls (use a large-holed needle and yarn to thread through the gumballs in order to hang them).

✧ Purchase a dozen or so helium balloons, several with Mother Goose characters on them. Tie them to the backs of chairs or place them in clusters around the room.

✧ Create a table centerpiece based on your theme. For example, if your theme is the nursery rhyme "Little Miss Muffett," sit a doll on a pillow with a giant spider suspended from the ceiling overhead. For "Mary Had a Little Lamb," use a doll with her arm around a stuffed lamb.

Amusements and activities

✧ Choose two or three activities from Chapter 7, such as:

✦ **Kazoo Marching Band.** The children can march to a recorded nursery rhyme. The younger children may not be familiar with kazoos, but they will catch on fast. Of course, the kazoos can be taken home as party favors.

✦ **Humpty Dumpty Says** (the same as "Simon Says").

✦ **Story Time.** Read several Mother Goose stories, and ask the children to act out the characters in the story. For example, "The Three Little Pigs" will need a cast of three pigs and a wolf.

✧ Some additional activities you might try are:

✦ **"Once Upon a Time..."**: Assemble the children in a circle, and compose a Mother Goose story or a fairy tale together by having each child in the circle say something to add to the story. Start the game by saying, "Once upon a time..." and let the next person in the circle continue the story.

✦ Show the video *Cinderella* or another favorite.

Edibles

✧ Make "magic wand snacks"—pretzel sticks dipped into peanut butter.

✧ Serve "Little Boy Blue's favorite treat"— macaroni and cheese, served with hot dogs dipped in ketchup.

✧ The birthday cake should be decorated to depict the party's theme—a cow jumping over the moon, Humpty-Dumpty sitting on a wall, etc.

✧ Make a "Goldilock's sundae" for each child —a scoop of ice cream with yellow candy sprinkles on top.

50

Teddy Bear Party (Ages 2 to 9)

Young children love the idea of bringing their teddy bears to a party, and once you have a room full of bears, your room has practically decorated itself!

Invitation ideas

✧ Attach tiny teddy bears to teddy-bear shaped invitations. Ask the children to bring their favorite teddy to the party. (If they don't have one, any stuffed animal will do.)

Attire

✧ The children will wear "teddy bear hats" during the party (see the first activity suggestion).

Ambiance

✧ Greet the children at the front door with a stuffed bear sitting in a lawn chair (made of a pair of overalls, shirt, tie, and boots stuffed with wadded-up newspaper, with the head of a real teddy bear sticking out from the shirt's collar).

✧ Round up all the teddy bears you can find. Tie ribbons around their necks and helium balloons to their wrists. Set them around the room—in a rocking chair, peeking out from behind a chair—or cluster three together as a table centerpiece.

Amusements and activities

✧ To make teddy bear hats, provide several colors of construction paper or light poster board, stickers, crayons, felt-tip markers, scissors, and glue. If the children are young, help them cut out crowns or hats, one for each child and one for the bear the child brought to the party.

✧ Play "pass the teddy." Divide the children into two teams. The first person in each line must put a teddy bear (the bigger the better) under his or her chin and pass it to the next person in line, who grabs it with his or her chin, and so forth, until it arrives at the end of the line. If the teddy is dropped, the team must start over. The first team to pass the teddy from the front to the back of the line without dropping it wins.

Edibles

✧ Provide a picnic lunch in the backyard or serve barbecued hot dogs, chili, and red gelatin salad.

✧ Serve teddy bear cookies (made from sugar cookie dough).

✧ Decorate the birthday cake with miniature teddy bears sitting with gifts in their laps (tiny wrapped sugar cubes).

51

THREE-RING CIRCUS (AGES 3 TO 6)

For this theme, you do your best to simulate a circus atmosphere for the kids—without the lion tamers, live elephants, and tightrope walkers, of course!

Invitation ideas

✧ Enclose invitations inside boxes of animal cookies, which can be hand-delivered or sent through the mail.

✧ Make copies of a picture of a clown. Print the invitation on the back of the copies. Cut the pictures into jigsaw puzzles and mail. (Cut the pictures into a few large pieces for small children and a dozen or more smaller ones for older children.) The child will have the fun of assembling the puzzle in order to read the invitation.

Attire

✧ Dress up as a ring master.

✧ Ask the children to come dressed as clowns or other circus performers.

Ambiance

✧ Set up a cardboard ticket booth at the front door.

✧ A circus theme needs lots of color, balloons, crepe-paper streamers, and stuffed animals (the bigger the better).

✧ Create a circus tent by attaching the center of a sheet to the center of the ceiling, suspending the corners of the sheet from the ceiling with fishing line. Add a cluster of balloons to each corner of the tent.

✧ Hang circus posters and banners.

✧ Provide triangular circus hats for each child, made by rolling a triangular-shaped piece of poster board into a cone and topping it with pom-poms made of yarn.

✧ Place the birthday cake in the center of the table and cover it with a "circus tent" made of crepe-paper streamers that hang down from the ceiling or light fixture above.

Amusements and activities

✧ Play circus calliope music during the party.

✧ Hire a professional clown (be sure to ask for references). Note: If your guests are 3 years old or younger, it may be a good idea to have the clown put on his costume and makeup in front of the children, so they won't be frightened by the finished product.

✧ Paint clown faces on the children, then take instant photos they can take home as party favors.

✧ Provide red clown noses for each guest to wear throughout the party, the noses may also be taken home as party favors.

✧ Have a circus parade around the house or yard.

✧ Near the end of the party, ask the guests to join you in playing a little joke on the birthday boy or girl. Come after the child with a bucket, and tell him or her that it's water and you're going to dump it on his or her head. Then, of course, the water turns out to be confetti.

Edibles

✧ Serve foods you would find at a circus—corn dogs, hot dogs, caramel corn, small doughnuts, peanuts, popcorn, and cotton candy (packaged cotton candy is available in the candy aisle in many grocery stores).

✧ Transform an ordinary round cake into a clown face. Draw a face using tubes of red, brown, and pink frosting. Squeeze on big, red, smiling lips, pink rouged cheeks, and brown bushy eyebrows. Crisscross small pieces of dark licorice over brown frosting eyes. Use a red strawberry, red ball, or a red clown's nose for the nose. Curl red crinkle ribbon for hair. Flatten a child's birthday hat for a hat. Make a collar from bright green, gathered tulle netting. Cut a bow tie from a child's birthday hat.

✧ Serve "clown cones" (upside-down ice cream cones served in saucers with jelly bean eyes and black licorice lips and eyebrows).

52

SAFARI PICNIC (AGES 3 TO 10)

A Safari Picnic can be held inside your house, in a backyard, at a park, or at a zoo (where it actually becomes a destination party).

Invitation ideas

✧ Attach the invitations to the wrists or necks of small stuffed animals, such as tiny brown bears. Ask each child to bring his or her favorite stuffed animal to the party.

✧ Send each child a mask that you have cut out of cardboard. Print the invitation on the back of the mask. Ask the children to decorate their masks to look like wild animals and to wear them to the party.

Attire

✧ Dress in bush gear: khaki shorts and shirts, hiking boots with thick socks, and pith helmets.

Ambiance

✧ Cover the front door with animal cage bars (hang strips of floor-length black crepe paper).

✧ Drape nets from the ceiling.

✧ Wind green and brown crepe paper vines around doorways.

✧ Hang posters of Africa and wild animals.

✧ Decorate the serving table and the room with stuffed animals—the bigger and wilder, the better.

✧ Set clusters of helium-filled animal balloons around the room or yard.

Amusements and activities

✧ The children can create their own "peanut zoos" by converting ordinary in-shell peanuts into animals. Provide each child with a sack of peanuts and 20 or 30 colored pipe cleaners. They can twist the pipe cleaners around the peanuts to make legs, horns, and tails. The faces of the animals can be created with felt-tip markers or poster paint. This project can get a little messy, so seat the children at a table covered with a plastic disposable tablecloth.

✧ Create a "wild animal obstacle challenge," an obstacle course for your wild animals (the children) to traverse. Each child needs to decide which wild animal he or she wants to be—a lion, elephant, tiger, etc. Then he or she is off to conquer the course. Send only one child through at a time so the others can enjoy watching. The course can begin in the house and extend onto the patio or into the yard. For obstacles, suspend wooden boards over make-believe dangerous rivers and around bushes and trees where dangerous animals (large stuffed animals) are lurking. Connect cardboard boxes for the children to jump over or into.

✧ Play animal charades. This game is played like regular charades except that the children must imitate an animal. Folded animal pictures are drawn from a basket. The first child who guesses what animal is being depicted gets to be the next contestant. The game goes on until every child has had a turn.

✧ Play "blind man's animal art," which is similar to animal charades except that the animals are drawn instead of acted out. You will need a blindfold, an easel, a large pad of drawing paper, and a felt-tip pen. Divide the group into two teams. Blindfold a member from one team at a time and have him or her try to draw a certain animal for team members to identify within three minutes. The teams alternate back and forth until each child has had a turn.

✧ Let the children make their own animal masks during the party if you didn't send cardboard masks as invitations. Provide colored construction paper or colored paper plates, yarn, wallpaper and fabric scraps, glue, scissors, etc.

Edibles

✧ Serve Make-Your-Own-Fruit Kabobs, Animal Sandwiches, and Dirt Pie (see Chapter 113).

✧ Animal crackers are a must. Put a box at each child's place setting.

53

LET'S PRETEND PARTY (AGES 3 TO 11)

Children love to play dress-up, so a Let's Pretend Party is a winning theme from the start. Kids like to pretend they are grown-ups, of course, but they also like to dress up as cowboys, Indians, astronauts, hula dancers, karate masters, or any movie or video game hero.

Invitation ideas

✧ Purchase a book of paper dolls, punch out the clothes, and print the invitation on the back of each outfit.

Attire

✧ As host or hostess, you should wear a humorous outfit in the spirit of "make-believe." For example, a female can don an evening gown, embellished with costume jewelry and a sparkly crown.

Ambiance

✧ Decorate with clothes racks full of dress-up clothes, plus baskets filled with hats, shoes, canes, umbrellas, shawls, scarves, wigs, ties, helmets, swords, bride's veil, capes, purses, etc. Raid a local goodwill or thrift store, or ask the children's parents to contribute to the cause. Be sure clothes and accessories from parents are identified with tags or markings so they can be returned after the party.

✧ Decorate the serving table with dolls that are all dressed up. Add a few extras, such as strings of sequins for Barbie and a tall black top hat for Ken.

✧ Provide one or two full length mirrors, decorated with balloons and streamers.

✧ Make a child's paper chain necklace for each guest. Place it in the center of each plate. Ask the guests to wear their necklaces during the party.

Amusements and activities

✧ The fun of this party is to play dress-up. To prolong the fun, take instant photos of each child in his or her outfit, but encourage the children to switch clothes so that each child has at least three photo ops. Send the photos home with the children as party favors.

✧ Provide stations manned by four of your friends who have agreed to serve as makeup artist, manicurist, hairstylist, and jewelry coordinator. Round up plenty of costume jewelry, makeup, nail polish, and fake nails, plus hot rollers and hair spray for exotic makeovers. The children will line up at each station, anxious to receive their mustaches, beards, long, decorated fingernails, glittery up-dos, glamorous jewelry, etc.

✧ To top it all off, walk around the room and spray the girls with perfume or cologne and splash a little after-shave lotion on the boys.

✧ Videotape the activities, and play the tape toward the end of the party so the children can see themselves in their outfits.

Edibles

✧ Serve grown-up party foods on grown-up serving platters, such as fancy appetizers, and serve ginger ale in long-stemmed, plastic champagne glasses.

✧ Decorate the birthday cake with paper dolls and their clothes.

Tip – One of my friends hosted a party for 5th grade girls. They modeled her nightgowns and baby doll pajamas, etc. She said it was the easiest party to plan because all she had to do was empty her dresser drawers. She did the girls' makeup using her own makeup supplies.

54

BRONTOSAURUS PARTY (AGES 4 TO 8)

Kids are just crazy about dinosaurs. Here's a party dedicated to all things prehistoric.

Invitation ideas

✧ Attach small toy dinosaurs to the invitations.

Attire

✧ Dress in cave man costumes, complete with clubs.

Ambiance

✧ Decorate the table with plastic toy dinosaurs standing amidst large rocks you've hauled in from your yard, plus old steak bones and a few dinosaur footprints cut from dark brown felt.

✧ Place stuffed toy dinosaurs around the room. Place the largest one at the front door to welcome the guests.

Amusements and activities

✧ Hold a brontosaurus play dough contest. Provide store-bought or home-made play dough (see recipe in Chapter 7) for the children to use to create their own take-home brontosaurus. Be sure to have several plastic or rubber dinosaurs available for them to use as models.

✧ Hold a dinosaur coloring contest. Purchase dinosaur coloring books. Let each child select one page to color. Give prizes.

✧ Have a dinosaur egg hunt, which is similar to an Easter egg hunt except that you hide dinosaur eggs—candies arranged in an egg shape and wrapped in cellophane.

✧ Videotape or photograph the children in their costumes.

✧ Show a rented "Flintstones" movie.

Edibles

✧ Serve "cave man finger foods," such as fried chicken, barbecued ribs, sandwiches, and crackers and cheese.

✧ Or serve "brontosaurus sandwiches"—peanut butter and jelly on white bread, cut into dinosaur shapes by using a dinosaur cookie cutter.

✧ Decorate the birthday cake with small plastic toy dinosaurs. Stick their legs down into the cake.

✧ Bake "brontosaurus cookies"—sugar cookies cut into dinosaur shapes with a dinosaur cookie cutter.

✧ Serve "volcano punch"—fruit punch with scoops of raspberry sherbet, topped with cold raspberry soda pop, which will make the sherbet fizz, creating a volcanic effect.

✧ Give each child a plastic bag full of "brontosaurus teeth" (candy corn) as party favors.

55

KING OR QUEEN FOR A DAY (AGES 4 TO 8)

A child absolutely loves the idea of being king or queen for a day. Go all out and take advantage of the theme to praise your child and build his or her self-esteem.

Invitation ideas

✧ Cut crowns large enough to fit around a child's head from yellow poster board. Glue the ends together. Cover with spray glue, and sprinkle with silver glitter. Handprint the invitation on the back of the crown, and mail in a padded envelope. Ask the children to wear their crowns to the party.

Attire

✧ Go to your fabric store and purchase a couple of yards of shiny gold metallic fabric, which can be fashioned into a regal cape for your child to wear throughout the party, along with a glittery crown and scepter.

Ambiance

✧ Create more sparkly yellow poster board crowns, and place them on dolls and stuffed animals. Arrange the dolls and stuffed animals into a "royal court" circle on a table.

✧ The children will wear their sparkly crowns (the party invitations), which will add even more glitter to the party. Have several extra crowns on hand for those children who forgot to bring their crowns to the party.

Amusements and activities

✧ Play "The Queen Says" or "The King Says," a variation of Simon Says. The birthday boy or girl reigns over this game, of course.

✧ Play "musical royal scepter," which is the same game as Musical Chairs (see Chapter 7), except that the children remain seated and pass around a scepter. When the music stops, the child holding the scepter is out of the game. Make the scepter by attaching a large star to the end of a 12-inch dowel, covering it with spray glue, and sprinkling it with silver glitter.

Edibles

✧ Serve a birthday cake decorated with a scepter made of icing and the words *Happy Birthday,* [child's name]—*King [or Queen] for a Day*.

✧ Serve "royal jewel treats," plastic cups of red gelatin topped with red and gold jellybeans.

✧ Make "royal punch," red fruit punch with raspberry sherbet, topped with cold lemon-lime soda.

56

LITTLE COWBOY OR COWGIRL BARBECUE (AGES 4 TO 8)

This is an easy party to plan—all you need is to add a few Wild West decorations to an ordinary barbecue lunch or dinner, and you'll have a real winner!

Invitation ideas

✧ Cut out invitations in the shape of cowboy hats, and handprint the party information on the back of the hats. You can also use a computer graphics program to create a customized invitation that includes clip art such as cowboy hats, cowboy boots, a cactus, a saddle, or any other appropriate icon.

Attire

✧ Dress in full western attire—jeans, boots, cowboy hats, red bandannas, even fake spurs, which you can find at a costume shop or novelty store.

Ambiance

✧ Decorate your home, yard, or patio with bales of hay, saddles, branding irons, and potted cactus plants.

✧ Cover your serving table with a red checkered tablecloth. Your centerpiece can be a hay-filled cowboy hat with a little cowboy or cowgirl peeking out (a doll wearing a cowboy hat and a red bandanna).

✧ Make favors by filling miniature cowboy hats, available from party supply stores, with trail mix made from of M&M's candy, peanuts, and raisins. Wrap in cellophane, and tie with a ribbon.

Amusements and activities

✧ Play Pin the Tail on the Donkey.

✧ Have a roping contest. Make a lasso by tying a rope into a slipknot. Have the children take turns trying to lasso the horns of a bull—that is, the handlebars of a bicycle. (Cover the bicycle with a blanket, leaving only the handlebars showing.)

Edibles

✧ Serve barbecued hamburgers and hot dogs, chili, potato chips and "cowboy or cowgirl hot chocolate"—hot chocolate served in a mug with a red bandanna tied around the handle. The children may keep these bandannas as party souvenirs.

57

Mr. Pumpkin Party (Ages 4 to 10)

A Mr. Pumpkin Party is great for a birthday during the month of October.

Invitation ideas

✧ Handprint the invitations on orange construction paper using black felt-tip markers. Roll them into scrolls, tie with black ribbons, and insert inside small plastic pumpkins (or attach to fresh pumpkins with a pushpin). Hand-deliver, or carefully pack and mail.

Attire

✧ Ask the children to come dressed as pumpkins—wearing orange clothing, green hats, and jack o' lantern faces painted on with black face paint. Encourage their parents to use their imaginations when helping the children get in costume!

Ambiance

✧ Decorate the room with orange balloons (with jack o' lantern faces drawn with black felt-tip marker), plus orange and black crepe-paper streamers.

✧ Place Mr. Pumpkins around the room (fresh pumpkins that have been cleaned out, carved, decorated, and lighted with candles).

Amusements and activities

✧ Hold a Mr. Pumpkin decorating contest. Provide one small pumpkin per child, along with felt, fabric scraps, felt-tip markers, construction paper, carrots, dried fruits, jelly beans, and plastic toothpicks. Give the children plenty of time to decorate their pumpkins. Give prizes for scariest, silliest, cutest, etc. Of course, the children can take their pumpkins home as party favors.

✧ Play "Mr. Pumpkin musical chairs." This is played the same way as the regular game (see Chapter 7), except that the children stay seated and pass a small decorated pumpkin around the circle as the music plays. The child who is caught holding the pumpkin when the music stops is out of the game. The last child left is declared the winner.

Edibles

✧ Make "Mr. Pumpkin sugar cookies" by decorating round sugar cookies with orange frosting and using black licorice to make eyes, a nose, and a mouth.

✧ Serve "Mr. Pumpkin punch." Fill a punch bowl with an orange drink and scoops of orange sherbet. Pour cold orange soda over the mixture, causing a spooky foaming effect.

✧ Have a birthday cake specially decorated with a picture of a jack o' lantern whose teeth form letters spelling out "Happy Birthday."

✧ Give one small plastic pumpkin filled with orange candy corn to each guest.

58

SOMEWHERE OVER THE RAINBOW PARTY (AGES 4 TO 11)

This theme is based on the movie *The Wizard of Oz*, opening a world of possibilities when it comes to decorating, food, games, and activities.

Invitation ideas

✧ Send invitations attached to small net bags filled with gold coin candies, or create your own invitations by drawing rainbows on the front of each, using colored crayons. (The colors of the rainbow are red, orange, yellow, green, blue, indigo, and violet.)

Ambiance

✧ Use butcher paper and tempura paint to create a giant rainbow, and drape it over the entryway door as the guests arrive.

✧ Create a rainbow and pot of gold as a table centerpiece. Run strips of colored crepe paper along the center of the table and into a small terra cotta flowerpot sprayed with gold paint and filled to overflowing with gold coin candies.

✧ Hang balloons and crepe-paper streamers in rainbow colors, or draw rainbows on plain white balloons, using wide felt-tip markers.

✧ Place a package of rainbow stickers at each place setting as party favors.

Amusements and activities

✧ Have a pot of gold treasure hunt. Create a treasure map that leads the children from one clue to another throughout the yard, until they finally come to the pot of gold—a small gold-sprayed coffee can filled with gold-foil wrapped coins or actual pennies, nickels, or quarters. When the children find the treasure, divide the coins up equally. (Count the coins ahead of time so everyone will get an even share.)

✧ Play "pin the pot of gold on the rainbow," which is played the same way as Pin the Tail on the Donkey.

Edibles

✧ Serve "rainbow sandwiches"—triple-deckers made by alternating white and pumpernickel bread with raspberry jelly and layers of blue whipped cream cheese (use blue food coloring). Slice each sandwich into four horizontal strips, and hold them together with food picks that have colored cellophane ruffles at the ends. Serve with potato chips.

✧ For dessert, serve "rainbow surprise"—a scoop of raspberry sherbet in a mug, with cold lemon-lime soda poured over the top. (The surprise is that the drink will foam.) Serve along with...

✧ "Rainbow cake." Bake a three-layer cake whose layers are each a different color (use food coloring). Using squeeze-tube frosting, create a rainbow on the cake that ends at a black pot topped with gold coin candies.

59

Swim 'n' Splash (Ages 4 to 12)

This is a great party theme for a hot summer's day. If you don't have a swimming pool, you can still provide lots of "splash" by using the ideas in this chapter.

Invitation ideas

✧ Wrap the invitations in swatches of beach towel material. Be sure to ask the children to wear their swimsuits to the party, along with a towel and a change of clothes for later.

Amusements and activities

✧ If you have a pool, the main activity will be swimming, of course. Kids will make their own fun—just provide plastic balls, Noodles (long foam tubes that curl up into pretzels), a net for water volleyball, rafts, and rings.

✧ If you don't have a pool, an alternate activity would be splashing and sliding down a long, wet, slippery plastic slide on the ground. You can buy one of these slides for about $15. You keep it wet and slippery by either attaching it to your garden hose or running the sprinkler over it.

✧ Have a water balloon contest. Draw a bull's-eye on your back fence, and let the children throw water balloons at it. Each child gets three tries. A prize goes to the child who hits the most bull's-eyes.

✧ Play water balloon volleyball. Of course, you'll need to have a supply of water balloons ready as they break throughout the game.

✧ Hold a "wet marble contest." Place 15 or 20 marbles in the bottom of a bucket or tub of water. Set your timer. Each child gets one minute to pick up as many marbles as possible with his or her *toes* and to place them on the ground. The child who manages to pick up the most marbles gets to keep all the marbles as a prize.

✧ Play "put out the fire." Divide the group into two teams, and designate a team leader for each one. Each team should line up single-file. Place a bucket of water in front of each team. Give each leader a metal cup that he or she must fill with water from the bucket and pass down the line to the last team member, who empties whatever water is left into a two-quart plastic bowl. Then the cup is sent back to the front of the line to be filled again. The process continues until one team's bowl is full; that team wins the game.

✧ Have a "water war." Convert empty plastic soda bottles into water guns by making holes in the plastic caps and filling the bottles with water. Provide each child with a water gun, and the children will be ready to squirt each other in a water war.

Edibles

✧ Serve birthday cake, along with Jell-O gelatin "jigglers," Peanut Butter Banana Dogs, and S'mores (see Chapter 113 for recipes).

60

SPACE AGE PARTY
(AGES 5 TO 9)

Your party may also be known as an Astronaut Party, a *Star Wars* Party, or a *Star Trek* Party, whatever is most appropriate for the age group.

Invitation ideas

✧ Spray-paint fist-sized rocks with silver paint. Write the words *Official Moon Rock* on each rock with black permanent marker. Wrap each rock in silver tissue paper, and mail it in a small square box with a party invitation.

Attire

✧ Ask the guests to come dressed as their favorite characters, depending on the party's theme. If it's an Astronaut Party, they can come dressed as astronauts, Martians, or any space creatures of their choice. If it's a *Star Wars* Party, they can come dressed as characters from the movie series, such as Ewoks, Darth Vader, Storm Troopers, or Princess Leah. If it's a *Star Trek* Party, they can dress as characters from the TV show, such as Spock, Captain Kirk, Scottie, or Mr. Sulu.

✧ Greet the children at the door dressed as your favorite character.

Ambiance

✧ Display a "moon rock," any large, impressive rock painted silver.

✧ Create the illusion of a night sky filled with stars and planets. Keep the lights low in your main party room, and illuminate the ceiling with a dozen or more strands of tiny white lights. To create planets, suspend various sizes of Styrofoam plastic foam balls, sprayed with liquid glue and sprinkled with silver glitter.

✧ Use sheets of wrinkled-up heavy-duty aluminum foil to cover the serving table and other tables in the room.

✧ Make spaceships by spraying toilet paper tubes with silver paint and adding white cone-shaped coffee filters as noses, facing skyward. Set the space ships amidst the aluminum foil.

✧ Greet your guests at the door with a life-sized Darth Vader, R2-D2, or Yoda, available through Advanced Graphics (see Resources).

Amusements and activities

✧ Show a *Star Wars* movie or a taped *Star Trek* program.

✧ Play the "flying saucer game." Place an upside-down Frisbee flying disc on the floor. Let the children take turns tossing six asteroids (small bean bags) into the flying saucer from 10 feet away. The contestant who lands the most asteroids inside the saucer is the winner. (Have a playoff in case of a tie.)

✧ If the party is at night, borrow a good-quality telescope. Have the children take turns viewing planets, including the planet's moons or rings.

✧ If fireworks are allowed in your city, purchase a supply of sparklers ahead of time. Light one sparkler for each child to twirl in the sky.

✧ Play background music from *Star Wars* or *Star Trek* during the party.

✧ Play the "I'm going to Mars" game, if the children are 8 or 9 years old. The children sit in a circle, and one says, "I'm going to Mars, and I'm going to take [any item of the child's choice] with me." The next child repeats what the first child said, adding another item. This continues around the circle, resulting in giggles as each child tries to remember all of the items the other children said.

✧ Have the children make play dough (see Chapter 7) creatures from outer space. Furnish odd buttons, pipe cleaners, wire, foil, bolts, washers, etc., for their creations. This will keep them occupied for about 20 minutes.

✧ A month or so before the party, save everything you can find that can be used for building spaceships: foil, frozen orange juice containers, paper towel and toilet paper tubes, small cereal boxes, etc. Divide the materials you've collected into three or four piles, adding tape, a stapler, scissors, paper clips, and felt-tip markers to each pile. Assign a group of children to each pile, and see which one can build the best spaceship.

Edibles

✧ Pass out Milky Way candy bars to eat while watching the video.

✧ Serve space food, such as powdered orange drink, dried fruits, beef jerky, or actual dried foods purchased from an outdoor recreation supply store.

✧ Decorate a cake to resemble the moon by spreading the frosting in a lumpy, wavy pattern. Sit a plastic astronaut figurine on top of the cake, beside a small American flag. If you have a spaceship to place next to the cake, all the better. Add small spray-painted silver rocks to the cake display.

61

FROSTY THE SNOWMAN PARTY (AGES 5 TO 9)

This is a popular party theme that will work whether you live in snow country or not.

Invitation ideas

✧ Cut a snowman out of heavy white paper. Decorate it by gluing on a miniature top hat, scarf, eyes, nose, buttons, etc. Handprint the invitation on the back of the snowman.

Attire

✧ If the children will be out in the snow, ask the parents to send along their warm snowsuits, hats, scarves, mittens, and waterproof snow boots.

Ambiance

✧ Build a real snowman in the front yard, ready to greet the guests as they arrive. If you don't live in snow country, or the party is during warm weather, place a store-bought snowman lawn ornament out in the yard. You can also create a snowman out of three tumbleweeds—a large one for the base, a medium-sized one for the middle, and a small one for the head of the snowman. Drop the tumbleweeds into place over a broomstick or tall post driven into the ground. Once the tumbleweeds are in place and have been mashed down onto each other, they need to be spray-painted heavily with white enamel paint, followed by a can or two of fake snow. When they're dry, decorate the snowman in the traditional way.

✧ Sprinkle fake snow or place a roll of cotton in the center of a serving table. Add tiny snowmen, each made of three small Styrofoam plastic foam balls glued together and dressed up in the traditional way.

✧ Place clusters of white helium balloons around the room.

Amusements and activities

✧ Divide the children into groups of three or four, and let them build small snowmen out of the snow in your yard (if there is any). Provide them with scarves, raisins, carrots, pieces of charcoal, large buttons, and so forth. Take instant photos of each guest standing next to his decorated snowman, and send the photos home as party favors. Give prizes to the team who made and decorated the funniest, most creative, or meanest-looking snowman. If you don't have real snow, the children can decorate tumbleweed snowmen.

✧ Have a snowball hunt. Hide fake snowballs (popcorn balls wrapped in cellophane) around the yard. Provide each child with a white decorated lunch bag for the hunt.

Edibles

✧ Provide a winter weather menu—serve "Frosty the Snowman chili" or "Frosty the Snowman stew" (chili or stew straight out of the can), hot dogs, chips, and hot chocolate served with plenty of miniature snowballs (mini-marshmallows) and snow (whipped cream).

✧ Decorate the birthday cake with a miniature Frosty the Snowman (made with giant marshmallows held together with a long cocktail or bamboo skewer).

62

SLUMBER PARTY (AGES 5 TO 10)

I hosted slumber parties for my daughter as she was growing up, and I have to say this: Anyone who decides to host a slumber party is either an insomniac, a serious night person, or a little bit nuts! Of all the parties included in this book, I must say—without a doubt—that this is my least favorite.

However, if you're one of those brave souls who thinks it's really fun to be up all hours with a bunch of hyperactive kids, this is the perfect party for you!

Invitation ideas

✧ Purchase inexpensive dolls from an everything-for-a-dollar store, and insert them into homemade sleeping bags, along with the party invitations. Mail in padded envelopes. (The sleeping bags can be as simple as narrow brown envelopes or quilted fabric sewn on your sewing machine.) In the invitation, ask each child to bring their sleeping bags, pillows, pajamas, robes, big fuzzy slippers, and a stuffed animal to the party.

Considering how long the children will be at your house and the fact that they'll go to bed as late as possible, you should probably have the party start around dinnertime or a little later (as opposed to mid-afternoon).

Attire

✧ Play clothes for the rowdy activities, and pajamas, of course, for the sleepover!

Ambiance

✧ You can't possibly improve on the natural ambiance of a sleepover scene, with all the colorful sleeping bags, pajamas, slippers, and stuffed animals.

Amusements and activities

✧ I highly recommend planning an exhausting activity early in the evening to wear the children out! You can have relay races in the backyard, a jump-rope contest, volleyball, or anything else you can think of—the rowdier, the better.

✧ Have a pillow fight—now there's a rowdy idea! (You might want to play this game outside on the lawn.) The children pair up and go piggyback, with one playing "horse" and the other "rider." The object is for a rider to knock as many other riders off their horses as possible, using a pillow. The last rider left on horseback wins.

✧ Consider wearing them out with an activity such as roller-skating, ice-skating, swimming, sledding, etc.

✧ Stage a pajama fashion show, using silly nightshirts and big fuzzy slippers.

✧ Videotape the evening's activities, and show the tape before (the ever elusive) bedtime.

✧ Speaking of bedtime, once you've exhausted the children as much as you can, snuggle them down into their sleeping bags in front of the TV, and let them watch as many rented movies it takes for them to get sleepy (ha!).

✧ The children are sure to amuse themselves with other activities at this point!

Edibles

✧ A slumber party requires lots of eats: a light supper and the birthday cake before or after the rowdy activities, followed by plenty of snacks during the movies, such as popcorn, pretzels, chips and dip, and decaffeinated soda (beware of sugary snacks!).

✧ After a good night's sleep (!@!#*#), you'll be in a great mood to fix a hearty breakfast: sausage, juice, pancakes, and the all-time slumber party favorite: hot chocolate with mini-marshmallows and whipped cream!

Tip – I'll pray for you!

SNOW PARTY (AGES 5 TO 10)

A snow party involves outdoor fun in the snow, followed by a warm, cozy indoor party. The object is to allow enough time for outdoor activities but not so much that the children are shivering in the cold.

Invitation ideas

✧ Attach invitations to small sleigh Christmas ornaments (available at year-round Christmas stores). Be sure to specify that the children need to bring warm, waterproof outdoor clothing.

Ambiance

✧ Make a snowman centerpiece out of Styrofoam plastic foam balls. Tie a bright scarf around his neck, top him with a black top hat fashioned from black construction paper, and draw a face with felt-tip markers. Set the snowman on a blanket of snow (a roll of cotton).

Amusements and activities

✧ Do the usual fun outdoor winter activities: Ice-skate at a neighborhood pond, go snow-sledding or tubing, build a snowman, and make angels in the snow. Be sure to provide plenty of props for decorating the snowman—hats, carrots, silk flowers, scarves, sunglasses, shawls, jewelry, raisins, etc.

✧ If the outdoor activities are cut short due to severe weather, choose one or two of the games from Chapter 7.

Edibles

✧ Serve Pineapple Boat Kebobs and Bean Boats (see Chapter 113).

✧ Serve vanilla Hostess Snowballs snack cakes with the birthday cake, along with plenty of hot chocolate with whipped cream and mini marshmallows.

LONG JOHN SILVER PARTY (AGES 6 TO 10)

A Long John Silver Party is a popular theme because children enjoy pretending they are pirates.

Invitation ideas

✧ Enclose a black eye patch (a round piece of black felt or poster board attached to a rubber band) with each invitation. Ask the children to wear their eye patches, along with pirate outfits—ragged shorts, vivid striped shirts, and bandannas tied around their foreheads.

Attire

✧ Using an eyebrow pencil, draw bushy eyebrows and facial scars on each guest once he or she arrives.

✧ You should be dressed as the fiercest, scariest pirate of them all. The kids will love it as you greet them at the door!

Ambiance

✧ Hang floor-length streamers of black crepe paper in the front entryway.

✧ Provide a pirate's sword for each child as a party favor. Purchase them at a party supply store or at an everything-for-a-dollar store, or make them out of heavy cardboard spray-painted with gold paint. Cover the handle with glued-on pieces of old costume jewelry or brightly colored jewel-like buttons.

✧ Decorate with homemade skull-and-crossbones flags or posters, made from black and white fabric or poster board.

✧ Draw a pirate's map on an 8 ½" x 11" piece of paper. Make copies to use as place mats.

✧ Set black and silver helium balloons in clusters of three on the serving table, as well as around the room.

✧ Make a treasure chest table centerpiece from a shoebox by spray-painting it with silver paint and embellishing it with foil and jewels (buttons or pieces of old costume jewelry). Fill the box with gold-coin candies, and leave the lid ajar so that they're visible.

✧ Use pieces of plywood or large cardboard appliance boxes to build a pirate ship. If the party will be held outdoors, use a swing set as its foundation. If indoors, convert an assembly of chairs and other furniture into a ship. Be sure to fly the skull and crossbones flag from the ship's mast!

Amusements and activities

✧ Gather the children in a circle on the floor as you read (or tell) them a scary pirate story. Visit the children's section of your local library for ideas.

✧ Have a treasure hunt. Create a treasure map that leads the children (individually or in teams) from one clue to another throughout the yard until they finally come to the spot of the buried treasure (a coffee can filled with jellybeans). Here are some sample clues:

1. Start at the back of the dog's house.
2. Take 10 steps forward until you see a red ribbon on the fence.
3. Follow a path that leads to a big rock. Look under the rock.
4. Take 20 hops backward until you come to a silver shed. Look inside for a tall shovel.
5. Attached to the top of the shovel is a map with an "X" marking the spot of the buried treasure.

Edibles

✧ Serve pirate's fare—a bucket filled with "Long John Silver's rum" (apple juice), barbecued chicken or turkey legs, potatoes roasted in the fire (whole potatoes baked with their skins on), bananas, and sliced pineapple.

✧ Provide pirates' daggers (forks with a swatch of a red bandanna tied to the handle) to use as utensils.

✧ Serve "hidden treasure" birthday cupcakes. Bake cupcakes with jellybeans or any type of candy inside. Add frosting, and top with lighted candles that must be blown out by the birthday child.

65

WILD, WILD WEST PARTY (AGES 6 TO 11)

Children enjoy dressing up as cowboys, pioneers, sheriffs, Indians, and Wild West characters such as Daniel Boone or Davy Crockett. Although this can be an indoor party, held in the garage or on the patio, it works best outdoors around a campfire.

Invitation ideas

✧ Attach the invitations to miniature cowboy hats, which can be purchased at party supply stores. Ask the guests to come dressed as Wild West characters, such as cowboys or frontiersmen, wearing boots, plaid flannel shirts, cowboy or coonskin hats, fringed leather jackets, and so forth.

Ambiance

✧ Give each guest a red bandanna or a toy star badge.

✧ Create a Wild West campsite, with Indian teepees (made from poles and brown butcher paper or burlap fabric), a campfire, bales of hay to sit on, cast-iron frying pans, blue enamel camping cups, bedrolls, real or cardboard cactus plants, a saddle, pairs of cowboy boots, etc.

Amusements and activities

✧ Gather around the campfire and tell scary or exciting Wild West stories. Visit the children's section of a library for ideas.

✧ Have the children make their own bows and arrows using three-foot lengths of bendable tree branches, string, sturdy plastic straws, tape, and cotton balls. Help the children make notches at the ends of each of the branches to secure the bowstrings. Use straws as arrows, but tape tiny cotton balls to the ends to prevent eye injuries.

✧ Sing cowboy songs, such "Home on the Range" and "Don't Fence Me In."

✧ Have a contest to see which child is the best "shot." Provide each child with a water pistol. Line up a row of lighted candles about 20 feet away from the children, and have a shootout. Give each child three tries, with three shots per try. Give a prize to the child who shoots out the most candle flames.

✧ Play "musical saddles," using stools or bales of hay as chairs. This is the Wild, Wild West version of Musical Chairs (see chapter 7), played the same way but with country-western music and different chairs.

✧ Have a roping contest. Make a lasso by tying a rope into a slipknot. Have the children take turns trying to lasso the horns of a bull—that is, the handlebars of a bicycle. (Cover the bicycle with a blanket, leaving only the handlebars showing.)

✧ Give horse or pony rides to the children.

Edibles

✧ Let the kids roast their own hot dogs over the fire. Top them with chili, and serve on hunks of French bread.

✧ Use camping mess kits as dishes, metal cups as glasses, and a couple of blue enamelware coffeepots as pitchers.

✧ Serve a Character Bundt Cake (see Chapter 113) with a cowboy inserted into the hole in the center of the cake.

66

DETECTIVE PARTY (AGES 8 TO 12)

This party theme gives children a chance to play detectives in a classic whodunit.

Invitation ideas

✧ Using narrow ribbon, tie the invitations to small magnifying glasses. Mail them in padded envelopes. (Instead of using actual magnifying glasses, you can use facsimiles cut from lightweight poster board.) Ask the children to come dressed as detectives and bring actual magnifying glasses (if not already supplied in the invitations).

Attire

✧ Greet the children at the door wearing a trench coat, sunglasses, and a hat pulled down over your eyes. Facetiously examine each child with a large magnifying glass before you allow him or her to enter.

Ambiance

✧ In the middle of your main party room, lay a large stuffed animal on the floor and cover it with a sheet to make it resemble a murder victim.

✧ Tape oversized newspaper headlines such as *Unsolved Mystery on* [name of street of party site] or *Police Have Suspect in Murder Case* to the walls. Handprint or computer-generate the headlines, or use actual newspaper headlines you have enlarged on a photocopy machine. Use newspaper photos, too, if any appropriate ones are available.

✧ Suspend toy water pistols from the ceiling using string, fishing line, or pieces of dental floss.

✧ If the children are in the lower end of the age range for this party, set a dozen or so suspects—dolls, stuffed animals, or monster figures—in a lineup.

Amusements and activities

✧ Play the "whodunit game." Explain to the children that one of the suspects in the lineup committed the murder. Send the children out on the case to gather clues. Write the clues on 3 x 5 cards, and hide them around the house or yard. Create clues that relate to your murderer. For example, if the teddy bear did it, here are a few suggested clues:

1. The footprints leading away from the crime scene showed that the murderer was barefoot.
2. A witness said she saw someone short and dark running away from the house after the murder.
3. Police discovered brown hair or fur stuck to the front gate.
4. Police reports show that the victim was hugged to death.

✧ For older children, play the "whodunit" game by dividing the children into teams of three or four, naming several famous movie or TV characters as suspects, and allowing each team to secretly pick one of the characters as the murderer. Each team writes its own clues about that character and gets a turn reading the clues aloud to all of the other teams. The children from the other teams have to guess which character is being described. The first child in each group who guesses a team's character is a winner.

✧ Play a round of the Clue board game.

✧ Challenge the children to a "super sleuth." Assemble them in a circle. Ask each child to draw a piece of paper from a hat. One of the pieces of paper should be marked with an "X"; the others should be blank. Explain to the children that the child who draws the "X" is the "murderer." He or she kills his or her victims by winking at them. When a player sees that he or she is being winked at, that player should play-act dying as dramatically as possible, falling into the center of the circle. The object of the game is for the rest of the players to try to figure out who the murderer is before they are "killed." The game ends when the murderer has finally "killed" everyone or when someone correctly identifies the murderer. (The game may be repeated by drawing from the hat again.)

✧ Show a mystery movie rented from a video store.

Edibles

✧ Serve movie food, such as hot dogs, chips, popcorn, and soda.

✧ Decorate the cake with a magnifying glass made of icing and the words *It's no mystery that we wish* [name of guest of honor] *a Happy Birthday!*

67

SCAVENGER HUNT (AGES 8 TO 12)

A scavenger hunt is a popular theme for children in this age bracket, whether it involves going door to door, searching in the yard, or scavenging inside your home.

Invitation ideas

✧ Attach a small flashlight to each invitation. Ask the children to bring their flashlights with them to the party.

Attire

✧ If the party is held outdoors, guests should dress appropriately for the weather.

Ambiance

✧ No special decorations are required for this party, other than normal birthday décor—balloons, streamers, party hats, etc.

Amusements and activities

✧ Of course, "scavenger hunt" is the theme of this party, so you need to have a good one. There are several ways to orchestrate a scavenger hunt:

✦ **Outdoors (weather permitting).** This is similar to an Easter Egg hunt, only the children are looking for specific items you have hidden in the yard ahead of time. For example, you can hide a large supply of wrapped candies, nickels wrapped in foil, and small party favors, such as wrapped bubble bath or toy cars (depending on the guests). Send the children on their hunt with instructions to bring back only one of each item. For younger children, hide the items in places that are easy for them to spot— for example, on a section of a tree limb at about their eye level. For older children, you can make the hunt more of a challenge by hiding items under the sand in the sandbox, inside a sack of dog food, or under the lid of the barbecue grill.

✦ **Indoors.** If the weather does not lend itself to an outdoor hunt, play the same game indoors.

✦ **Door to door.** This is the traditional form of a scavenger hunt, in which each child is given a list of items to retrieve from neighbors. The children go knocking on doors, trying to find someone who has at least one of the items. This works best if the items are things that don't need to be returned to the neighbors. You can make up your own list of items or borrow ideas from this list:

- A piece of chewing gum.
- A plastic spoon.
- A rubber band.
- A glove.
- A piece of foil.
- A sock.
- A nail.
- A roll of toilet paper.
- A candle.
- A clothespin.
- A magazine.
- A drinking straw.
- A penny.
- An empty tin can.
- A Band-Aid adhesive bandage.
- A key chain.
- A golf ball.
- A spool of thread.
- A day-old newspaper.
- A stick from an ice cream treat.
- A red paper plate.
- A toothpick.
- A refrigerator magnet.
- A cookie.
- A peanut butter and jelly sandwich.
- A red pencil.

Edibles

✧ Serve Jell-O gelatin "jigglers," Mini-Pizza, and Rocky Road Sandwiches (see Chapter 113).

Tip – If the hunt takes place door-to-door, you'll need several adults to help supervise and keep the children safe, especially when crossing streets.

Part 6

Special Ideas for Teen Parties

"Build a teen's self-esteem—plan a party to honor his or her achievements!"

There are three things all successful teen parties have in common:
1. They must have plenty of food.
2. They must be somewhat loose and unstructured.
3. They must be a lot of fun (as all parties should be).

In the chapters that follow you'll find ingenious ways to keep teenagers entertained—not an easy task, mind you! In addition to giving you tips for successful teen birthday parties, this section is loaded with information on parties that are unique to teenagers—Quinceañeras, Bar or Bat Mitzvahs, Graduation Parties, Prom Parties, Team Parties, and parties to celebrate all manner of teen achievements—acceptance to college, scholarship awards, election to class president, and so forth.

68

AT-HOME BIRTHDAY PARTIES

You have several options for this type of party, depending on the preferences of your child. Your daughter may want to have her female friends over to swim in your pool, play video games, watch rented movies, or have a sleepover. She'll probably appreciate a couple balloon bouquets, a decorated serving table, and a personalized birthday cake. Your son, however, will probably prefer a destination party, so he can get away with his male friends to do fun stuff. If you decide to plan an at-home party for him, be sure you talk it over with him first so that you are on the same page as to what's in and what's out. For example, balloons, streamers, and a cutesy birthday cake are definitely out for male teen parties. (In fact, they'll probably embarrass your son to death!) What's in? Unchaperoned activities, such as swimming, volleyball, video games, darts, or rented movies. As for decorations, cover your table with plenty of eats!

Co-ed parties are more appropriate for older teens. Add dancing to the activities just mentioned, especially if you have a good stereo system and an area that lends itself to dancing. If the teens can drive, they may also enjoy a Video Scavenger Hunt (see Chapter 92), an Agatha Christie Party (see Chapter 91), or a Karaoke Party (see Page 96). They may also enjoy a food-oriented party (see the themes in Part 7, such as a Hawaiian Luau and a Big "D" Barbecue). For a co-ed party, go light on decorations for your son's birthday and heavier on them for your daughter's, or decorate according to the theme.

Edibles

Teen parties require lots of food, such as a few of these teen favorites:

- ✦ Pizza.
- ✦ Hamburgers.
- ✦ Chili.
- ✦ Lasagna.
- ✦ Plenty of cold soda.
- ✦ Make-your-own tacos and burritos.
- ✦ Bean Boats (see Chapter 113).
- ✦ Spaghetti.
- ✦ Hot garlic bread.
- ✦ Ice cream sundaes and banana splits.
- ✦ Chips, dips, and Party Gorp (see Chapter 107).

69

DESTINATION PARTIES FOR TEENS

A destination party is easier to plan than an at-home party because the burden of orchestrating events to keep teens occupied is no longer on your shoulders. You can't go wrong if you plan a Destination Birthday Party for your teenager, as long as your child is in on the plans and approves of the destination. Here are a few favorites:

- ✦ Going water-skiing.
- ✦ Frolicking on the beach—swimming, playing volleyball, and tossing a Frisbee flying disc.
- ✦ Going white-water rafting or tubing
- ✦ Playing miniature golf.
- ✦ Taking a hay ride, or sleigh-riding.
- ✦ Partying at a rented summer camp facility after camp season is over.
- ✦ Going cross-country or downhill skiing.
- ✦ Attending a special movie, followed by a trip to a pizza parlor.
- ✦ Having a tailgate party before a professional football, basketball, or hockey game (see Chapter 85).
- ✦ Attending a live theater or concert performance.
- ✦ Spending the day at a family fun center or an amusement park.
- ✦ Going ice-skating or roller-skating
- ✦ Going on an outing to a famous tourist attraction—for example, riding the ferry to the Statue of Liberty if you live near New York City or eating lunch at the top of the Space Needle if you live near Seattle.
- ✦ Partying on a houseboat for a day, with swimming and a barbecue.

Attire

✧ Be specific about the activities involved so the teens can dress accordingly.

Ambiance

✧ Ask your teenager whether he or she would like a few balloons and a birthday cake at the destination site; many teens prefer not to make a big deal of their birthdays in public.

Edibles

✧ The eats will be easy to plan once you've decided on a destination. For example, if you'll be cross-country skiing, plan a campfire and barbecue at the end of the trail, or combine miniature golf with a trip to a nearby pizza parlor.

Tip — Involve your teen in the plans. For help with ideas, sit down together and look through the yellow pages for destination sites.

70

Sweet 16 Parties

When a girl reaches her 16th birthday, she may be honored with a special celebration called a Sweet 16 Party. Many people consider turning 16 years old a milestone, signifying the division between childhood and womanhood. The party is usually hosted by the girl's parents, grandparents, or an aunt and uncle.

This party can be an all-girl party, which many girls prefer, or one to which boys are invited. Often the party is a dressy affair that includes dinner and dancing, with a live band or a D.J. Other options include a destination party (see Chapter 69) or a special night out to a live concert, a theater performance, or an exhibition ice-skating show. Offer your daughter several options—the choice is up to her.

Invitation ideas

◇ A formal party, such as a dinner dance, calls for formal invitations (see Chapter 4). For a co-ed party, you can invite the guests to bring dates.

◇ An informal, at-home party, such as a sleepover (see Chapter 62 for ideas), gives your daughter the option of extending invitations by word of mouth or over the telephone.

Attire

◇ A dinner dance requires formal or semiformal attire.

◇ A sleepover requires pajamas, robes, and slippers.

◇ Guests should dress appropriately for a novelty party—for example, a party that includes a hay ride or, on the opposite side of the spectrum, a live theater performance.

Ambiance

◇ If this is to be a formal dinner dance, it may be held in a hotel ballroom, at a country club, or a hall, in which case more elaborate decorations will be required (see Chapter 5).

◇ Wherever the party is held, you can create a table centerpiece with an arrangement of 16 candles in candleholders of various heights. Tie candles at their bases with narrow satin ribbon.

Amusements and activities

◇ A dinner dance or special event will provide its own entertainment.

◇ For an informal party's entertainment, have a makeup consultant do makeovers for the girls.

◇ Watching the birthday girl open her gifts will be the focal point of any Sweet 16 Party.

Edibles

◇ See Chapters 86 and 109 for menu ideas for a formal dinner party.

◇ Pizza, salad, and sourdough French bread are hits at sleepovers. Top them off with a special dessert, such as Magic Mountain Sundaes (see Chapter 112).

◇ A late-night supper or light dessert buffet may be served at home after attending a special event.

◇ Be sure to include a few of the birthday girl's favorite dishes.

◇ A Sweet 16 birthday cake is a must, complete with 16 candles, of course!

71

QUINCEAÑERA

A Quinceañera (pronounced *keen-see-an-yeah-ra*) is a significant and memorable event that celebrates a Latino girl's passage into womanhood and her debut to society. This lavish celebration is a significant event for the girl and her relatives, usually taking place on the girl's 15th birthday. (Many Latinos, including those in the northeastern United States, often hold the party at 16 years old instead, calling it a Sweet 16 Party.) The event is taken very seriously, often requiring 18 months to 2 years of preparation. The girl usually wears a beautiful gown and even has maids of honor. Families of varied financial means observe the event.

Expenses for this Cinderella affair can total anywhere from $1,000 to more than $100,000, which is why sponsors, known as padrinos, often contribute financially to the celebration. Padrinos are friends and family members who not only help out with the costs but agree to fulfill one or more of the many responsibilities involved with the planning.

A Quinceañera celebration may be preceded by a Catholic or Protestant religious service. This service is often considered an important element of the Quinceañera and often includes scripture readings, renewal of baptismal vows, a prayer of thanksgiving, the presentation of 15 red roses, and the blessing and presentation of Quinceañera gifts to the girl by her family and sponsors.

The Quinceañera reception usually includes a formal ball that is choreographed as follows:

✦ Presentation of the girl in a formal entrance ceremony.

✦ The girl's first dance with her father (during which, tradition says, she passes into womanhood for the first time).

✦ The girl's first dance with her escort.

✦ A speech of thanks by the girl to her family.

✦ General dancing, usually including a traditional Quinceañera waltz.

And here are just a few party services and items a sponsor may agree to pay for:

✦ The girl's gown, tiara, accessories, jewelry, or bouquet.

✦ A professional choreographer (to incorporate a theme and plan the presentation of the girl at her entrance ceremony).

✦ Cushions for the girl to kneel upon during the religious ceremony.

✦ A videographer.

✦ A photographer to take photographs of the event as well as formal portraits.

✦ Invitations to the prospective members of the girl's "court" (often 15 girls and 15 boys), invitations to the celebration, reception and reply cards, pew cards, thank-you scrolls and thank-you notes, place cards, programs, and menu cards.

✦ Transportation services, often including a limousine or carriage.

✦ Musical entertainment, including a mariachi to play at the church and/or reception.

✦ The reception site, including lavish and abundant food and drink.

✦ An exquisitely decorated multi-tiered cake (with a gazebo, fountains, and dolls that represent the honored girl and the girls in her court).

✦ Decorations and flowers for the home, church, and reception site.

✦ Ceramic souvenirs to be given to the guests.

✦ A gold ring for the girl.

✦ Toasting glasses for the girl, her escort, members of her court, and her sponsors.

✦ A prayer book, Bible, or rosary.

✦ Rental of tables, tents, chairs, a portable dance floor, flower baskets, a decorated arch, and a candelabra.

Tips — In lieu of the traditional celebration, gifts such as a trip abroad, a cruise, or a new car are often accepted. As a matter of fact, cruise lines, such as Carnival Fun Ships, offer party packages that includes a debutante ball, a candlelight ceremony, and the traditional Quinceañera waltz.

— A traditional Quinceañera celebration can be more complex, elaborate, and expensive than the average wedding. Therefore, it should come as no surprise that entire books have been written on the subject. My personal favorite, which I highly recommend, is *Quinceañera, The Essential Guide to Planning the Perfect Sweet Fifteen Celebration* by Michele Salcedo (see Resources).

BAR OR BAT MITZVAH

72

When Jewish boys and girls turn 13 (sometimes 12 for girls), this "coming of age" is marked with a celebration to observe the Bar Mitzvah ("son of the covenant") or Bat Mitzvah ("daughter of the covenant"). The religious commemoration is typically noted at a Saturday morning (Sabbath) service in which a portion of the Torah is recited. Most families continue the celebration with a party of some sort. The party may be anything from a casual luncheon with no theme at all to a novelty destination affair, such as a riverboat cruise or a hayride, to an all-out formal dinner dance with no expense spared.

In addition to the Saturday morning service and the party later that day, it is quite common to involve an entire weekend, from Friday evening through Sunday brunch.

Invitation ideas

✧ Formal parties require formal invitations (see Chapter 4). Invitations for informal parties may be extended by word-of-mouth or with commercial store-bought invitations.

Attire

✧ From casual to black-tie attire, depending on the formality of the scheduled events.

Ambiance

✧ Although it is not imperative to have a theme, it has become popular to honor the Bar or Bat Mitzvah child with a theme related to one of the child's interests or talents. For example, if she is the star of her soccer team, you can decorate with soccer balls, soccer nets, large posters created from photos of the girl in her soccer uniform, and so forth.

Amusements and activities

✧ Choose a gift for each individual child in attendance, matching the gift to each child's special interest or hobby.

✧ Hire a band or small group of musicians to entertain, especially if you plan to host a formal dinner dance.

✧ If the festivities span the weekend, you may want to plan a few physical activities, such as skating, hiking, swimming or bowling.

Edibles

✧ If the festivities extend from Friday evening through Sunday brunch, you'll need to plan several menus, or in the case of a large sit-down luncheon or a formal dinner, you may prefer to hire a caterer. That way you'll feel more relaxed and be able to enjoy your guests.

Tips — Why not splurge and hire a limousine and driver to transport the honored child and his guests to and from the scheduled events?

— Prepare a gift basket for each out-of-town guest. Deliver the baskets to the guests' hotel to be placed in their rooms, or place them in the guest bedroom in your home or that of nearby relatives.

73

HIGH SCHOOL GRADUATION PARTY

A high school graduation party theme can be based on the school colors, an interest, or a hobby or goal of the graduate, or use one of the food-oriented party themes included in Part 7—luau, barbecue, etc.

Invitation ideas

✧ Send diploma invitations—rolled-up parchment scrolls tied with narrow ribbon with the invitation printed inside.

✧ Make color copies of a photo of the school mascot or the honored guest as an elementary student. Write the invitation on the back.

Attire

✧ Invite all to dress casual.

Ambiance

✧ If you're planning on hosting the party with other parents and you expect a big crowd, this might be one of those times you want to splurge and rent a tent, unless you live in California where you can be pretty sure it won't rain in June.

✧ Decorate with oversized rolled-up diplomas and mortarboards, complete with dangling tassels.

✧ Decorate the serving table with high school memorabilia—prom photos, textbooks, pom-poms, pennants, yearbooks, etc.

✧ Enlarge the graduate's yearbook photo to display on an easel.

✧ Splash the school colors around the room with crepe paper or Mylar polyester film streamers and helium balloons.

Amusements and activities

✧ Ask the school mascot to make a surprise appearance.

✧ Ask the graduates present to tell what they will remember most about their high school years and their friendships with the guest of honor.

✧ Watch videotapes of senior proms, school sports events, and the graduation ceremony.

✧ Play a roving reporter—with videotape in hand, go up to guests and ask how they would complete the following phrase about the graduate(s) standing next to them: *most likely to....*

Edibles

✧ Choose an appropriate menu from Part 11, or serve traditional teen favorites, such as make-your-own tacos, spaghetti, pizza, barbecued hamburgers with all the trimmings, or giant deli sandwiches.

✧ Inject humor into the party by converting your kitchen counter into a school cafeteria and labeling dishes with names such as "Mystery Casserole," or serve the refreshments in school lunch boxes or brown lunch bags.

Tips – It's important to involve your graduate in the party plans.

– Don't serve alcohol at a high school graduation party.

74

POST-PROM PARTY

Once teens have found their dates to the prom, purchased their gowns or rented their tuxedos, and secured their transportation, the issue of utmost importance becomes what to do *after* the prom. Many teens of driving age choose to caravan to hotels or vacation homes at area beaches and spend the weekend enjoying the surf and sand. Others keep it as simple as a late-night snack at a local diner. Some teens prefer to extend the gala with an after-prom shindig. If you plan to host a party for the kids after the prom, you can continue with the formal tone of the evening or host a more laid-back get-together. In any case, the kids will appreciate being able to prolong the fun of the evening by having some place to go to reminisce and enjoy special eats and each other's company.

Invitation ideas

✧ Send formal or informal invitations, depending on the type of party (see Chapter 4).

Ambiance

✧ Line luminaries (see Chapter 5) along the driveway and the entryway to your home.

✧ For a formal affair, set a table with long-stemmed toasting glasses or mugs custom-engraved with an appropriate logo, such as, "Evening in the Park— Harding High Senior Prom." Give the glasses or mugs to the guests to take home as mementos of their prom night. (Such glasses and mugs are available from Anderson's Prom and Party Catalog. See Resources.) Make or order an elegant floral arrangement as a centerpiece for the serving table. Turn the lights down low and illuminate the room with candles.

✧ Sprinkle the table with metallic confetti in the letters *p*, *r*, *o*, and *m* or in the shape of a dancing couple (also available from Anderson's Prom and Party Catalog).

✧ For an informal affair, add balloon bouquets and colorful streamers to the ambiance.

Amusements and activities

✧ Take an instant photo of each couple. Send the photo home in a frame you have constructed beforehand from poster board.

Edibles

✧ Depending on how late you plan the party, serve a Midnight Buffet or a Breakfast Buffet (see Chapters 108 and 109 for menu ideas). Stay away from any foods that are drippy or messy.

Tip   – Don't serve alcoholic beverages.

75

End-of-Season Team Party

Whether it was a winning season or not, it is always a bit of a let-down when the season is finally over. What better idea than to perk things up and celebrate the end of the season by getting the team together for bonding and reflection?

Invitation ideas

✧ Cut appropriate shapes from heavy paper, representing the sport, such as a football, soccer ball, baseball, etc. Use a black felt-tip marker to handprint the invitation on the back of the ball, then mail.

Attire

✧ Encourage the team to wear their uniform shirts, sans pads in the case of football.

Ambiance

✧ Decorate with cheerleading pom-poms, megaphones, and sports paraphernalia, such as soccer balls, football helmets, or field hockey sticks.

✧ Place a mum plant in the center of the serving table, embellished with a pennant with the team's name on it (made from a poster board triangle stapled to a dowel).

✧ Borrow a few photos taken at season games from other parents and display them on a bulletin board.

✧ If you have a scanner hooked up to your computer, enlarge players' photos into poster-sized pictures that can be displayed around the room.

Amusements and activities

✧ Take instant photos of the team members as they arrive. Display them on small easels as part of the table art.

✧ Videotape the party, and play the tape toward the end of the party, along with tapes showing outstanding plays from a few of the team's games.

✧ If weather permits, provide a few outdoor activities: volleyball, badminton, horseshoes, and a basketball shooting competition. If you have a swimming pool, you won't need anything else!

✧ An End-of-Season Party definitely calls for toasts (use ginger ale or soda)— to the coach, to the team, to certain players. The toasts can be serious or humorous, just so they give tribute.

✧ You don't need to worry too much about amusing the guests—they will entertain themselves as they enjoy the relaxed team camaraderie and relive their season.

Edibles

✧ Serve plenty of appetizers—chips and salsa, bowls of freshly popped, buttered popcorn, pretzels, etc.

✧ Serve pizza, hamburgers, hot dogs, or spaghetti, along with green salad and plenty of soda.

✧ Make or buy a cake decorated with pictures of appropriate sports-related items and a saying such as "Congratulations on a Winning Season" or "Way to Go, Cougars!"

Tip – Be sure to involve your teen in the party planning, and ask what types of food and entertainment he or she would enjoy most.

76

ACHIEVEMENT CELEBRATIONS FOR TEENS

A teenager deserves to be congratulated and pumped up a little when he or she has achieved something great, so why not throw a party to celebrate? Make a big deal out of any achievement you can, including:

+ A college scholarship.
+ An award for excellence in academics or sports, for winning a school debate contest, for doing community service, for dedication to an after-school activity, etc.
+ Induction into the National Honor Society.
+ Receiving a driver's license.
+ Buying his or her first car.
+ Being elected president of his or her class, most likely to succeed, most valuable player, queen or king of the prom, etc.
+ Getting braces removed.

Invitation ideas

✧ Send customized computer-generated invitations heralding your teen's achievement and the details of the celebration.

Ambiance

✧ Rent a neon "Congratulations" sign for your front window. (To find a rental outlet, see the headings "signs" and "neon signs" in the yellow pages.)

Amusements and activities

✧ Use one of the destination party ideas in Chapter 69 or party themes from Part 7 or 8, or celebrate by inviting the teen's friends over for a fun at-home party (see Chapter 68 for ideas).

Edibles

✧ Pull out all the stops and serve anything your teen suggests, even if it's barbecued steaks on the grill. Cater to his or her every whim, which will prove to him that you're really impressed with the achievement and want to honor him or her at the party.

✧ If it's a "braces off" party, you might suggest serving all those goodies that couldn't be enjoyed for so long, such as corn on the cob or candied apples.

Tip   – Ask your teen what type of party he or she would prefer.

Part 7
Food-Oriented Parties

"Food is the way to everyone's heart!"

At some parties, the type of food served is the main attraction—even the theme itself. It's interesting to note that food is secondary when it comes to children's parties, but at adults' parties, food is the thing! As we get older, we usually become more adventurous about the foods we'll try, and sometimes we like the new culinary territories we've wandered into so much that we feel the need to dedicate a whole party to them! This section offers ideas on how to plan a terrific food-oriented party—a traditional luau, a progressive dinner, an international feast, and much more.

HAWAIIAN LUAU

I've found the Hawaiian Luau to be the most popular party theme of all. I'm not sure why, but it may be because it reminds people of their carefree, romantic Hawaiian vacations, or perhaps this type of hang-loose party is just a refreshing escape from their everyday lives.

Invitation ideas

◇ Tie the corner of each invitation to a colorful Hawaiian lei or shell necklace, and mail in a padded envelope. Ask the guests to wear their leis or necklaces to the party.

◇ Or attach each invitation to the corner of an Hawaiian travel brochure.

Attire

◇ Appropriate attire includes grass skirts and halter tops; flowers in women's hair; Hawaiian shirts, sarongs, or muumuus; colorful leis, beads, or shell necklaces; and on the feet—nothing!

Ambiance

◇ Whether your party is held outdoors, which is ideal, or indoors due to inclement weather, here are some appropriate decorations:

✦ Brochures and travel posters of Hawaii (visit your friendly travel agent).

✦ Fishnets hanging from ceilings or doorways.

✦ Displays of sand (use sandbox sand), seashells, and driftwood.

✦ Live or silk plants, as tropical-looking as possible.

✦ Arrangements of large, colorful fresh or silk flowers.

✦ Display a mural that has a Polynesian theme, such as one of several available from Anderson's Prom and Party Catalog (see Resources.)

+ Outdoor tiki torches (available through party rental establishments or in home and garden sections of major department outlets).
+ Large palm fronds or grass mats as place mats.
+ Large round fish bowls, with live goldfish, as centerpieces.
+ A rubber raft filled with colorful silk or fresh flowers and lighted votive candles, floating in a swimming pool.
+ A lava fountain, tiki statues, and Hawaiian masks (borrow or rent).
+ Grass hula skirts (wrap them around coolers and buckets of iced drinks).

Amusements and activities

◇ Play Hawaiian background music throughout the party.

◇ If you didn't send Hawaiian leis with your invitations, greet your guests at the door with a lei and a kiss on each cheek.

◇ If the party takes place around a pool, include swimming as an activity.

◇ Hold a hula contest. Purchase inexpensive hula skirts from your favorite import store, or make them with strips of green crepe paper or plastic garbage bags. Tie skirts around a few of the guests (be sure to include a few men), play recorded Hawaiian music, and see how well they can hula. (Keep your camera or video cam ready!)

◇ Hula lessons, whether amateur or professional, are always fun.

◇ Provide each guest with flowered Hawaiian fabric, plus scissors and safety pins. Set a timer, and see who can come up with the most clever Hawaiian garment—scarf, headband, belt, hat, halter top, short sarong skirt—in five minutes.

◇ Ask a talented male to lip-sync Don Ho's recordings of "Tiny Bubbles" and "Pearly Shells." This is really effective, especially if he can mouth the Hawaiian words well.

◇ Have someone play a ukulele and sing "Lovely Hula Hands," accompanied by a woman who hulas with exaggerated hand motions.

◇ Add an interesting "twist"—have a hula hoop contest.

◇ Of course, the main amusement is enjoying the Luau menu.

Edibles

◇ Serve an authentic Hawaiian Luau menu, which includes:
  + Roast pork.
  + Grilled fish.
  + Fresh pineapple slices, soaked in teriyaki sauce and lightly grilled.
  + Fresh strawberries.
  + Melons.
  + Papayas.

✦ Roasted bananas (peel, dip in melted butter and sprinkle with sugar, wrap in aluminum foil, roast for 20 minutes, and serve with a drizzle of rum).

✦ Sweet Hawaiian bread.

✦ Bowls of sweet, fresh coconut.

✦ Boiled sweet potatoes.

✦ Fresh green salad with tomatoes, onions, raw zucchini, cucumbers, and plenty of ripe avocado slices.

✦ Hawaiian fruit salad, made by combining 1 cup sour cream, 1 cup shredded coconut, 1 cup pineapple tidbits (drained), 1 1/2 cups Mandarin oranges (drained), and 1 1/2 cup miniature marshmallows. Let chill in refrigerator overnight. Sprinkle with freshly ground nutmeg just before serving.

✦ Bowls of macadamia nuts.

◇ Serve "Hawaiian volcano punch"—fruit punch and scoops of raspberry sherbet, with cold raspberry soda or ginger ale poured over mixture, making it foam with a volcanic effect.

Tip – Traditional luau food should be served from one long buffet table.

78

Big "D" Barbecue

This is a country-western barbecue where everything is *big*—nothing skimpy about this party! Drag out your cowboy boots, 10-gallon hats, and bandannas, and encourage your guests to get into the spirit by wearing their western outfits, too.

Invitation ideas

✧ Make big invitations by cutting the shape of Texas out of 16" x 22" poster board. Draw a star over the spot where the city of Dallas would be and handprint your invitation above and below the star.

✧ You can also brand the invitation onto pieces of leather. Buy leather scraps from a craft shop, and brand the invitation onto the leather using a wood-burning tool, or write it on using an indelible fabric marker.

Attire

✧ Everyone should wear western-style outfits—jeans, cowboy boots, western shirts, bolo ties, bandannas, ten gallon cowboy hats, and big belt buckles (preferably in the shape of Texas!).

Ambiance

✧ Hang up pictures of big cattle and big oil wells.

✧ Decorate your home, yard, or patio with bales of hay, saddles, branding irons, wagon wheels, spurs, cowboy hats, and potted cactus plants.

✧ Cover your serving table with a red checkered tablecloth.

✧ Create a centerpiece by filling a 10-gallon hat with hay and wild flowers.

✧ Tie the silverware with red bandanna napkins.

✧ Use blue enamel pie tins as plates and Mason jars as glasses.

- ✧ Decorate your tables with "Mason jar luminaries." Fill a Mason jar with three inches of sand and place a candle or votive in the sand.

- ✧ Drag out your child's old erector set, and build an oil rig beside a galvanized tub filled with ice, canned soda, and beer.

- ✧ Make party favors by filling miniature cowboy hats with trail mix (M&M's candy, peanuts, and raisins), wrapping them with cellophane, and tying a ribbon around them. Miniature cowboy hats are available at party supply stores.

- ✧ If you know anyone who lives on a ranch or a farm, take advantage of it and have the party there!

Amusements and activities

- ✧ Welcome the guests with their favorite country-western music, such as recordings by Willie Nelson, Garth Brooks, or Waylon Jennings.

- ✧ Have a country-western sing-a-long, singing such down-home tunes as "Deep in the Heart of Texas."

- ✧ Have a roping contest. Make a lasso by tying a slipknot in a piece of rope. Take turns trying to lasso a tree stump or stake in the ground.

- ✧ Rent a dance floor for a little country-western dancing (hire an instructor to teach the guests a new line dance or square dance). Hire a country-western band, or play recorded music.

Edibles

- ✧ Serve barbecued hamburgers, steaks, baby back pork ribs, spareribs, or chicken (do not skimp on the quality of the meat!).

- ✧ Make roasted "Big 'D' potatoes"—split potatoes sprinkled with garlic salt and sprayed with butter-flavored oil, then cooked in heavy-duty foil over hot coals for 30 minutes.

- ✧ Serve "husky corn on the cob." Soak the corn (husk and all) in water for about 15 minutes. Then place the corn, still in its husks, over the hot coals for about 20 minutes, turning constantly.

- ✧ Dole out plenty of warm garlic French bread roasted over the coals.

- ✧ For dessert, dish out hot apple pies and watermelon.

Tips – Appetites soar as guests savor the aroma of food cooking over a barbecue, so plan on a little more food per guest than normal.

– Invite the guests to help with the grilling. This will get them involved in the party and give them a chance to be sure their steaks are cooked exactly the way they like them.

79

Good Old-Fashioned Picnic

In spite of all the latest trendy party themes, the tried-and-true, good old-fashioned picnic is still a favorite. Your guests will not only enjoy the food but the traditional games as well. After all, when was the last time they competed in a three-legged race?

Invitation ideas

✧ Informal, of course—via telephone, e-mail, fax, a handwritten note, or a handcrafted novelty card (for example, a miniature basket lined with a tiny piece of red-checkered fabric, with the invitation tucked inside).

Attire

✧ Totally casual and comfortable!

Ambiance

✧ Reserve a designated area in a public park, or rent a private park. If you have enough property, you can also hold the picnic in the backyard.

✧ Cover picnic tables with disposable red and white checkered tablecloths or old quilts.

✧ Tie balloon bouquets to the ends of the picnic tables.

✧ Create a watermelon centerpiece by inserting the stems of fresh flowers into a watermelon that has been cut in half lengthwise.

Amusements and activities

✧ Have a watermelon-seed spitting contest—a surefire way to get your guests loosened up! Contestants should line up single-file and take turns trying to spit a watermelon seed into a bucket 20 feet in front of them. If more than one contestant gets a seed in the bucket, keep holding more rounds, moving the bucket farther away each time until only one person has the lung power to ring it!

✧ Play old-fashioned 4th of July or Sunday School picnic games, including traditional favorites such as a nail-pounding contest, a horseshoe competition, an egg toss or water balloon toss, a sack race, a three-legged race, or a wheelbarrow race.

Edibles

✧ Serve traditional picnic fare:

✦ Fried chicken and cold boiled lobster, or barbecued steak, chickens, swordfish, lamb chops, or hot dogs.

✦ Potatoes and fresh corn on the cob smothered in butter and cooked on the grill in aluminum foil.

✦ Potato salad.

✦ Coleslaw.

✦ Baked beans.

✦ Watermelon.

✦ Seedless grapes.

✦ Potato chips.

✦ Chocolate cake or cupcakes.

✦ Homemade ice cream.

✦ Plenty of ice-cold beer and soda.

Tip — Do not forget to bring these picnic essentials:

- Disposable tableware (plates, cups, etc.).
- Paper towels and paper napkins.
- Disposable tablecloths.
- Potholders or barbecue mitts.
- Plenty of trash bags.
- Serving spoons and forks.
- Utensils (tongs, skewers, etc.).
- Supplies for games and sports.
- Sharp cutting knives.
- A bottle opener.
- Plenty of ice.
- Matches.
- Aluminum foil.
- A grill.
- Blankets.
- Sunscreen.
- Salt, pepper, catsup, mustard, relish, olives, pickles, seasonings, and any other condiments of your choice.
- Folding lawn chairs and/or stadium seats with back rests.
- Insect repellant.
- Citronella candles to ward off the insects in the first place!

80

ELEGANT GOURMET PICNIC

A picnic, of course, doesn't have to be about scarfing down messy barbecued spareribs and playing games that cause you to get grass stains all over your clothing. If you want the lighthearted fun of a picnic but with a little more finesse (for celebrating a romantic anniversary, for example, or entertaining professional colleagues), then the Elegant Gourmet Picnic is a nice way to surprise your guest(s) with a special treat.

Invitation ideas

✧ Informal invitations are acceptable—invite your friends via telephone, e-mail, or fax.

✧ Or go all out and send formal invitations. They will set the stage for the surprising gourmet lunch to follow.

Attire

✧ Formal or not, you do need to wear something that will be comfortable as you sit on a blanket.

Ambiance

✧ Reserve a designated area in a public park, or rent a private park.

✧ Lay a soft, print blanket across a nice stretch of plush grass.

✧ Set your "table" in style—cover the blanket with a white linen tablecloth, set out stoneware plates (no need for fine china), glassware (not paper cups), and stainless steel utensils. Provide linen napkins.

✧ Set a sturdy but attractive pitcher or vase filled with freshly cut flowers in the middle of your table.

✧ If the picnic will continue past dusk, set votive candles on the tablecloth.

✧ Lounge on lace-trimmed eyelet pillows (you're going for elegance!).

✧ Be sure to provide wine or champagne glasses for toasts.

Amusements and activities

✧ The fun is in the novelty of having a gourmet picnic complete with champagne and toasts.

Edibles

✧ The menu consists of elegant continental fare, such as:

✦ Sourdough French bread.

✦ Vichyssoise (see Chapter 109).

✦ Gourmet cheeses.

✦ Chilled shrimp cocktail.

✦ Fresh fruits (served on silver trays), including seedless grapes and large ripe strawberries sprinkled with powdered sugar.

✦ Sliced meats, such as smoked turkey, ham, and beef.

✦ Delicacies, such as pickled herring and imported Russian caviar.

✦ Crudités with a variety of dips.

Tip – If you and your friends are planning to attend a free outdoor concert or another event in a public park, use it as an opportunity to enjoy this type of picnic. You should arrive early at the park, bringing tables, chairs, linen tablecloths and napkins, crystal champagne glasses, tall candlesticks, large floral centerpieces, and so on. Set up in a choice spot. When your guests arrive, you can all enjoy your meal, then watch the concert as you recline leisurely in your chairs.

81

WINE-TASTING PARTY

Wine-tasting is a great excuse for a party! This type of party will be a lot of fun for all your wine connoisseur friends; it gives them a chance to taste a variety of fine wines and pretend they are wine judges. However, give careful thought to your guest list—not everyone appreciates the special qualities of fine wines.

Invitation ideas

✧ Send full-sized or miniature empty wine bottles with computer-generated labels announcing the party. Or just send the invitation on computer-generated labels you have made to look like wine labels, with your last name as the name of the wine. You may invite each guest to bring a bottle of his or her favorite wine for the wine-tasting, or provide the wine yourself.

Attire

✧ A wine-tasting party usually inspires the guests to dress nicely.

Ambiance

✧ Decorate with empty wine bottles filled with fresh or silk flowers.

✧ Create a centerpiece by arranging breads, cheeses, strawberries, and grapes on a large breadboard.

Amusements and activities

✧ The main event? A wine-tasting contest, of course. Ask your guests to serve as judges as they rank each wine according to color (clear? pale? rich?), bouquet (fruity? delicate? pungent?), and taste (dry? smooth? full-bodied?).

Here is a guide to the qualities of different types of wine to assist with judging (photocopy this list for each guest):

1. Table wines—red

- **Dry:**
  Bordeaux (soft taste; excellent flavor).
  Burgundy (full body; full flavor).
  Cabernet Sauvignon (Bordeaux-like qualities).
  Chianti (round, full flavor).
  Claret (Bordeaux-like qualities with a soft flavor).
  Pinot Noir (warming Burgundy-like qualities; pleasant flavor).
- **Medium-dry:**
  Lambrusco (fruity, mellow flavor).
  St. Emilion (Bordeaux-like qualities; full body; soft flavor).
  Zinfandel (fruity, delicate flavor).

2. Table wines—white

- **Dry:**
  Chablis (medium body; crispy flavor).
  Gewürztraminer (spicy flavor).
  Graves (soft, light, pleasant flavor).
  Moselle (light, delicate flavor).
  Rhine (light body.)
  Verdicchio (very light body).
- **Medium-dry:**
  Chenin Blanc (soft, fruity flavor).
  Johannesburg Riesling (fresh, flowery, soft flavor).
  Liebfraumilch (Rhine wine, with touch of sweetness).
  Soave (refreshing flavor).
  Vouvray (delicate, fresh flavor).
  White Bordeaux (smooth, refreshing quality).
  Zeller schwarze Katz (light, refreshing quality).
- **Medium-sweet:**
  Sauterne (medium body; fruity, mellow flavor).
- **Sweet:**
  Asti Spumanti (champagne-like qualities).
  Haut Sauternes (full body).

3. Rose wines

- **Dry:**
  Rose d'Anjou (light body and flavor).
  Tavel Rose (pleasant, clean taste).
- **Medium-dry:**
  Mateus (bubbly taste; soft flavor).

- ✧ If you should be so fortunate as to have a legitimate wine connoisseur among your guests, take advantage of the person's expertise by having him or her introduce the wines as they are served, explaining their origins and qualities.

Edibles

✧ Serve six to eight fine wines (if each guest furnishes a bottle, all the better). Always serve the wines one at a time. Furnish each guest with a supply of plastic wine glasses for wine-tasting and two or three glass wine glasses for actual drinking.

✧ Serve hors d'oeuvres and finger foods (see Chapter 107 and 108).

✧ Serve breads and crackers in baskets.

✧ Provide fresh strawberries and seedless grapes.

✧ Offer a variety of cheeses to accompany the wines. Here is a list of popular cheeses and the wines they best accompany:

   ✦ Appenzeller (Burgundy).
   ✦ Bel paesi (Moselle, Rhine).
   ✦ Blue (Chianti, Burgundy, Bordeaux).
   ✦ Brie (Chianti, Burgundy, sherry).
   ✦ Camembert (Burgundy, Chateauneuf).
   ✦ Cheddar (Bordeaux, Burgundy).
   ✦ Edam (Bordeaux, Burgundy, medium-dry sherry).
   ✦ Feta (Chianti, Burgundy, Bordeaux).
   ✦ Fontina (Beaujolais, Moselle).
   ✦ Gouda (Beaujolais, Graves, Chablis).
   ✦ Gruyère (Burgundy).
   ✦ Jarlsberg (Burgundy).
   ✦ Liederkranz (Burgundy).
   ✦ Muenster (Bordeaux, Chablis).
   ✦ Provolone (Burgundy).
   ✦ Swiss (Burgundy, Bordeaux).
   ✦ Tilsit (Chablis).

✧ Serve a fancy dessert and coffee (see Chapters 111 and 112).

Tips — Be sure to serve each wine at its required temperature. For example, Burgundy wine should be served at room temperature, while white wine should be chilled but not icy. Red wines should be opened an hour or more before serving, allowing them to breathe.

— If you really want to impress your guests with your knowledge of wines, visit the Web site www.smartwine.com to read about the latest trends in the wine industry.

82

TAILGATE PARTY

Most of us don't think about having a Tailgate Party until we pull into a stadium parking lot for a concert or sports event and notice other people clustered around their cars having a great old time—eating barbecued chicken, enjoying beer and refreshments, and listening to the concert performer's music or watching the pregame show on portable TVs. Why not plan ahead and get there early yourself so you can have a great party with your friends?

Invitation ideas

✧ Use postcards showing a picture of a car, or take a photo of your car with the tailgate down or the trunk open, with a blanket or checkered tablecloth spread out, topped with picnic basket, ice chest, etc. Write the invitation on the back of the postcard or photo and mail.

Ambiance

✧ A tailgate party needs no ambiance—the excitement of the event is enough. However, it has become trendy to "dress up" a tailgate party with candlesticks, serving trays and utensils, crystal wine glasses, white linen tablecloths, flower bouquets, and any other decorations you would like to include, such as trailing ivy to frame the tailgate or trunk.

✧ Or you can use color-coordinated or team-emblem plastic plates, cups, serving bowls, and tablecloth.

Amusements and activities

✧ Bring a boom box and tapes or CDs, or a portable TV to watch pregame coverage.

Edibles

✧ Set up your portable barbecue, and cook steaks, hamburgers, hot dogs, roasted potatoes, or corn on the cob.

✧ Or bring heroes or cold-cut sandwiches.

✧ Bring an ice chest filled with fried chicken, macaroni salad, cold veggies and dips, cheeses, imported beers, and soda.

✧ Serve potato chips and cookies, and bring insulated containers of hot coffee or hot chocolate.

✧ Don't forget the condiments—catsup, mustard, mayonnaise, steak sauces, relish, pickles, olives, butter, cream, sugar, salt, and pepper.

✧ A few TV trays will come in handy.

Tip – If you and your guests arrived in separate cars, park them in a semicircle to create the ultimate bonding experience.

– Bring plenty of utensils, barbecue tools, a bottle opener, a sharp carving knife, steak knives (if applicable), serving forks and spoons, and cloth napkins or paper towels.

– Bring lots of blankets and folding lawn chairs.

– Bring plenty of garbage bags—don't litter!

83

BEACH PARTY

Take the party to the beach. It doesn't have to be an ocean beach—it can be any beach, alongside a river, stream, or lake.

Invitation ideas

✧ Attach the invitations to postcards with a beach scene or travel brochures for an island destination.

Attire

✧ Come prepared to swim or sunbathe.

✧ Provide each guest with a beachcomber hat, available for less than $2 from Anderson's Prom and Party Catalog (see Resources).

Ambiance

✧ Decorate the serving table with shells, driftwood, or pieces of coral.

✧ On a folding table, create a centerpiece of cut flowers set in a piece of floral foam that has been inserted into a large conch shell.

✧ Bring candles to light at dusk.

Amusements

✧ Toss a Frisbee flying disc, play beach volleyball, swim, sail, fish, or have a sandcastle-building contest.

✧ Relax on comfortable folding lawn chairs.

Edibles

✧ Place a grill over a roaring campfire or bring your portable barbecue to cook the following:

- ✦ Steaks.
- ✦ Hamburgers.
- ✦ Hot dogs.
- ✦ Lobster.
- ✦ Chicken.
- ✦ Baked potatoes and corn on the cob, buttered and cooked in foil.
- ✦ Garlic French bread, buttered and cooked in foil.

✧ Bring an ice chest filled with fried chicken, macaroni salad, sandwiches, potato salad, cold veggies and dips, cheeses, beer, and soda.

✧ Serve potato chips, cookies, and iced tea from an insulated container.

✧ Don't forget the condiments—catsup, mustard, steak sauces, relish, pickles, olives, butter, cream, sugar, salt, and pepper.

✧ Bring plenty of utensils: barbecue tools, bottle opener, sharp carving knife, steak knives (if applicable), serving forks and spoons, plenty of cloth napkins or paper towels.

Tip
- — Don't forget the matches!
- — Bring plenty of blankets and beach towels.

84

PROGRESSIVE BREAKFAST, LUNCH, OR DINNER

This is an easy, affordable way for several couples to co-host a party. A progressive meal, of course, is one in which guests travel from home to home, eating one course at each. The couples get together to plan the menu and decide on the decorations and entertainment, if any.

Invitation ideas

✧ Design the invitation as if it were a restaurant menu, listing the courses and where each will be served. Be sure to include a street map that marks the locations of each of the homes.

Attire

✧ Unless you decide to have a theme for the progressive meal, you and the guests should wear what you would normally wear to someone's home for dinner.

Ambiance

✧ Decorations should fit the theme, if any. Otherwise, each host or hostess may decorate his or her home and table any way he or she would like or use ideas from Chapter 5.

Amusements and activities

✧ A progressive meal is entertainment in and of itself—giving the guests a chance to see each other's homes.

✧ You may include a few games at the final stop.

Edibles

✧ Of course, each meal—breakfast, lunch, and dinner—requires a different menu. For a Progressive Breakfast, I recommend the following foods, served in the order indicated.

✦ At the first home: juices, fresh fruits, and coffee.

✦ At the second home: continental breakfast cuisine (light croissants, sliced nut breads, small slices of coffee cake, etc.).

✦ At the third home: the main breakfast course—waffles with all the extras, omelets, crepes, flavored pancakes, breakfast potatoes, sausage, bacon, etc.

✧ A Progressive Lunch usually has fewer courses than a progressive dinner, so you may want to spread it out over three sites. I recommend the following menu.

✦ At the first home: soup and crackers.

✦ At the second home: hot sandwiches and potato salad.

✦ At the third home: dessert and coffee.

✧ For the main course of a Progressive Dinner, you can go gourmet, use an international menu, or cook the foods included in Part 11. Whatever you choose, be sure the other courses go nicely with your main course. Here is a suggested menu:

✦ At the first home: appetizers and cocktails.

✦ At the second home: soup and salad.

✦ At the third home: the main course.

✦ At the fourth home: dessert and coffee.

✧ At the fifth home: fruit, cheeses, and liqueurs.

Tip — If you are mingling with other guests during a course that is just before the course you're hosting, be sure to leave that home early enough so that you are prepared to welcome guests at your home for the next course. Choose dishes that can be delayed, just in case the soup and salad take longer than you estimated, and so forth.

85

INTERNATIONAL FEASTS

Host an international party that features one ethnic cuisine or several. Ask your guests to dress in appropriate costumes or to wear colors representing the flags of the countries represented at your feast.

Invitation ideas

✧ Trim your invitations with flags or travel brochures representing the country or countries whose cuisine will be featured at your party.

Attire

✧ Everyone should wear costumes or colors representing the countries being featured at your party.

Ambiance

Decorate according to the colors and items associated with the country you choose. Here are some ideas:

✧ **Italian**

  ✦ Decorate the food dishes with tiny Italian flags.
  ✦ Use red and white checkered or red, white, and green print tablecloths.
  ✦ Hang Italian travel posters and flags.
  ✦ Display lighted, dripping candles in Chianti bottles.
  ✦ Create a centerpiece with an arrangement of breadsticks in a wicker basket tied with red and green ribbons.

✧ **German**

  ✦ Hang German flags and travel posters.
  ✦ Use a tablecloth and napkins in the colors of the German flag (black, red, and gold).

- ✦ Arrange flowers in German beer steins.
- ✦ Decorate the table with cuckoo clocks and Hummel figurines.

✧ **Scandinavian**

- ✦ Display miniature Viking ships, Viking hats, and Swedish horses.
- ✦ Hang or wear a Swedish apron.
- ✦ Line your dinner table with Swedish table runners.
- ✦ Display Scandinavian travel posters.

✧ **Chinese**

- ✦ Hang China travel posters.
- ✦ Display Chinese paper lanterns, kites, masks, dragons, fans, wooden cricket cages, chopsticks, and anything decorative made out of bamboo.
- ✦ Purchase take-out cartons from a Chinese restaurant or a restaurant supply store. Spray-paint the cartons red, and fill them with live or silk plants. Insert pairs of gold-sprayed chopsticks.
- ✦ Create displays of borrowed Oriental tea sets.
- ✦ Scatter fortune cookies down the center of the table.

✧ **Mexican**

- ✦ Display large, colorful paper flowers.
- ✦ Decorate with red, white, and green balloons and crepe-paper streamers.
- ✦ Hang Mexican flags, sombreros, travel posters, and piñatas.
- ✦ Arrange dozens of candles and strings of colored lights along tables.
- ✦ Miracle candles, those wonderful, tall candles that sit inside a painted glass. These are usually carried by Mexican grocery stores, if you can locate one in your area, or in the ethnic foods section of grocery stores.

✧ **Irish**

- ✦ Haul in the biggest rock you can carry and set it on a bed of crushed green tissue. Label it "Blarney Stone," and encourage your guests to kiss it.
- ✦ Create a pot of gold by covering an empty half-gallon ice cream container with gold foil and filling it with gold foil-wrapped chocolate coins.
- ✦ Hang Irish travel posters.
- ✦ Decorate with shillelaghs, shamrocks, leprechauns, clay pipes, and rubber snakes (St. Patrick is said to have chased the snakes out of Ireland).

Edibles

✧ Serve authentic Italian, German, Scandinavian, Chinese, Mexican, or Irish cuisine. (See Chapter 110 for recipes.)

Tips — Plan an "Around-the-World" Feast as a progressive or potluck dinner; each person can provide food and decor for a different country.

86

FORMAL LUNCH
OR DINNER PARTIES

I love being invited to one of these parties because I know everything about it will be special—a cordial host or hostess, charming ambiance, exquisite cuisine, and congenial conversation.

Formal lunch parties

Many formal lunches are hosted and attended by women. Here are two common formal lunch themes:

+ **A Proper Tea Party.** Despite its name, there is no reason for this elegant affair to be starched or stuffy. It can still be an enjoyable, relaxed time for your guests. The most common time for a tea party is on a weekend (usually Saturday) afternoon around 2 p.m. You can set the tone for the afternoon with a gentle, gracious, relaxed attitude. Tea parties actually originated in England, so the cuisine has a distinctive British flair: high-quality tea, tea sandwiches, tarts, scones, and dream puffs (see Chapter 109 for the recipes).

+ **A Country Garden Party.** This type of party works best outdoors in an actual garden setting, but you can still create a garden atmosphere indoors by decorating with pots of flowers, silk ficus trees, park benches, birdbaths filled with floating candles and gardenias, a white trellis entwined with paper flowers, a low white picket fence, and patio tables with umbrellas and potted geranium centerpieces. You can serve a formal afternoon tea (see Chapter 109) or a formal lunch menu, which usually consists of the following courses, served in this order: fruit or soup served with hot breads or rolls; fowl or meat; salad; and dessert.

Invitation ideas

✧ Invitations are always formal (see Chapter 4).

Attire

✧ A dress or nice pants suit is appropriate.

Ambiance

✧ See Chapter 5 for centerpiece and table decoration tips, including napkin-folding techniques and place card ideas.

✧ Lighted candles are not usually considered appropriate for formal lunches.

Amusements and activities

✧ Relaxing classical or semiclassical music is an appropriate background for the pleasant conversation.

Tips – When planning a formal menu, the emphasis should be on quality, not quantity. In order words, serve exquisite dishes, though they may be few in number.
– Be sure the serving plates or platters are dressed up with lace doilies, garnishes, or fruits for the party.
– Usually, only one type of wine is served during a formal lunch.

Formal dinner parties

The menu for a formal sit-down dinner is usually quite elaborate and served plate service or French service (see Chapter 109). And because the meal is so elaborate and has so many courses, it takes up most of the evening.

Invitation ideas

✧ Invitations are always formal (see Chapter 4). By the way, it is said that the ideal number of guests for a formal dinner party is no more than six to eight, the perfect number for gathering comfortably around most dining room tables.

Attire

✧ Formal, semiformal, or casual-formal attire is required. The latter includes a elegant, dressy pants suits for women.

Ambiance

✧ The rule of thumb for a formal dinner is to present an exquisite table, which includes folding napkins in a special way (even if that means simply slipping a fresh flower into each napkin's folds or tying each napkin with an elegant satin ribbon). See Chapter 5 for centerpiece and table decoration tips, including napkin-folding techniques and place card ideas.

✧ Light up the table and the room with candles to create an elegant, impressive ambiance.

Amusements and activities

✧ You may decide to engage the services of professional musicians, such as a stringed trio, to perform during the meal service. If you really want to impress your guests as they enjoy their after-dinner coffee, arrange for a soloist or instrumentalist to present a mini-concert.

Edibles

✧ See Chapter 109 for a suggested menu and recipes for appetizers, vichyssoise, fruit salad, filet of beef, buttered red potatoes, asparagus tips with Hollandaise sauce, rolls, dessert, and dessert cheeses, and after-dinner mints and chocolate truffles.

✧ A formal dinner party usually requires the serving of alcoholic or nonalcoholic champagne, plus fine wine, liqueurs, and specialty coffees (see Chapter 112).

✧ A truly proper formal dinner menu consists of the following courses, served in this order:

1. Fresh fruit cup, soup, melon, or shellfish.
2. Seafood course.
3. Main course (usually beef or fowl) served with vegetables.
4. Salad.
5. Dessert.
6. Coffee.

Tips – Proper formal dinner etiquette is to have someone other than the host or hostess serve the meal. Hired servers are a nice touch if you can afford them. However, a dinner is usually considered formal as long as it is elegantly presented, using fine silver, china, and crystal.

– As a special touch, place a menu card—a fine-quality linen card with the menu written on it in calligraphy—between every two place settings.

– Don't rush the meal. One of the most charming qualities of a formal dinner is its nice, slow pace. There should be air between the courses, giving the guests time to breathe and enjoy pleasant conversation. In other words—drag it out and milk it for all it's worth!

87

INFORMAL LUNCH OR DINNER PARTIES

Most of the people I interviewed for this book prefer informal entertaining, but it's not because they don't know how to handle a formal event. They just feel more comfortable when hosting an informal gathering. I tend to agree with them, not only because I feel more relaxed when hosting a less structured party, but because my guests usually sense that I'm enjoying myself, and they loosen up, too.

Invitation ideas

✧ Send an informal invitation, such as a handwritten note, or simply give your guests a call.

Ambiance

✧ If your lunch or dinner party has a theme, decorate your table accordingly. Otherwise, use any of the informal table art suggestions in Chapter 5.

Amusements and activities

✧ Have easy-listening background music playing during the meal, but keep the volume low enough to enjoy the pleasant conversation.

Edibles

✧ Serve your tried-and-true favorites.

✧ Use lunch, dinner, and dessert recipes from Part 11.

✧ Have a barbecue bash with steak kabobs, grilled corn on the cob and red potatoes, one or two salads, and hot garlic bread. (See Chapter 78 for additional barbecue menu suggestions.)

✧ For a Hawaiian theme, see the menu suggestions in see Chapter 77.

Tips
- If you're planning to invite more than eight guests, you may want to serve the meal buffet-style, which is the easiest way to serve a large crowd, especially if you don't have any help.
- A potluck meal makes for extra-easy entertaining because you have the fun of getting together without all the work.
- Informal entertaining lends itself to guest participation, especially when preparing certain types of food. For example, a Chinese meal can become a "hot wok party" in which the guests help stir-fry the ingredients. Or guests can barbecue their own meat over a grill or help prepare the pastas and sauces for an Italian meal. Cooperative cooking adds to the fun of the party.

88

DESSERT PARTIES

A dessert party is one of the easiest parties to host. Instead of a full meal, all you need to serve is dessert and coffee. A dessert party is also versatile. It can be fancy or casual, you can serve one dessert or several, and you can add a little entertainment or just let everyone enjoy each other's company.

Invitation ideas

✧ If the party is formal, such as a Candlelight and Roses Dessert Party (see Chapter 32), you can send formal invitations (see Chapter 4). Otherwise, just call people and ask, "Would you like to come over for dessert and coffee Friday night?"

Ambiance

✧ The decorations can be as elaborate or as simple as you want them to be. If you're hosting a formal Candlelight and Roses Dessert Party, you can create a romantic ambiance by turning off most of the lights in the room and decorating with candles, fresh roses, antique lace, swirling tulle netting, delicate satin ribbons, and tiny white lights. Otherwise, see Chapter 5 for decorating suggestions.

Amusements and activities

✧ For a formal dessert party, you may limit the entertainment to soft background music and good conversation. For an informal dessert party, you can include a couple of games (see Chapter 6).

Edibles

Prepare one or two of your favorite dessert recipes, purchase them from a bakery, or use a few of the recipes from this book. The following is a list of possible party themes and desserts from Chapters 110 and 111 that might be appropriate.

- ✧ International Dessert Buffet (see Chapter 110 for recipes):
  - ✦ Swedish Macaroon Tea Cakes.
  - ✦ Mexican Sopaipillas.
  - ✦ Irish Appleberry Crunch.
  - ✦ Cappuccino Cookie Float.

- ✧ Old-Fashioned Ice Cream Social:
  - ✦ Magic Mountain Sundaes (see Chapter 111).
  - ✦ Banana splits.
  - ✦ Ice cream floats.
  - ✦ Special ice cream and yogurt party drinks (see Chapter 112).

- ✧ One Spectacular Showy Dessert (see Chapter 111):
  - ✦ Raspberry Lemon Trifle.
  - ✦ Baked Alaska Cake.

89

COCKTAIL PARTIES

The traditional cocktail party has had a resurgence in popularity and is considered a great way to entertain large, mixed groups of people. Usually a stand-up affair, it can be a happy, lighthearted way to mingle and meet new friends. The beauty of a cocktail party, however, is that it can be whatever you want it to be—a large gathering of 50 to 75 guests, an intimate get-together with six to eight close friends, an Open House (see Chapter 102) with no time limits, or a structured party with specified arrival and closing times.

Invitation ideas

◇ The invitations may be formal or informal (see Chapter 4). They usually give a specific beginning time and ending time, unless they're for an Open House, in which case they'll tell guests the hours during which they can drop by. (Note: An average cocktail party is two to three hours long.)

◇ To prevent a crowded or stuffy environment, don't invite more guests than your venue can hold.

Attire

◇ Unless you state otherwise, a cocktail party is usually somewhat dressy.

Ambiance

◇ Set up a mini-bar, complete with the staples listed below, plus bar tools:

- ✦ Juice squeezer.
- ✦ Swizzle sticks.
- ✦ Fancy toothpicks.
- ✦ Ice pick.
- ✦ Corkscrew.

- ✦ Ice crusher (one pound ice per person).
- ✦ Shot glass.
- ✦ Sharp knife and cutting board.
- ✦ Measuring cups.
- ✦ Bottle opener.

✦ Blender.

✦ Cocktail shaker.

✦ Coasters.

✦ Strainer.

✦ Martini pitcher and stir rod.

✦ Cocktail napkins (three per person).

✦ An assortment of glasses (all-purpose, highball, sherry, wine, champagne, brandy, liqueur, martini).

Amusements and activities

✧ Provide background music for the noisy, happy chatter between the guests, which provides its own entertainment.

✧ Or dance to the tunes of a live band or D.J.

Edibles

✧ Usual fare at a cocktail party consists of alcoholic and nonalcoholic beverages. These are the staples usually found in a well-stocked home bar:

✦ Club soda.

✦ Cola.

✦ Tonic water.

✦ Bourbon.

✦ Gin.

✦ Scotch.

✦ Tequila.

✦ Lemons and limes.

✦ Olives.

✦ Tabasco sauce.

✦ A variety of fruit juices.

✦ Vodka.

✦ Ginger ale.

✦ Blended whiskey.

✦ Brandy.

✦ Light and dark rum.

✦ Dry sherry.

✦ Flavored liqueurs.

✦ Fresh cream.

✦ Alcoholic and nonalcoholic wines.

✦ Chilled soft drinks.

✧ See Chapter 112 for popular nonalcoholic drink ideas.

✧ You may also serve hors d'oeuvres and desserts buffet-style. Be sure the food is in bite-sized portions that can be eaten with the fingers (see Chapters 107 and 108 for ideas).

Tips – A crowded party generates its own heat, so be sure the room is well ventilated. It doesn't hurt to turn on the air-conditioning system and cool the room down before the party begins.

– In many states a host is legally responsible for seeing that guests do not drive home intoxicated. Limit the number of drinks per person over a three-hour period to two full-strength drinks, or the equivalent (for example, one full-strength drink followed by two weak ones, each containing half as much alcohol; four weak drinks; or four small drinks, each containing half as much alcoholic as a full drink).

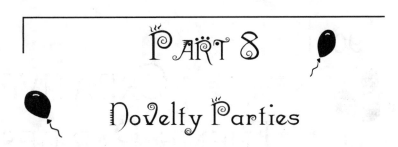

Part 8

Novelty Parties

"There is no idea too silly or bizarre to work as a party theme."

Most parties are celebrations of some special life event—an engagement, a birth, a wedding anniversary, or a birthday—or a holiday, such as the Fourth of July or Christmas Day. The truly great hosts and hostesses of this world, however, don't need a reason to throw a party. They just love to come up with creative new ways to entertain their friends. The parties described in this section are some of their favorite themes, and they may become your favorites, too!

90

CREATIVE
THEME PARTIES

If you're tired of the same old party themes, maybe you need a new idea to whet your creative appetite. Here are a few silly party themes that may appeal to your sense of whimsy, beginning with two hatched from the creative mind of a quintessential hostess named Mary Christensen. Mary's one of those marvelous hostesses who just thinks up stuff! My kind of gal!

Eat, Drink, and Be Messy

How Mary ever came up with this idea, I can't imagine, but it has become so popular that she's hosted this party eight times. Here's what you need to do:

✧ Buy a thick piece of fine-grade clear plywood, sand it, edge it with quarter-round molding, and varnish it. Place the plywood on top of your dining room or eating table.

✧ Set the table with a wooden spaghetti fork and a large bib for each person—no plates, no centerpiece, and no decorations.

✧ Before the guests arrive, sterilize the table by washing it with red wine.

✧ Wear a full-length apron and chef's hat during the party.

✧ When the guests arrive, ask them to sit at the table. Place wooden salad bowls at each place setting, and serve a giant green salad.

✧ When the guests have finished their salads, clear the table of everything except the wooden spoons.

✧ Now comes the big surprise. You or a co-host should stumble into the room and fake a clumsy accident—tripping and dumping a huge pot of cooked pasta onto the middle of the table. Don't let on that this is an act.

✧ Next, you or your co-host should stumble and accidentally dump a bowl of spaghetti sauce on top of the pasta. By now, the guests will begin to catch on.

✧ Instruct the guests to help themselves to pasta and sauce. Invite them to place a portion in front of them on the bare table and dig in with their wooden forks. Serve red wine, Parmesan cheese, and hot garlic bread.

✧ After the main meal, the guests should adjourn to the living room as you wash the table, cover it with a sheet of plastic, and top it with a fine linen tablecloth. Set the table with your finest china and silverware, in addition to a beautiful floral centerpiece and lighted candles.

✧ Invite the guests back to the table to enjoy an exquisite dessert.

Tip — Mary designed the party invitation in the shape of a bib.

Health and Wellness Party

This is another one of Mary's ingenious ideas. Whenever she was around a certain group of friends, she realized that the main topic of conversation was the state of their health: their latest operations, illnesses, aches and pains, etc. Therefore, she decided to host this party, which goes something like this (you'll need a couple of co-hosts to pull this off)...

✧ Attach real Band-Aid adhesive bandages to the front of the invitations, which should ask each guest to bring a healthy dish or food item to the party and to wear workout clothes.

✧ The party room is decorated with medical paraphernalia, plus flowers arranged in a hot water bottle.

✧ When the guests arrive, they are greeted at the front door by someone in a nurse's uniform who has each guest draw a folded piece of paper from her nurse's cap. These pieces of paper assign a certain illness to each guest, such as impotency, constipation, heart problems, etc.

✧ The guests then have their blood pressure taken and proceed to the doctor's clinic (a designated part of your home) where they are prescribed medicines to cure their illnesses. Each guest receives a prescription bottle filled with a cure. For example:

Illness	Cure
✦ Impotency.	Rock candy.
✦ Ulcers.	Garlic cloves.
✦ Eye problems.	Sliced carrots.
✦ Valley Fever.	Bed rest, preferably with your spouse.
✦ Heart problems.	Candy hearts.
✦ Kidney problems.	Kidney beans.
✦ Constipation.	Brown M&M's candy.

✧ Once the guests have been medicated, they select a healthy activity from a list you hand out—such as aerobic exercise led by an aerobics instructor on the patio, running laps around a course in the backyard, or putting into a putting cup on the lawn.

✧ As the guests participate in these strenuous activities, they are served health drinks from a juice bar set up in your kitchen, and they receive relief from their aches and pains from you or a co-host, offering them Ace elastic bandages and Ben-Gay analgesic ointment.

✧ Finally, everything settles down and the guests enjoy eating the potluck dishes they have brought.

✧ Give awards for silly achievements, such as "most recent doctor's appointment," "most recent operation," and so forth. Give a seven-day pillbox to the guest who comes closest to guessing the correct number of aspirin in an aspirin bottle.

✧ The door prize is something leftover from a hospital stay, such as booties and hat worn during surgery.

Winter Beach Party

This is a fun idea for the cold winter months, especially if you live in the Northeast and Midwest, where temperatures dip into the teens.

✧ Turn the thermostat up to 78° or higher.

✧ Ask the guests to wear beach attire—swimsuits, cover-ups, beach shoes, and hats.

✧ Roast hot dogs and marshmallows over the fire (use your fireplace), add a few old-fashioned picnic dishes (see Chapter 79), and serve cold beer and soda from a tub filled with ice.

✧ Decorate the room with palm trees cut out of poster board, embellished with green paper fronds, and travel posters of warm beach destinations.

✧ Play island music, such as Caribbean or Hawaiian melodies.

Backward Party

✧ Send invitations with the words written from right to left.

✧ Wear clothes backward.

✧ Have guests enter the party walking backward.

✧ Serve refreshments in reverse order (the dessert first, etc.).

Blackout Party

Reminiscent of the great New York blackout of November 9, 1965, the party takes place in the dark (well, almost) with only candles to light the room.

✧ Guests wear black and white attire.

✧ Serve appetizers and finger foods that are easy to see in the dark, along with cocktails or soft drinks.

✧ Slow dance to romantic music.

Noah's Ark Party

✧ Pairs of guests come dressed as pairs of animals.

✧ Build a wooden ramp leading up your front steps.

✧ Play one of those soothing, "sounds of nature" CDs or cassette—one of rain and thunderstorms.

✧ Light the room with candles and oil lamps.

✧ Decorate with pairs of stuffed animals (two bears, two dogs, two cats, etc.).

✧ If hosting the party as a couple, greet your guests dressed as Noah and his wife.

Glitzy Fashion Brunch

This all-girl party is a tongue-in-cheek spoof of the filthy rich. The guests arrive ready to model showy attire.

✧ Send elegant, engraved invitations, trimmed with rhinestones and jewels and sprinkled with gold glitter.

✧ Guests arrive wearing hoity-toity garb—evening gowns with mink or ostrich feather stoles, gobs of diamond jewelry, highest heels, and several ankle bracelets.

✧ Decorate with gaudy, jeweled knickknacks, shiny satin or sequined fabrics, gold lace and braiding, and, of course, your glitziest silver and crystal, plus floral arrangements dripping with jewels and sequins.

✧ The fashion show is the highlight of the party as the hostess describes each outfit being modeled. (Give prizes for most glamorous, most glitzy, most creative, etc.)

✧ Serve an informal or formal lunch (see Chapter 108 or 109).

✧ Hire a violinist or harpist to provide upscale background music for this prestigious affair.

Sadie Hawkins' Old-Fashioned Box Social

This theme is great for a singles' group because it offers an innocent way to pair up couples at a dinner.

✧ Each gal furnishes a beautifully decorated box containing a sumptuous picnic for two.

✧ The men arrive empty-handed and pay for their supper by bidding on the boxes, winning the right to share the food and the company of the box's owner.

✧ The money raised by the auction may be contributed to charity.

✧ In the spirit of an old-fashioned Sadie Hawkins' Day, everyone can dress up in their favorite western attire—men in jeans, boots, western shirts, and cowboy hats; women in eyelet blouses and full cotton print skirts.

✧ Hire a live caller for square-dancing.

✧ Or invite a country-western band or play recorded country-western music for a little country swing or line dancing.

White Elephant Party

A "white elephant" is any ugly, impractical, or humorous item you received as a gift or somehow ended up with—one of those best-forgotten objects (a hideously ugly vase, a gaudy necklace, a terribly tacky tie) you stashed away in the closet or basement years ago.

✧ Ask everyone to bring one or two gift-wrapped white elephants. Stack them together, and let each guest select a gift from the pile. Ask the guests to open the gifts, one at a time. After a guest has opened a gift, give him or her the option of keeping the gift, selecting another from the pile, or "robbing" another guest of his gift. Each guest has three "steals" until the last gift has been opened. Or auction off the white elephants as a mock fund raiser.

✧ Make it a dessert party (see Chapter 88).

Tips – Use the party themes in this chapter as inspiration for crazy ideas of your own!

– More silly excuses for a party:
  ✎ January 22—Feast Day of St. Vincent, Patron Saint of Wine Growers.
  ✎ February 1—Beginning of Potato Lovers' Month.
  ✎ February 18—Day the Planet Pluto Was Discovered (1930).
  ✎ March 11—Johnny Appleseed Day.
  ✎ March 19—Day Swallows Fly Back to the Mission of San Juan Capistrano, California.
  ✎ April 14—Chicken Strut in Bethune, South Carolina.
  ✎ May 18—Jumping Frog Jubilee in Angels Camp, California.
  ✎ May 31—End of Pickle Week.
  ✎ June 10—Chicken Festival in Milford, Delaware.
  ✎ June 28—Mel Brooks' Birthday.
  ✎ July 16—National Ice Cream Week.
  ✎ July 21—Garlic Festival in Gilroy, California.
  ✎ August 11—Popcorn Festival in Van Buren, Indiana.
  ✎ September 8—Kickoff of National Rub-a-Bald-Head Week.
  ✎ September 30—Oyster Festival in Oyster Bay, New York.
  ✎ October 5—International Balloon Fiesta in Albuquerque, New Mexico.
  ✎ November 4—Kona Coffee Festival in Kailua-Kona, Hawaii.
  ✎ December 1—Catfish Stomp in Elgin, South Carolina.
  ✎ December 12—Crossword Puzzle Day.
  ✎ December 23—Night of the Radishes in Mexico.

91

Agatha Christie Party

Mystery becomes a winning party theme when the guests are invited to participate in—and are even *suspects* in—a make-believe murder mystery. The fun of one of these get-togethers is trying to figure out "whodunit." If you plan your party well, no one will know until the last minute which guest is actually the "murderer."

Invitation ideas

✧ Most mystery party games are designed for a total of eight to 10 people, so plan your guest list accordingly. Decorate your invitations with fingerprints (press your finger on an ink pad). Give each guest a copy of a script for the murder mystery you will stage, and ask each guest to play a certain character (see the heading "Amusements and activities" for information on murder mystery games).

Attire

✧ You and your guests will be dressed as the characters in the plot. You can rent your costumes, or you may find what you need at a thrift shop.

Ambiance

✧ Hang enlarged photocopies of the front covers of murder mystery books.

✧ Decorate the table with toy magnifying glasses and weapons.

✧ Spray canned Halloween cobwebs in ceiling corners and doorways and on light fixtures.

✧ Scatter a generous supply of lollipops (remember *Kojak*?) on the tables.

✧ Draw the outline of a body on the floor using black crafting tape.

✧ Tape off the crime area using yellow plastic ribbon.

Amusements and activities

✧ Purchase a murder mystery party game from your local party supply store, or order from the Lighter Side Catalog (see Resources). Generally, mystery party games are set up for a party of 10 people. The guests are told that someone has been murdered and that the murderer is present in the room. Then, the guests are furnished with questions to ask each other to try to determine the identity of the murderer.

✧ Award prizes for most authentic costumes.

Edibles

✧ A sit-down dinner is often served as an integral part of the mystery itself. This meal can be catered and served by maids or servants dressed in appropriate costume, depending on the era in which the murder takes place. For example, if the murder takes place during the Victorian period, the maids should be dressed in Victorian-style maid costumes.

✧ You may choose to serve an informal meal or dessert buffet instead.

Tips – Many dinner theaters, bed-and-breakfast inns, and hotels offer murder mystery entertainment packages, which usually include a dinner as part of the evening's activities.

92

VIDEO SCAVENGER HUNT

This is one of the most popular party themes going these days, and one of my own personal favorites. The reason I love Video Scavenger Hunt parties is that, no matter how many of these parties you host or attend, they're different every time.

Divide the guests into teams of four to six people (enough to fill one car). Each team must have a video camera and a tape (in your invitations, you can ask guests to bring these supplies). The teams compete to be the first to return to the original party site with a videotape that shows them completing every task from a list provided in advance. You may also include this list in your invitations.

Invitation ideas

✧ Obtain enlargements of a photo of a humorous stunt or scene. Write the invitation on the back of each enlargement, and mail in a photo mailer.

Attire

✧ Dress is casual and comfortable, for performing the stunts required.

Ambiance

✧ Set up folding chairs, theater-style, in front of your TV.
✧ Tie a couple of balloon bouquets to the chairs.

Amusements and activities

Your list of required stunts and activities to be videotaped by the teams can be as creative as you want it to be. The list should contain no more than 15 or 20 stunts because each carload will have only an hour and a half to videotape as many as they can. Here are some ideas from actual Video Scavenger Hunt parties to get you started:

+ One of the members of the team standing in front of (or sitting on) a statue.

+ Several members of the team joining a street entertainer in his or her act.

+ A stranger singing the national anthem.

+ One or more members of a team standing under a public clock at an exact time (such as 7:21 p.m.).

+ A member of the team singing a 1970s song on a stage.

+ A member of the team singing "I Wish I Were an Oscar Meyer Wiener" while standing in the hot dog section of a local grocery store.

+ A member of the team standing on a surfboard.

+ Any stranger from the state of [name any state other than your own].

+ Depending on the season of the year, members of the team standing in front of a lighted outdoor Christmas tree, or waving an American flag, or offering candy from a box of Valentine's candy, or carrying an Easter basket while pretending to search for Easter eggs, etc.

+ A friend or acquaintance "abducted" and brought back to the party.

+ A team member helping to carry a stranger's groceries.

+ A stranger trying to spell *potato* [or any other word].

+ A team member opening a door for a stranger while asking for a tip.

+ A stranger reciting the names of all the continents.

+ One or more members of the team singing at a karaoke bar.

+ A couple dancing to department store or elevator music.

+ A team member reading a book or reciting a poem to a stranger.

+ A team member going to a department store and trying on a shirt or dress that is several sizes too small, then asking the clerk if it fits.

+ A stranger who has been to [a particular tourist attraction of your choice].

+ A stranger demonstrating the Macarena.

+ A stranger named Bob.

+ A stranger who knows your state flower.

+ A stranger who can imitate John Wayne.

+ A policeman drawing a chalk line on the ground around one of the team members.

+ A team member filling a stranger's car with gas, washing the car's windows, and checking the oil.

+ One or more team members standing beside a tombstone.

+ A team member sitting on a fire truck with a fireman.

+ Road kill (an animal that has been run over on the highway).
+ A team member standing by the greeter at a Wal-Mart and greeting the customers.
+ A team member asking a hardware store clerk to explain the difference between a flat head and a Phillips head screwdriver.
+ Team members standing in a row arranging their bodies so that they spell a certain word.
+ A team member washing dishes at a restaurant.
+ Team members singing an Elvis song while standing under a neon sign.
+ A team member holding a chicken.

These are examples of the types of stunts you'll need to add to your list, but I'm sure you can come up with dozens more of your own.

The guests should be given an exact time to return to the party venue. If not back on time, the team is disqualified. Once everyone has returned, the video-tapes are played. The guests vote on the stunts presented in each videotape as follows:

+ **1 point:** The stunt was completed, whether done well or not.
+ **2 points:** The stunt was completed with creativity.
+ **3 points:** The stunt was exceptionally creative.

Five bonus points are awarded to any team that comes up with an original stunt and tapes it. For example, at one Video Scavenger Hunt party, a team's videotape showed a big, husky male team member walking into a department store and trying on bras in the middle of an aisle as other team members, with straight faces, critiqued the way each one fit.

The team with the most points wins.

Edibles

✧ Serve snacks, appetizers, and cold or hot beverages before the hunt and while the game rules are being explained.

✧ Set up a self-serve ice cream sundae station for the guests to enjoy while watching the videos (see Chapter 111). Decorate your ice cream bar with balloons and colorful plastic bowls and napkins.

Tip — It's a good idea to serve nonalcoholic beverages because driving is required.

93

TACKY PARTY

A Tacky Party is a party at which everything is done as gaudily or tastelessly as possible—the invitations, the decor, the attire, the refreshments. This is a chance for everyone to leave their troubles at home, loosen up, and enjoy acting out.

Invitation ideas

✧ In order to have the proper degree of tackiness, the invitations will need to be handcrafted. Include misspelled words, small embellishments that have been glued on crooked, smudges, and torn corners. Mail in old envelopes that have had the old addresses blacked out and new stamps attached.

Attire

✧ Guests should wear the tackiest outfits they can come up with—unlaced combat boots with an evening gown, long white gloves with a denim dress, a fancy hat with jeans and a flannel shirt, balled-up polyester pants suits, and so forth. Encourage them to stop by local garage sales and thrift shops for articles of clothing.

✧ Greet the guests at the door wearing a ratty nightgown or pajamas, an old, faded robe, mismatched socks, your hair in curlers, etc.

Ambiance

✧ Your guests may be greeted with a dozen or so pink plastic flamingos standing in the front yard.

✧ A garage is a wonderfully suited venue for a tacky party!

✧ Decorate in the gaudiest, tackiest way possible: toilet paper streamers, a dirty tablecloth, paper towels as napkins, metal and plastic tableware mixed, and an assortment of odd glasses, some with lipstick and dirty fingerprint marks on them. Use empty soup cans as cups. Hang broken Christmas ornaments on silk or fresh plants, and serve drinks in cups and glasses with company logos on them. Hang a huge black velvet toreador picture on the wall.

✧ Create a tacky centerpiece for the table—a drippy paint can filled with weeds and dying flowers, or a perfectly awful vase filled with dusty, plastic flowers.

Amusements and activities

✧ Everyone should act as tactlessly as possible, adopting sloppy eating habits, scratching themselves in obnoxious places, using their pinky fingers to clean out their ears, etc.

✧ Exchange tacky, tasteless gifts, such as an enema kit, wrapped in old holiday paper, newspaper, or bags with logos.

✧ Give prizes for the tackiest outfits and the tackiest behavior.

Edibles

✧ Serve tacky food in tacky containers, such as bologna slices and hard bread, along with real food served on decent paper plates (see Chapters 107, 108, 110, and 111 for ideas).

✧ Serve generic brands of beverages.

✧ For dessert, serve Twinkies and Hostess cupcakes.

94

DECADE PARTIES

A Decade Party is one whose theme is a certain decade in our history. Once you've chosen a decade as your theme, plan everything else around it—decorations, attire, food, music, and activities.

Here are three examples:

40s Canteen

The 1940s are remembered as the war years, the days of the stage door canteens, or USO clubs, where the military men and women were provided with refreshments, dancing, and entertainment.

✦ Enclose homemade dog tags (the metal IDs worn around the necks of servicemen) inside the invitations.

✦ Decorate your room like a stage door canteen, with a bar serving refreshments, bandstand, dance floor, and revolving mirror ball.

✦ Hang Uncle Sam posters, U.S. flags, and 40s movie posters, along with other memorabilia.

✦ Scatter ration coupons along the serving bar.

✦ Dress in 40s attire, including military uniforms (check vintage clothing shops or costume rental stores).

✦ Play background music of 40s hits by the Andrews Sisters, Glenn Miller, etc.

✦ Sing 40s songs, such as "Don't Sit Under the Apple Tree."

✦ Dance to recorded 40s hits

✦ Serve typical canteen refreshments—sandwiches, coffee, punch, doughnuts, and ice cream.

50s Sock Hop

The 50s were the days of shake, rattle, and roll, Bobby socks, saddle shoes and poodle skirts.

✧ Glue black musical notes on the front of the invitations, voice-mail the invitation to background music of a 50s hit, or mail old LP records with the invitation printed on a new record label.

✧ Men can wear blue jeans, black leather jackets, and tight white T-shirts with a pack of cigarettes rolled up in one sleeve.

✧ The women can wear poodle skirts, white off-the-shoulder blouses, bobby socks (socks that barely reach over the ankle), saddle shoes, and ponytails in their hair.

✧ Decorate the walls with Elvis posters or a mural of a '57 Chevy (available from Anderson's Prom and Party Catalog—see Resources).

✧ Rent a jukebox.

✧ Pull back the rug or rent a dance floor so the guests can enjoy dancing to a few of the romantic oldies.

✧ Have a dance contest that includes dancing the Stroll, the Mashed Potato, and the Twist.

✧ Display life-sized cardboard figures of James Dean, Elvis Presley, or Marilyn Monroe (available from Advanced Graphics—see Resources). Take a photo of each guest with his or her arm around a figure.

✧ Use ponytail holders as napkin rings.

✧ Borrow someone's classic car from the 50s to park in your driveway. Decorate with fuzzy dice, pom-poms, school pennants, or a cluster of helium balloons tied to the antenna. See if you can talk the owner of the classic car into offering rides around the block.

✧ Play background music by 50s favorites—Bill Haley & the Comets, Chubby Checker, Elvis, and so forth.

✧ Have a hula hoop contest.

✧ Serve 50s soda fountain favorites—hamburgers, hot dogs, French fries, ice cream sodas, root beer floats, cherry cokes, and brownies a la mode.

Surfin' 60s

The 60s was the decade of the Beatles, the Beach Boys, the surfing craze, the *Ed Sullivan Show*, Peter, Paul, and Mary, and, of course, hippies.

✧ Record the invitation onto cassette tapes with Beatles music playing in the background.

✧ Dress in 60s attire—tie-dyed T-shirts, bell bottoms, sandals, crocheted vests, headbands, dark sunglasses, and bead necklaces.

- ✧ Decorate Beatlemania-style, displaying Beatles posters, photos, and records, pictures of yellow submarines, and so forth. Play an album of Beatles hits. Ask the guests to come dressed as one of the Beatles.

- ✧ Hang mobiles of old 45 records.

- ✧ Create a beach scene on your patio if weather permits or indoors. Arrange a beach chair and umbrella, swim towel, huge white-framed sunglasses, and a straw beach hat.

- ✧ Play background music by the Beatles and the Beach Boys.

- ✧ Stage an episode of the *Ed Sullivan Show,* with someone portraying Ed Sullivan and others lip-syncing to songs from the 60s, juggling, or performing other novelty acts.

- ✧ Serve healthy snacks and natural foods, such as pastas, raw fruits and vegetables, and brown rice on a surfboard placed on top of the serving table or on vintage album covers.

- ✧ Serve fresh-squeezed fruit and vegetable juices.

TV and Video Parties

Plan a party around the television set, whether you're watching the Olympics, the Grammy Awards, the Indy 500, NBA finals, the Soap Opera awards, the Oscars, the Super Bowl, the World Series, or a rented movie or travelogue.

Invitation ideas

✧ Invites are informal—via telephone, e-mail, or word of mouth.

Attire

✧ Encourage everyone to dress appropriately for the event being viewed—for example, a referee's shirt and whistle for the NBA finals, a racing jumpsuit for the Indy 500, a football jersey for the Super Bowl, etc.

Ambiance

✧ Display banners, sports equipment, pennants, movie posters, sports magazines, etc., depending on the event or movie.

✧ If the party centers on a sports event, lay a narrow carpet of synthetic turf from the front door to the TV room. If it's a movie, use a red carpet.

Amusements and activities

✧ The event or movie on TV is the main attraction. Arrange benches as bleacher seats or chairs as theater seats, all facing the television set.

Edibles

✦ Corn dogs.
✦ Chips.
✦ Personal pizzas.
✦ Egg rolls.·

✦ Giant bowls of freshly popped popcorn.
✦ Snacks and appetizers from Chapter 107.
✦ Soda or beer served in large plastic cups.
✦ Magic Mountain Sundaes (see Chapter 111).

96

KARAOKE PARTY

Everyone enjoys the novelty of karaoke. A karaoke machine provides the words and professional accompaniment for popular songs, which helps almost anyone sound well when they give it a try.

Invitation ideas

✧ Attach the invitation to a child's toy microphone, and mail in a padded envelope.

Attire

✧ Ask the guests to dress as if they are contestants on *Star Search*—wearing sequined gowns, snazzy suits, etc.

Ambiance

✧ Create a marquee for your entryway that announces the names of the people "auditioning." Use a heavy black marker to write the names on poster board. Surround the poster with flashing white Christmas bulbs.

✧ Hang enlarged copies of sheet music.

✧ Suspend CDs and glittery stars from the ceiling with fishing line.

✧ Display real or toy drum sets and other instruments around the room.

✧ Create a stage setting by placing folding chairs in rows in front of a spotlighted stage.

Amusements and activities

✧ Rent a karaoke machine (check listings under "disc jockeys" or "party rentals" in the yellow pages).

✧ Interview the "celebrities" before they sing.

✧ Encourage as many guests as possible to give it a try Usually, with just a little encouragement, one or two guests who have used a karaoke machine before will be glad to demonstrate how the concept works. The next thing you know, they're really enjoying themselves, which will encourage the rest of your guests to give it a try.

✧ Invite guests who don't want to sing to act as judges. The judges can vote to have contestants removed from the stage, as well as award prizes for the most professional, most creative, most bizarre, or funniest performance.

✧ Videotape the evening's performances, and show the tape at the end of the auditions.

Edibles

✧ During the performances, you can serve bags of buttered popcorn and over-sized drinks, followed later in the evening by a light supper or dessert buffet (see Chapters 108 and 111).

97

AMATEUR NIGHT

Remember when the best thing about summer camp was Amateur Night, when kids performed skits, sang, played instruments, told jokes, recited poems, or demonstrated some amazing one-of-a-kind talent? Well, you can relive those times with this theme. Just remember that what makes these parties a success is to incorporate as much humor as possible—this is not the time for a serious piano recital.

For example, one Amateur Night party featured three guys who sang their own version of "I Left My Heart in San Francisco." Their act was hilarious not only because of their original lyrics, but because none of the three could carry a tune! Then six gals came out to compete in a hula hoop contest, followed by a hillbilly band that performed with kazoos, sandpaper blocks, a broomstick bass, pots as drums, pot lids as cymbals, and a musical saw. Every guy in the band wore a goofy hat and kept a straight face during the entire performance.

Amateur Night should be all tongue-in-cheek—as light and silly and fun as it can be!

Invitation ideas

✧ Call the people you plan to invite ahead of time to find out if they can perform. Then print the invitations on the back of programs that facetiously announce the guest performers, so-called awards they have won, how they are known all around the world for their talent, and so forth. (Also, be sure to assign guests to the following roles: master of ceremonies, ushers, and audience.)

Attire

✧ Performing guests should wear their stage costumes.

✧ A master of ceremonies who introduces each act should wear a tux and top hat.

✧ Ushers should be dressed in suits and ties.

✧ The audience (nonperforming guests) can wear semi-formal out-to-the-theater attire.

Ambiance

✧ Create a program of the evening's entertainment on a white poster board using a black marker. Set the program on an easel at the room's entrance for the guests to see as they arrive.

✧ Set up chairs as if in a theater-in-the-round setting. Darken the room and have ushers use flashlights to lead guests to their seats.

✧ Make a hand-operated, poster board "laugh-o-meter" to measure the applause for each act.

Amusements and activities

✧ Decide the order of the acts in advance—for example, karaoke singing, then performing in a kazoo or hillbilly band, then a stand-up comedy routine, and so on.

✧ Remember that there are no rules for these parties. Anything goes!

✧ Present awards for best musical group, most creative, etc.

Edibles

✧ Serve bags of buttered popcorn and large-sized drinks during the performances, followed later in the evening with a self-serve ice cream sundae bar.

Tip – This type of party needs a big crowd to be successful—at least 30 guests.

98

CASINO PARTY

Everyone seems to like a Casino Party, even without the real money. The games played can include bingo, poker, bridge, or even a board game (such as checkers or backgammon).

Invitation ideas

✧ Send decks of new cards with invitations inserted inside the wrappers.

Attire

✧ As the host or hostess, wear dealer's attire—black slacks, white shirts with black bow ties, green visors, etc.

Ambiance

✧ Display giant dice, giant playing cards, token-filled cups, and a money wheel.

Amusements and activities

✧ Before the games begin, supply the guests with plenty of play money.

✧ You can have a few games going on at once—poker at one circular table, bridge and board games at several card tables, bingo on the patio or in another part of the house (it's a noisy game!), etc.

✧ The guest with the most play money at quitting time wins a lottery ticket.

✧ Top the evening off with an auction of worthless white elephant gifts. Let the guests go wild spending whatever play money they have left.

Edibles

✧ Serve finger foods (see Chapter 107). Arrange them on small tables spread around the rooms.

99

BIG APPLE PARTY

Treat your guests to an evening in Manhattan, without having to travel—what an exciting theme for a party!

Invitation ideas

✧ Visit the *New York Times* Web site (www.nytimes.com/yr/mo/day/), and print out copies of the page to use as invitations. Paste a headline over each page that reveals the party information. Ask the guests to come dressed as stereotypical Manhattan characters—bag ladies, cab drivers, Broadway show characters, Wall Street bankers, and so forth.

Attire

✧ You'll have an array of interestingly attired characters at your party. Of course, you'll want to wear something fun yourself.

✧ If the guests don't come in costume, order top hats and canes for each (available from Anderson's Prom and Party Supply Catalog—see Resources).

Ambiance

✧ Decorate with travel posters, playbills, and a mural of the Manhattan skyline (also available from Anderson's).

✧ Set up a hot dog or souvenir vendor cart on your patio or front porch.

✧ Show a travelogue video of New York City (borrow it from a library, video rental store, or travel agency).

✧ Rent a karaoke machine so the guests can take turns singing Broadway show tunes.

✧ Throughout the party site, have several small television sets showing different movies inspired by Broadway hits, such as *My Fair Lady, Brigadoon, Les*

Miserables, and *Mame* (available from the "classics" section in video rental stores). Play the movies simultaneously throughout the evening, with the volume turned low.

✧ Turn your dining room into Tavern on the Green by surrounding the table with silk or live trees entwined with tiny white lights.

✧ Or serve your dishes from the hot dog vendor's cart.

✧ Be sure to take plenty of instant photos and videotape the evening's activities. Watch the video toward the end of the party.

Amusements and activities

✧ Play instrumental versions of Broadway hits. Give a prize to the guest who can name the most correct titles.

✧ Why not splurge and hire a horse and carriage to give rides to your guests?

Edibles

✧ If you use the Tavern on the Green idea, serve an elegant sit-down dinner (see Chapters 86 and 109).

✧ If you use the vendor cart idea, serve hot dogs, hot pretzels, roasted chestnuts, chips, and bottled fruit juices, right off the cart itself.

Part 9
Just-for-the-Fun-of-It Parties

"Make someone feel good—invite him or her to a party just for the fun of it."

Why not host a party just for the fun of it? No one *expects* you to organize a Block Party or welcome the new family across the street with a Welcome Neighbor Party, but what the heck! Why not? It's a great excuse for a party!

100

BON VOYAGE PARTY

Everyone loves the idea of a Bon Voyage Party, especially the guest(s) of honor. When someone has scraped and saved for years, looking forward to that Caribbean cruise or Hawaiian holiday, they deserve a party! Don't you agree?

Invitation ideas

✧ Slide the invitations inside luggage tags, and attach the tags to travel brochures for the destination of the guest(s) of honor. (Luggage tags are available at airports and where luggage is sold.)

Attire

✧ Ask the guests to wear clothing appropriate to the destination, such as Hawaiian garb for Hawaii or sombreros for a cruise to Mexico.

✧ Or have the guests come dressed as tacky tourists, wearing such things as plaid shorts, knee-high brown socks, black dress shoes, several cameras around their necks, oversized sunglasses, straw hats, etc.

Ambiance

✧ Use the destination as your decorating theme. For example, display tiki torches, conch shells, orchid leis, and grass skirts for a Hawaiian vacation or sombreros, serapes, and Mexican flags for a cruise to Acapulco. If Paris should be the destination, create a replica of the Left Bank with unfinished paintings on easels, baskets of fresh or silk flowers, and sidewalk cafes. You get the idea!

✧ Or transform your living room into the deck of a cruise ship by laying out a shuffleboard game, adding canvas-backed deck chairs, and colorful life jackets and buoys.

✧ Display travel brochures and posters of the destination.

✧ Enlarge a map of the destination, attach it to a poster board, and display it on an easel.

Amusements and activities

✧ As guests arrive, play background music that fits the destination, such as Don Ho songs if the destination is Hawaii.

✧ Rent or borrow a travelogue of the destination, and play it continuously during the evening. Turn the volume low, or off, if appropriate.

✧ Play one or two games suggested in Chapter 6.

✧ Purchase a foreign language phrase book for the travelers, if they'll need one where they're going. Play a game in which you recite translations for common statements such as "Where is the rest room?" and "Where is the subway?" and have guests repeat after you. When you're done, quiz the guest(s) of honor.

✧ Ask the guests to tell their most humorous travel experiences.

Edibles

✧ Serve food and drink you would find at the couple's destination (see Chapters 77 and 110 for menus and recipes).

Tips – The party doesn't have to take place in a home—you can have it in the airport (get permission to use one of their lounges) or in the stateroom or lounge aboard the cruise ship before it embarks.

– Purchase a supply of colorful postcards and have the guests address them to themselves during the party. Give them to the guests of honor to write on and mail back home during their trip.

101

BLOCK PARTY

A block party is one in which a certain block or cul de sac is closed to traffic to provide an open-air venue for a neighborhood get-together. The purpose of this party is for neighbors to get to know each other better and have a good time. It can include anything from a potluck supper to an elegant sit-down candlelit dinner at nicely decorated picnic tables. It can have a theme or just be an informal means of socializing. There are no rules for this event. Often, however, block parties are holiday-oriented—celebrating Independence or Memorial Day with a picnic (see Chapter 79), a barbecue (see Chapter 78), a luau, complete with authentic Polynesian entertainment (see Chapter 77), or a Tacky Party (see Chapter 93).

Here's how to go about planning your own Block Party:

◇ **Step 1.** It takes a minimum of four people to assure stress-free planning, so enlist three neighbors to join you on a planning committee. Set up a time to get together for a one-hour meeting to talk about theme ideas, possible dates, food, entertainment ideas, and admission fees (if you decide to charge one). (This fee should cover the minimal out-of-pocket expenses your committee may have in the way of brochures, decorations, or prizes, etc.) Design a flyer to hand-carry to each neighbor requesting input.

◇ **Step 2.** As soon as you've heard from at least half of the neighbors, you'll have a good idea of how many are interested in having a block party and when most will be available. At this point the committee needs to get together once more and decide on a firm date, in addition to the theme (if any), type of food, activities and party attire.

◇ **Step 3.** Call the local police department to get permission to block the streets during the party. (Make this call early in case there are forms that need to be filled out, etc.)

◇ **Step 4.** Design and distribute flyers announcing the date and details of the party, in addition to reminders to be distributed two or three days before the party. (You'll find that many people don't take an invitation to a block party as seriously as they would an invitation to a more formal affair.)

◇ **Step 5.** A second committee member is put in charge of coordinating the food, portable barbecues (if required), tables, chairs, tubs of ice for the beverages, etc. Basically, this entails calling each neighbor asking for a firm commitment on what they will furnish.

◇ **Step 6.** A third committee member plans the activities and entertainment. If there will be dancing, you'll need recorded or live music, if there are sports competitions or games for the children, you'll need to round up the gear, such as a volleyball net for street volleyball, if the theme calls for entertainment, you'll need to locate (or enlist) hula dancers, square dancers, or line dancers. You can provide prizes for the loudest shirt, the craziest hat or the tackiest outfit, depending on the theme of the party.

◇ **Step 7.** The fourth committee member is in charge of street decorations, including helium balloons attached to street lights, crepe paper streamers tied to utility poles, colorful disposable table coverings, candlelight or lanterns (for an evening party), and so forth.

Tips – If the weather doesn't cooperate, be prepared to transport the party into someone's garage or onto a covered patio, or if there is a huge crowd, turn it into a progressive party, traveling from home to home.

– Don't forget to include the pets! You can even have a pet parade with prizes for the scruffiest, silliest, cutest, etc. This is a great way to get the children involved.

– Ask everyone to dress according to the theme, if you have one. For example, if it's a Big D Barbecue, suggest jeans, cowboy boots, ten-gallon hats, bandannas, etc. Or, if it's a Polynesian party, you'll have no problem enticing everyone to drag out their Hawaiian clothes, leis, and shell necklaces.

– You may want to increase the admission fee to include a professional videographer to immortalize the event, or to pay for portable cameras at each table.

– Solicit the local merchants for goods or gift certificates to use as prizes or favors.

– Allow at least eight weeks to plan the party—three months is even better.

102

OPEN HOUSE

An Open House—a party without a set schedule of events, to which guests stop in at their convenience—may be the least stressful way to celebrate the holidays, meet your new neighbors, or show off you new home.

Invitation ideas

✧ Invitations may be written on informal note paper, extended over the telephone, or sent via store-bought fill-in invitations.

Attire

✧ Dress somewhere between formal and casual so that your guests will feel comfortable however they are dressed.

Ambiance

✧ Light the fireplace and a few candles, and place floral arrangements around the serving area. Also, burn scented candles in the bathrooms.

Amusements and activities

✧ Be prepared to give tours of your house. However, while you're showing off your master bedroom closet, be sure someone is on duty to greet other guests at the front door as they arrive.

✧ If you receive a few housewarming gifts, set them aside to open later. If everyone brings a gift, open the gifts as part of the festivities.

Edibles

✧ An Open House may be a cocktail party, a dessert party, or a light hors d'oeuvre buffet. Keep the food fresh and appetizing as the party goes along.

103

WELCOME NEIGHBOR PARTIES

There is no better excuse for a party than to welcome new neighbors. You may have brought a casserole dish or freshly baked pie to the poor bedraggled creatures on the day they moved in, but it's still nice to give them an official welcome to the neighborhood. A party will not only give you a chance to become acquainted with the newcomers, but it will mean more to them than you realize. (If it's been a while since you made a major move, you may have forgotten how bereft it feels to be plopped in the middle of a foreign land.)

Invitation ideas

✧ Handprint or computer-generate personalized invitations. Here's a sample:

Have You Met the New Kids on the Block?

Tom and Ginny Hanson are the proud new owners of 731 Walnut.
Tom is an engineer with Tyro Corporation, and
Ginny is currently looking for a position as a legal secretary.
They have two children: Brad, age 10, and Mandy, age 7.
Come help us welcome our new neighbors at a dessert social

Monday, June 11
at 7 p.m.
at our house, 711 Walnut.
Bill and Carol Williamson
RSVP: 555-1198

Attire

✧ Be sure everyone dresses casually for this get-together so the honored guests will feel relaxed and comfortable.

Ambiance

✧ Jazz up the serving table with a helium balloon bouquet.

✧ Hang a computer-generated banner that personally welcomes the honored guests—for example, "Welcome to the neighborhood, Tom, Ginny, Brad, and Mandy!"

✧ Furnish name tags to help the honored guests learn the names of their new neighbors.

Amusements and activities

✧ With everyone sitting or standing in a circle, have each person say his or her name, occupation, hobbies, and one thing people might be surprised to know about him or her.

✧ Allow plenty of time for moving around the room and socializing.

✧ Pass around a sheet of paper on which the guests can fill in their names, addresses, and telephone numbers. Give this to the new neighbors to take home with them.

Edibles

✧ If it's a Dessert Party, ask each neighbor to bring a special dessert to be shared, serve your specialty, or use one or two of the recipes from Chapter 111.

✧ If it's a Saturday morning breakfast, a casual luncheon buffet, a barbecue on the patio or a progressive meal, it's meaningful for all the neighbors to contribute to the menu, because that way the new neighbors will realize that everyone participated in making them feel welcome. If you feel uncomfortable asking for help with this get-together, host it yourself, but keep it affordable and manageable by serving a light and easy menu.

Tips – Gifts are appropriate, such as plants or shrubs for the new neighbors' yard or anything decorative for their home.

– If you decide to bring the party to the new neighbors' home as a surprise, you can set up a buffet table with sawhorses and plywood in their garage.

PART 10

Business Functions

"Don't forget: A little praise oils the wheels of progress and productivity."

Generally speaking, there are two types of business get-togethers: those for entertaining clients and those for entertaining co-workers. What I would like to emphasize in this section is the latter. There is tangible value in getting together with your co-workers on a regular basis. Whether for a birthday party, a baby shower, a retirement party, or a simple supper at the end of the workweek, gathering with your work mates is healthy for a number of reasons. It will help you get to know each other better, it will release office tension, and it can result in feelings of camaraderie that will make the workday run more smoothly with higher productivity.

In the chapters that follow you'll find helpful guidelines for planning three types of business get-togethers: a business breakfast, lunch, or dinner; an office celebration; and a holiday party.

104

BUSINESS BREAKFAST, LUNCH, OR DINNER

A business breakfast, lunch, or dinner can take place on a workday (if the reason for the gathering is work-related) or over the weekend (if the meeting is more for socializing).

Business breakfast

There are two kinds of business breakfasts: breakfasts with clients and breakfasts with co-workers. Breakfast with a client has become preferable to meeting for lunch or dinner because it doesn't interrupt the flow of the business day. Breakfast with your co-workers is also a smart idea, for a number of reasons:

✦ You and your work mates want to do a little problem-solving before a 9 a.m. meeting with your manager.

✦ You want to fuel up together as a group before attending a grueling all-day conference or training session.

✦ Breakfast may be the only time you can all get together just to socialize.

You can meet at your favorite restaurant, reserving a banquet room if necessary, or everyone can contribute toward a breakfast buffet held in a conference room at work.

As a more relaxing alternative, you might want to invite your co-workers to your home for a Saturday morning breakfast or a lazy Sunday morning brunch, which is the time to wow them with something wonderful! How about an elegant Champagne Breakfast buffet? (See Chapter 109.)

Business lunch

There are two types of business luncheons, as well: "power lunches" with clients and get-togethers with co-workers.

Again, you can meet at your favorite restaurant, reserving a banquet room if necessary. Alternatively, everyone can contribute toward a lunch buffet held in a conference room at work, or you can just plan to meet in the company cafeteria. Again, your lunch gathering may be work-related (perhaps you all need a midday stress reliever), or it could be strictly about socializing. You may also invite co-workers to your home for a buffet luncheon on the weekend. If you do decide to entertain at home, serve a special menu, something a little out of the ordinary, to get your work buddies out of the daily-grind mode (see **Chapters** 107, 108, 110, and 111 for ideas).

Business Dinners

✧ If you're taking a client to dinner, choose a quiet, upscale restaurant where you can have a private conversation.

✧ When socializing with your co-workers, how about a TGIF meal in a casual restaurant after work on Friday night? What a great time to relax and do a little bonding, especially if your company allows dress-down Fridays.

✧ A weekend get-together in your home can be a simple potluck barbecue on your patio or something special like an International Feast (see Chapters 85 and 110).

✧ How about a dinner/concert outing on a Saturday night?

✧ If several employees live reasonably close to each other, a Progressive Dinner would be a nice way to see each other's homes and get to know each other's families.

✧ Always try to warm up employee get-togethers with a little humor!

Tip — Even though you may be the busy, overworked boss, it doesn't hurt to initiate an employee get-together once in a while. It can be a catered luncheon buffet in the conference room, or you can splurge and take the gang out to dinner. Use the time to get to know your employees better. Ask them about their families and hobbies. Go one step further—praise each person for something you appreciate about him or her as an employee. The results will be a relaxation of office tensions and an increase in productivity.

105

OFFICE CELEBRATIONS

There are all kinds of office celebrations—baby showers, wedding showers, promotion parties, birthday parties, retirement parties, parties to celebrate reaching a company goal or winning an award, and so forth.

An office party needs very little in the way of planning, decorating, or expense—it's the thought that counts. Set out extra-special bakery treats or a decorated cake, plus a few helium balloons, in a meeting room or someone's office. It doesn't get much easier than that!

Another option is to bring the party to a nearby restaurant where everyone can order lunch and split the costs evenly. On the other hand, how about ordering box lunches from a local deli and carrying them to a nearby park?

Send out informal invitations in advance, in the form of cleverly worded office memos. For example, for a baby shower, the subject of your memo could be "A new arrival is expected in our in-box."

On the following page is a sample invitation that can be faxed, e-mailed, or dropped in staff in-boxes.

You may decide to take up a collection for a joint gift. You can plan entertainment, if you like—sing a familiar song with lyrics adapted to the occasion, recite a poem, read a tribute, or make a toast. In the case of an Over-the-Hill Party (see Chapter 45) or a Retirement Party (see Chapter 41), humorous gifts may also be in order.

Tip   – It's a nice gesture to invite the honored guest's spouse, especially if the party is a life event celebration.

Office Memo

To: All employees

From: Beverly Matson

Date: April 5

Re: New Arrival Expected in Our In-Box

═══

Join us for a Baby Shower Luncheon at

Uptown Restaurant

Over the Lunch Hour

on Wednesday, April 20

in Honor of Mommy-to-Be

Angie Gray

Hint, hint: She's expecting a girl!

RSVP: Bev at x337

106

HOLIDAY PARTIES

The heyday of the holiday office party that no one left sober has long since passed. Today's parties have evolved into more mature celebrations at which employees relax and enjoy themselves in a social setting, usually at the boss's expense. In those rare cases where management is too Scroogey to throw a holiday party, department heads often plan parties for their underlings. The party may celebrate any holiday—Independence Day, New Year's Day, and Hanukkah or Christmas, with parties for the latter generally held the afternoon or evening before the holiday break.

A holiday party may be held in an office meeting room if it's an afternoon get-together, or at a local restaurant if it will be held in the evening. In either case, there should be a host who stands at the door to greet the guests.

When planning an office holiday party, you'll need to assign the following responsibilities to other people, or take on a few yourself:

✦ Select the menu and/or party site.
✦ Make speeches and/or toasts.
✦ Purchase any employee gifts or awards.
✦ Present the gifts or awards.
✦ Order floral arrangements, balloons, and other decorative items.

Tips – Decide whether employees may bring along spouses or significant others. Note that if you do allow this, employees may tend to be on better behavior and drink less. On the other hand, either the employees may completely exclude their spouses or significant others from conversations with co-workers or they may totally cling to them. If spouses or friends are invited, make sure you plan festivities that keep everyone involved.

– Try to monitor the amount of alcoholic beverages served. This will prevent a world of disasters.

Part 11

Party Menus

"Although food is secondary at a children's party, it is primary at an adult party."

This section contains menus and recipes for just about any type of party you decide to have. The type of food you serve depends, of course, on the time of your party, your theme, and your budget.

You will find popular recipes for: snacks and appetizers; formal, informal, and international meals; trendy party drinks, such as smoothies and specialty coffees; festive desserts; and children's party menus.

Have fun as you plan your menu. And remember, don't plan more than you can handle. After all, you want to have fun at the party, too!

107

Snacks and Appetizers

You make snacks and appetizers look appealing by serving them on large trays layered with lace doilies. The trays can be arranged on one large table or scattered around the room on several smaller tables. The advantage of the latter is that it will help your guests get to know each other as they cluster around the food. Here are a few party snacks and appetizers for your consideration:

Baked Brie
Hollow-out a round loaf of French bread. Pack the hole with Brie cheese. Bake at 350° for 10 minutes. Serve with small hunks of French bread.

Fruit and Cheese Tray
Arrange fresh fruits and cheeses on a tray. Strawberries, melons, and grapes are popular choices because they hold up well and look colorful and attractive. Also, use specialty cheeses such as French Brie, American Liederkranz, American Camembert, Gouda, Edam, and Gruyère.

Mexican Nachos
Combine shredded jack cheese and shredded cheddar cheese three parts jack to one part cheddar, and microwave on high for two minutes, stirring halfway through. Serve with large tortilla chips.

Apricot Nut Surprise

1 pound dried apricots	3 ounces softened cream cheese
1 tablespoon finely chopped nuts	2 tablespoons lemon-flavored yogurt
1 teaspoon lemon juice	1 tablespoon confectioner's sugar

Whip together the cream cheese, yogurt, lemon juice, and confectioner's sugar. Fold in the chopped nuts. Use a sharp knife to cut a pocket in each apricot. Fill each apricot with one teaspoon of the filling. Refrigerate for at least an hour, and sprinkle with confectioner's sugar before serving. Makes 60 servings.

Jalapeño Pinto Pinwheels

1 8-ounce package of cream cheese
cup finely chopped red onion
1 cup sour cream
2 finely chopped jalapeño peppers
1 15-ounce can pinto beans, drained
1/2 cup chopped black olives
One small bottle chunky salsa
1 cup shredded Monterey Jack 1/3
cheese
1/2 teaspoon seasoned salt
1/8 teaspoon garlic power
1/4 cup chopped pimentos
5 large flour tortillas

Blend everything together except the beans and tortillas. Cover and refrigerate for at least three hours. Whip beans in a food processor until smooth. Spread each tortilla with a thin layer of beans, covered with a thin layer of the refrigerated mixture. Roll up the tortillas tightly, wrap in foil, and refrigerate for one hour. Cut into one-inch slices, and serve pinwheel side up on plate garnished with salsa. Makes 15 servings.

Parmesan Mushrooms

3 pounds large fresh mushrooms
3/4 cup finely chopped green onions
1/2 cup nonfat mayonnaise
1 teaspoon garlic power
4 tablespoons grated Parmesan cheese
6 tablespoons extra virgin olive oil
2 cups finely chopped red bell pepper
1/4 cup Dijon mustard
1 tablespoon red wine

Remove mushroom stems. Roll mushrooms in oil, and broil caps right side up for six to eight minutes or until tender. Chop the mushroom stems, and add them to the onions and bell pepper. Sauté in oil for four minutes, add wine, and sauté for another minute. Add the mayonnaise and mustard. Stir mixture well, and spoon one teaspoonful into each mushroom cap. Sprinkle with the Parmesan cheese, and broil until brown. Makes 12 servings.

Party Gorp

If you want an irresistible snack that's easy to prepare, mix these ingredients together, and serve in bowls or baskets:

Peanuts
M&M's candy
Chopped dates
Raisins
Sunflower seeds
Chocolate chips

Crumbled Heath candy bars (tap them with a hammer while still in wrapper)

Snack Mix

1 box Wheat Chex cereal
1 box Corn Chex cereal
1 large jar peanuts
1 pound butter
1 tablespoon onion salt
1 box Rice Chex cereal
1 large can of mixed nuts
1 package of thin pretzels
2 tablespoons chili powder
1/4 cup Worcestershire sauce

Pour the cereals, nuts, and pretzels into a flat metal baking pan. Melt butter and seasonings together over a low heat. Pour over the cereal/nut mixture, and bake in 250° oven for 45 minutes.

Dips for chips

Along with any kind of sturdy chips, serve one or more of these home-made dips:

Guacamole Dip

4 ripe avocados
3/4 cup chopped green onions
1/2 cup drained jalapeño pepper slices
2 cloves garlic
1/2 cup chopped tomato
Salsa

1 16-ounce carton of low-fat cottage cheese
1/4 cup lemon juice
2 teaspoons chili powder
8 sliced black olives

Put aside half of the onions, plus the chopped tomatoes, olives, and salsa. Blend the rest in a blender or food processor until smooth, adding salsa until the mixture is soft enough to be dipped without breaking the chips. Scoop the mixture into a bowl and garnish with remaining onions, tomatoes, and olives. Makes 12 servings.

Horseradish Crab Dip

2 1/2 cups imitation crab meat, shredded
1 1/2 cups undiluted evaporated skimmed milk
1 teaspoon garlic salt

3 8-ounce packages of light Neufchatel cream cheese, softened
1/2 cup finely sliced green onions
1/2 cup finely chopped red bell pepper
2 teaspoons prepared horseradish

Whip the milk and cream cheese together. Stir in rest of ingredients. Cover and refrigerate for two hours. Makes 6 cups.

Creamy Spinach Dip in a Bread Bowl

3 large round loaves of sourdough French bread
1/2 cup reduced-calorie mayonnaise
2 packages of dry onion soup mix

4 cups low-fat yogurt
2 10-ounce packages frozen chopped spinach, thawed and squeezed dry

Mix together the yogurt, spinach, mayonnaise, and onion soup mix. Cover and chill in the refrigerator for up to four hours. Use a sharp knife to hollow out the loaves of French bread. Fill the bread bowls with the spinach mixture, and serve with the scooped-out bread pieces, which can be used as dippers. Makes 20 servings.

Cilantro Bean Dip

2 15-ounce cans of drained black beans
1 cup low-fat sour cream
1/4 cup chopped cilantro
1 teaspoon garlic powder

1 cup nonfat mayonnaise
2 4-ounce cans of chopped green chilies, drained
2 teaspoons chili powder
2 teaspoons hot sauce

Mash beans with a fork or use slow speed in food processor. Mix in remaining ingredients, cover, and refrigerate for one hour. Makes 5 cups.

Clam Cocktail Dip

4 cups low-fat sour cream
1/2 cup chopped green onions,
   save out half
1/2 teaspoon black pepper

3 6 1/4-ounce cans of minced clams,
   drained
1/4 cup Worcestershire sauce

Mix the ingredients together, and chill in the refrigerator for at least two hours. Serve in a brightly colored bowl. Add remaining onions as garnish. Makes approximately four cups.

Easy Appetizers

Strawberry Ring: Arrange large fresh strawberries in a ring around a bowl of confectioner's sugar for dipping.

Shrimp Cocktail: Arrange large cooked shrimp in a ring around a bowl of cocktail sauce.

Oysters on the Half Shell: Wash oysters in shells. Chill, open, and arrange halves on a plate of crushed ice, in a ring around a bowl of cocktail sauce with lemons on the side.

Broiled Cocktail Sausages: Cut a cabbage into two halves, and place cut-side down on two plates. Broil cocktail sausages. Skewer them with long wooden or plastic party picks, and stick them into the cabbages, capping each pick with a black olive.

Ham and Cream Cheese Rolls: Spread thin ham slices with pineapple cream cheese. Roll and skewer with short plastic party picks.

108

INFORMAL CUISINE

This chapter contains menu suggestions for informal parties, including recipes for hearty favorites, a breakfast or lunch buffet, and a barbecue bash. These recipes have been party-tested and are sure to please.

Breakfast buffet

A note regarding buffets, breakfast or otherwise: The latest trend is to serve food from several food stations rather than from a traditional buffet table. For a breakfast buffet, for example, hot dishes are served from one station, pastries and fruit from another, and drinks from yet another.

Basic breakfast menu

+ Bacon, ham, or sausage.
+ Hot buttered biscuits.
+ Orange juice.
+ Coffee and tea.

+ Scrambled eggs.
+ Heated Danish pastries.
+ Fresh strawberries, raspberries, or boysenberries.

Pancake or waffle breakfast menu

+ Bacon, ham, or sausage.
+ Hot maple syrup.
+ Orange juice.
+ Coffee and tea.

+ Pancakes or waffles.
+ Blueberry and boysenberry syrups.
+ Fresh strawberries, raspberries, or boysenberries.

Note: For a more formal breakfast, see the Champagne Breakfast menu in the next chapter.

Lunch buffet

It's important for a buffet to offer varied dishes—from light foods to rich foods, from mild flavors to spicy flavors. Again, you may want to consider serving your lunch buffet from several food stations.

Antipasto tray

Place a glass or mug in the middle of a large, circular tray, and fill it with breadsticks. Arrange the following ingredients on the tray, and serve. Provides 24 servings.

8 ounces of sliced oven-roasted turkey breast

1 8-ounce package of sliced salami

8 ounces Provolone cheese slices

8 ounces jalapeño-flavored Monterey Jack cheese, cut inch-sized cubes

1 7-ounce jar of baby corn cobs, drained

Deviled eggs topped with anchovies

Cherry tomatoes, radishes, and scallions

1 large can of jumbo pitted black olives, drained

1 8-ounce package of sliced prosciutto

1 6-ounce jar of pimiento-stuffed green olives, drained

3 6-ounce jars of marinated artichoke hearts, drained.

Marinated mushrooms

Celery stuffed with chicken salad, cream cheese, deviled ham, or prepared cheese spreads

Fancy Party Sandwiches

Lay out bread and crackers—see the following list for types and portions—and begin making the sandwiches using the other ingredients from the list. First, moisten the slices of bread with mayonnaise and/or mustard. Then lay two or three ingredients on each sandwich, being as creative as possible so that each one looks like a different work of art. To show the sandwiches off, arrange them on the darkest tray you can find—preferably black. Provides 40 servings.

40 slices of party rye

1 large can of tuna, drained and flaked

1/2 medium cucumber, thinly sliced

1/4 cup Dijon mustard

Caviar

Small tomato slices

Steamed, fresh asparagus tips

Dill sprigs

40 small endive or butter lettuce leaves

1/2 pound frozen cooked bay shrimp, thawed

1 cup nonfat mayonnaise

Pimento strips

Sliced green onions

Jumbo, pitted black olives, halved

Steamed, frozen pea pods

Peach Coleslaw

4 cups shredded cabbage

1 large can sliced peaches, drained

1 1/2 cups miniature marshmallows

1/2 cup chopped bell pepper

1 cup chopped celery

Enough mayonnaise to moisten

Combine ingredients, mix well, and chill. Makes 10 servings.

Tossed Green Salad

Tear your favorite lettuce into bite-sized pieces, and combine with sliced tomatoes, green onions, artichoke hearts, fresh sliced mushrooms, canned garbanzo beans, and slices of avocado. Serve with a variety of dressings on the side.

Creamy Waldorf Salad

4 cups diced red Delicious apples	2 tablespoons sugar
2 cups diced celery	1 teaspoon lemon juice
2 cups walnut pieces	A dash of salt
1/2 cup mayonnaise	1 cup whipped cream

Mix together the mayonnaise, sugar, lemon juice, salt, and whipped cream. Add apples, celery, and walnuts. Chill before serving. Makes 12 servings.

Tomato Flower Potato Salad

12 extra-large chilled tomatoes	2 teaspoons salt
12 medium potatoes	1/2 teaspoon pepper
1/2 cup finely chopped red onion	1/2 cup Italian salad dressing
1 cup chopped celery	1 cup mayonnaise
4 hard-boiled eggs, cut up	2 tablespoons mustard
1 head red leaf lettuce	1 small can of sliced ripe olives

Boil potatoes in salted water until tender. Drain, cool, and peel. Cut potatoes into small cubes. Combine with onion, celery, and eggs. Combine salad dressing, mayonnaise, mustard, salt, and pepper, and add to potato mixture. Cover and refrigerate for three to four hours. Cut off stem ends of chilled tomatoes, to give them flat bottoms for stability. With cut-side down, cut each tomato into sixths, cutting through within a half-inch of the bottom. Carefully spread the sections apart, forming a flower. Fill tomatoes with chilled potato mixture, top with olives, and serve on large platter lined with red leaf lettuce.

Note: Several of the Snack and Appetizer recipes in Chapter 107 may be added to your luncheon buffet, such as Apricot Nut Surprise, Jalapeño Pinto Pinwheels, or any of the Easy Appetizers. Many of the international dishes included in Chapter 110 or the luau menu in Chapter 77 will also work, whether your party has an ethnic theme or not.

Barbecue Bash

In addition to the usual hot dogs, hamburgers, steaks, chicken, or turkey fillets, here are a few interesting alternatives:

Turkey-Ginger root Kabobs

3 medium zucchini squash	3 large red bell peppers
1 cup red wine vinegar	2/3 cup corn syrup
1/4 cup soy sauce	2 tablespoons grated ginger root
3/4 teaspoon garlic powder	3/4 teaspoon pepper
1 1/2 pounds turkey breast tenderloin steaks	

Combine vinegar, corn syrup, soy sauce, ginger root, garlic powder, and pepper for marinade. Rinse turkey and pat dry, cut lengthwise into one-inch strips. Soak in marinade for one hour in the refrigerator. Cut zucchini and red peppers into one-inch pieces, and thread onto twelve skewers, alternating with turkey strips leave space between each piece. Place on grill for 10 to 12 minutes, marinating frequently. Makes 12 servings.

Grilled Corn on the Cob

Soak the corn husk and all under water for about 15 minutes. Then lay the corn, still in its husks, over the coals for about 20 minutes, turning constantly.

Grilled Red Potatoes

Split potatoes, sprinkle with garlic salt, and spray with buttered-flavored oil. Wrap in heavy-duty foil, and place over hottest coals for about 30 minutes.

Steak Kabobs

3 pounds lean round steak	3 red bell peppers
3 green bell peppers	1 1/2 cups steak sauce
4 cloves garlic	2 cups beer
2 teaspoons cornstarch	2 teaspoons ground cumin

Crush the garlic, and add it to the beer, cornstarch, and cumin, stir well. Cut the round steak into strips three-fourths of inch thick, place in a glass bowl, and cover with the garlic-beer marinade. Refrigerate for three to four hours. Remove steak from the marinade save the marinade. Cut the bell peppers into two-inch pieces. Thread the steak and pepper pieces alternately onto 12 skewers leave space between each piece. Place the remaining marinade in a pan, add the cornstarch, and bring to a boil. Place the kabobs on the grill, and cook for approximately 15 minutes, turning and brushing with marinade frequently. Makes 12 servings.

Note: If you don't have barbecue skewers, you can use heavy-duty wire coat hangers.

Hearty favorites

If you've got some hearty eaters at your party—and chances are, you will, especially if men are on your guest list—they may not be too crazy about finger sandwiches and stuffed apricots. But they will appreciate these tried-and-true, homestyle favorites:

Reuben Sandwiches

Black rye bread	Swiss cheese
Corned beef, cooked & sliced	Canned sauerkraut
Butter	Thousand island dressing
Hot mustard	

For each sandwich, butter all sides of two pieces of bread. On inside of sandwich, spread hot mustard on one piece of bread and the dressing on the other. Drain sauerkraut well. Place a layer of corned beef, a layer of sauerkraut, and a layer of Swiss cheese. Grill sandwich on medium heat until cheese is melted.

Potato Salad

Use the potato salad recipe in this chapter or the Hot German Potato Salad recipe in Chapter 118.

Chili and Extra-Sourdough Bread

Make it easy on yourself by purchasing the giant-sized cans of hot chili con carne. I've tried this and found that I can't make it any better from scratch!

Hamburger Pie

2 pounds ground round	2 cans of condensed tomato soup
2 onions, chopped	10 boiled potatoes, mashed
1 teaspoon salt	1 cup warm milk
1/2 teaspoon pepper	2 cans of cut green beans, drained
2 eggs, beaten	1 cup grated cheddar cheese
2 baked pie shells	

In a large skillet cook meat and onion until meat is brown and onion is tender. Add salt and pepper. Add drained beans and soup. Pour mixture into the pie shells. Mash potatoes while they are still hot, add milk and eggs. Spoon mounds of mashed potatoes over the meat mixture. Sprinkle potatoes with the grated cheese. Bake at 350° for about 25 minutes. Makes eight man-sized servings.

109

Formal Cuisine

This chapter contains three elegant formal party menus: Champagne Breakfast, Proper Tea Party, and Formal Sit-Down Dinner.

Champagne Breakfast

A Champagne Breakfast is more formal than the breakfast buffet described in the last chapter. It will require your finest linen tablecloth and napkins, china, crystal and silver tableware, champagne flutes, and a silver wine cooler, if possible. Serve these foods and refreshments:

✦ Chilled tomato and orange juices.

✦ Canadian bacon.

✦ Scrambled eggs (cooked with one tablespoon cream per egg) with sautéed mushrooms and green onions.

✦ Large fresh strawberries with freshly whipped cream.

✦ Thinly sliced nut, banana, orange, and raisin breads, with butter and cream cheese.

✦ Hot croissant rolls with berry preserves.

✦ Regular coffee, specialty coffees (see Chapter 112), and, of course, chilled champagne.

Proper Tea Party

What should be on the menu for this type of party?

Tea, of course

The secret to an excellent cup of tea is to start with cold water, bring it to a roaring boil, and drop in a tea filter filled with fresh tea leaves. It helps to warm up the teapot in which you'll serve the tea by keeping it filled with hot water until serving time. (It is impractical to repeat this process continually if you have a large group, so keep a large carafe of hot water available.)

There are many kinds of tea—herbal, black, spiced, orange pekoe, and, of course, hundreds of scented and blended teas, each with their own exotic brand names. A liqueur may also be added, such as amaretto or crème de menthe. As hostess, you may serve any tea of your choice.

Tea sandwiches

These sandwiches differ from the party sandwiches described in the last chapter because they are smaller, fancier, and more time-consuming to make. Start with thinly sliced breads, such as rye, pumpernickel, or a low-fat, low-calorie bread. Instead of mayonnaise and mustard, start with softened butter, which will keep the fillings from making the bread soggy. What follows is a list of some of the most popular fillings, but always remember to butter the bread first, regardless of which garnishes you add.

- Ham and Swiss—thinly sliced ham and Swiss cheese slices, garnished with Dijon mustard.
- Turkey and cranberry—thinly sliced turkey, garnished with a mixture of whole cranberry sauce and Dijon mustard.
- Salmon and cream cheese—a layer of softened cream cheese, thinned with cream and fresh dill, and a thin layer of smoked salmon.
- Egg and black olive—eight hard-boiled eggs that have been crumbled and mixed with 1/4 cup mayonnaise, 1/4 cup plain yogurt, 3 teaspoons curry power, and one small can of chopped black olives.
- Walnuts and cream cheese—one package of softened cream cheese whipped until smooth with 1/4 cup cream, mixed with 1/2 cup finely diced celery and 1/2 cup chopped almonds or walnuts.
- Pineapple and cream cheese—one package of softened cream cheese, whipped until smooth with 1/4 cup cream and mixed with 1 cup well-drained crushed pineapple. (This is my personal favorite, especially when served on Boston brown bread.)
- Chicken and bacon—chopped chicken breast and finely crumbled bacon combined with whipped butter that has been blended with a splash of lemon juice, a half-teaspoon of Dijon mustard, and 1 tablespoon of mayonnaise.
- Apricot and cream cheese—thinly sliced ham and a spread made of 1 cup of apricot preserves mixed with 1 cup of softened cream.
- Cucumber and watercress—now here's something really British!—thinly sliced cucumbers, sprinkled with vinegar and salt, alternating with layers of watercress.

To make each sandwich, first (as I mentioned before) cover each piece of bread with butter, put the sandwich elements together, wrap, and refrigerate. Shortly before serving, remove from the refrigerator, trim off the crusts, and cut into shapes—rectangles, triangles, squares, rounds, and hearts or any other shape that can be cut with a cookie cutter. (The bread cuts cleanly when cold.)

Tarts

Make your own tart shells from fillo dough (found in the frozen food section of supermarkets), or buy ready-to-use tart shells from your bakery. Fill with any kind of fruit preserve and top with freshly whipped cream.

Scones

Scones are light, tender biscuits, best served hot from the oven. Here's a recipe for tasty scones:

4 cups flour	1 cup cream
2 eggs	1/3 cup butter
1/2 teaspoon salt	1/2 cup sugar
1 1/2 tablespoons baking powder	

Sift the dry ingredients together, and cut in butter until crumbly. Add the eggs and cream. Knead the dough for about 45 seconds. Roll the dough into a 1/2-inch thick layer, and cut into triangles. Bake at 400° for about 15 minutes. Serve with butter and preserves. Makes 20 servings.
Variations: Add raisins, berries, molasses, nuts, or dried currants.

Tip — If you don't want to go to all the work of making scones from scratch, pick up a box of scone mix from the supermarket. (I won't tell!)

Dream Puffs

These tasty pastries are served cold, but they will go like hot cakes!

1 cup flour	4 eggs
1/2 cup softened butter	1 cup water
1/4 cup sugar (optional)	1/2 teaspoon salt

Combine water and butter in a saucepan, and bring to a boil. Remove from heat and add flour, sugar, and salt all at once. Stir quickly, forming mixture into a thick, smooth ball. Beat the eggs together thoroughly, and add them to the ball a little at a time. Spoon the dough onto greased cookie sheets, about 2 inches apart. Bake at 400° for about 10 minutes, then at 350° for 10 more minutes, until crisp.
Fill with chicken, tuna, or shrimp salad, mincemeat pie mix, or any fruit pie filling. Makes 25 servings.

Tip — You can save yourself a lot of work by purchasing ready-to-use frozen puff pastries from your supermarket.

Formal Sit-Down Dinner

You can have this type of dinner catered or hire a server so that you don't need to spend the meal running back and forth from the kitchen to the table (some say this diminishes the formality of the affair). However, if you do decide to prepare and serve the dinner yourself, here is an elegant menu:

Appetizers
Choose snack and appetizer recipes from Chapter 107.

Vichyssoise
This elegant French soup is actually quite easy to prepare if you use instant mashed potatoes (no one will ever know!). And, of course, it can be cooked ahead of time and left in your refrigerator until served.

2 small yellow onions, grated	2 tablespoons instant chicken
2 cups water	bouillon
1/2 teaspoon salt	4 cups whole milk
2 1/2 cups instant dry mashed	2 cups cream
potatoes	Chopped chives

Combine onion, bouillon, water, and salt in large kettle. Heat to boiling. Reduce heat, cover, and simmer for 15 minutes. Remove from heat. Add milk and instant potatoes. Whip until fluffy. Gradually stir in remaining milk, heat just to boiling point, and remove from heat. Cover and chill in refrigerator. Just before serving, stir in cold cream, beating vigorously with a fork until blended. Serve topped with chopped chives. Makes 12 servings.

Grapefruit, Melon, and Avocado Salad
This delightful combination will make your guests' mouths water.

2 large Crenshaw melons or	3 large ripe avocados
cantaloupes	2 cans of grapefruit pieces
1 cup mayonnaise	1 tablespoon sugar
Orange juice, enough to thin	2 heads of butter lettuce
mayonnaise	

Place lettuce leaves on salad plates. Cut melon slices into inch-wide half-moon shapes, and arrange three slices on each plate. Drain grapefruit, and arrange pieces next to melons. Cover with plastic wrap, and chill in refrigerator until ready to serve. Combine mayonnaise, sugar, and enough orange juice to form a thin dressing. Chill dressing until ready to serve. Just before serving, slice each avocado into eight half-moon pieces, and arrange them on the salad plates next to the grapefruit, two pieces per plate. Drizzle dressing over the salad before serving. Makes 12 servings.

Fillet of Beef With Mushroom Sauce
A delicious delicacy.

6 pounds tenderloin of beef	1 pound bacon

Place bacon strips on top of beef, and roast at 325° until internal meat thermometer reads 170° (approximately two-and-a-half hours). Cut into thick slices to serve.

To make mushroom sauce, add one pound of fresh, sliced sautéed mushrooms to one large bottle of mushroom sauce. Heat thoroughly in a pot, and pour over beef slices before serving. Makes 12 servings.

Buttered Red Potatoes

This simple recipe yields 12 servings.

12 small red potatoes, peeled and quartered	1/2 cup melted butter Chopped parsley

Boil potatoes until tender. Serve covered with butter and parsley.

Asparagus Tips With Hollandaise Sauce

This elegant dish is so easy it's embarrassing!

3 pounds frozen asparagus tips   2 bottles of Hollandaise sauce

Cook asparagus according to directions on package. Pour Hollandaise sauce into your prettiest gravy server, and dribble over asparagus as it is served onto guests' plates. Makes 12 servings.

Parker House Rolls

Purchase from your local bakery. Heat before serving.

Dessert

Serve Raspberry Lemon Trifle (see Chapter 111).

Dessert Cheeses

Once the dessert has been served, bring out a tray of dessert cheeses, such as French brie, American Liederkranz, American Camembert, Gouda, Edam, and Gruyère.

After-Dinner Mints and Chocolate Truffles

Visit a gourmet chocolate shop, and splurge on melt-in-the-mouth mints and truffles.

Tip – If you really want to impress your guests, present the main course on an elegantly decorated serving cart that can be rolled over to each guest for French service. (French service is serving guests their dishes one at a time from a cart. Plate service is serving guests their dishes from the kitchen two at a time.)

110

INTERNATIONAL CUISINE

This chapter contains a collection of my favorite recipes for ethnic foods to serve at International Feasts or to complement any informal meal.

Scandinavian smorgasbord

+ Swedish meatballs.
+ Marinated herring with sour cream sauce.
+ Marinated anchovy fillets.
+ Potato sausage korv.
+ Fish balls.
+ Potato casserole.
+ Deviled eggs.
+ Light and dark dessert breads.
+ A bowl of fruit balls and berries.
+ Havarti cheese.

Recipes for Swedish meatballs, fish balls, and potato casserole follow. The herring and anchovy fillets are sold in the supermarket, although you may want to add a little more sour cream, a squirt of lemon, and a few capers to the marinated herring before serving. The potato sausage can be ordered through most delicatessens. Traditionally, the fish foods are set at one end of the table and the meats at the other, with the other dishes arranged in between.

Fish Balls

4 pounds salmon	1/2 teaspoon nutmeg
1 teaspoon salt	1/2 teaspoon mace
1 teaspoon pepper	Milk and butter as needed

Remove bones and grind salmon with a meat grinder. Add seasonings and enough milk to form into balls. Fry in butter. Makes 20 servings.

Swedish Meatballs

2 pounds ground chuck
1 pound ground pork
2 eggs, slightly beaten
2 tablespoons cornstarch
1 cup hot milk
2 tablespoons flour
1 teaspoon pepper

1/2 cup butter
2 yellow onions, minced
1/2 teaspoon nutmeg
1/2 teaspoon ground ginger
3 teaspoons salt
1/4 teaspoon allspice

Mix meat, eggs, milk, and cornstarch together. Add the rest of the ingredients, except for the flour and butter. Form mixture into small balls, and brown in the butter. Add a little water, and simmer slowly for about 40 minutes. Remove the meatballs from the pan. Add flour and enough water to the drippings to make a medium-thick gravy. Makes 20 servings.

Potato Casserole

4 pounds cooked, mashed potatoes
2 pounds canned Danish bacon
6 medium yellow onions
Chopped parsley

2 teaspoons salt
1/2 teaspoon white pepper
4 cups cubed pickled beets

Dice bacon and onions, and sauté them in butter until onions are tender. Add seasonings to the mashed potatoes. Place potatoes in large casserole dish, and pour the drained bacon and onions over the top. Bake in 300° oven for 10 minutes. Garnish with pickled beets and parsley. Makes 20 servings.

Note: See Chapter 111 for a special Swedish dessert—Swedish Macaroon Tea Cakes.

German cuisine

Lentil Soup

4 cups dried lentils
Large ham bone
2 large yellow onions, minced
1/4 cup each butter and flour for thickening if desired

6 stalks celery, chopped
2 sprigs parsley
1 teaspoon each salt and pepper

Soak lentils in water overnight. Place lentils, ham bone, onion, celery, parsley, and seasonings in large kettle filled with 6 quarts of water. Bring to a boil, cover, and simmer for about five hours, until lentils are tender. Thicken, if desired, with 1/4 cup butter and 1/4 cup flour. Makes 16 servings.

Fried Bratwurst

Purchase one bratwurst per guest. Fry the bratwurst in butter, turning frequently until golden brown on all sides. Cover the bratwurst with water, and simmer uncovered for 20 minutes. Serve with hot mustard or sour cream.

Sauerbraten

4 pounds lean boneless top round beef steak, cut with the grain into 2-inch strips, then cut across the grain into 1/4-inch thick slanting slices

1 cup each dry white wine and white vinegar	1/4 cup dark brown sugar
1 teaspoon each pepper and ground cloves	4 dry bay leaves
	1/4 cup salad oil
4 cups thinly sliced carrots	4 red onions, thinly sliced
4 cloves garlic, minced	2 cups thinly sliced celery
1 cup crushed ginger snaps	1/2 cup water
	Sour cream, optional

In a bowl, mix wine, vinegar, brown sugar, bay leaf, pepper, and cloves. Stir in meat, and let marinate for one hour. Drain meat, reserving marinade. Remove bay leaves. Place wok or heavy skillet over high heat. Add oil. When oil is hot, add meat and stir-fry until meat is browned about two minutes. Remove meat, and add onion and carrots. Stir-fry for one minute. Add celery and garlic. Stir-fry for one minute. Add water, cover, and cook until carrots and celery are tender, about three more minutes. Return meat to wok, and add marinade and ginger snaps. Stir until sauce thickens. Serve garnished with dollops of sour cream. Makes 16 servings.

Hot German Potato Salad

12 medium-sized potatoes, boiled in skins, peeled, and sliced thin	14 slices of bacon, fried until crisp and broken into pieces
1 1/2 cup diced yellow onion	1 teaspoon celery seed
1/4 cup flour	1 teaspoon pepper
1/4 cup sugar	1 1/2 cups water
3 teaspoons salt	1 cup vinegar
1 tablespoon chopped chives	

Cook onion in bacon fat. Mix in all dry ingredients. Add water and vinegar, and cook until mixture boils. Simmer for three minutes. Pour over potatoes. Add most of the bacon pieces. Cover and let stand until ready to serve. Garnish with remaining bacon and minced chives. Makes 12 servings.

Chinese cuisine

Shrimp Fried Rice

3 cups cold cooked rice	2 tablespoon peanut or olive oil
1/4-pound cooked shrimp	1/4 cup light soy sauce
2 eggs	3 green onions, chopped
1/4 cup sliced water chestnuts	1/2 cup peas

Blend eggs with 2 tablespoons water, and set aside. Heat oil in a wok, or heavy skillet over medium heat. Add green onions, and stir-fry for 30 seconds. Add eggs, stirring until firm. Stir in rice, and cook until heated through. Add shrimp, peas, water chestnuts, and soy sauce, stirring until blended and shrimp is heated through.

Chinese Chicken Salad

4 whole chicken breasts, cut into thin strips
8 scallions, sliced thin
1 teaspoon dry mustard
1/2 teaspoon salt
1/2 cup sesame seeds, toasted
1/3 cup plum sauce
Virgin olive oil
2 heads of lettuce, shredded
1 cup chopped parsley
1 teaspoon sugar
1/2 teaspoon dry ginger
1 cup slivered almonds, toasted

Stir-fry chicken strips in 2 tablespoons of oil until cooked through. Allow chicken to cool.

Toss lettuce, onion, and parsley together in a large salad bowl. Add cooled chicken.

Combine 4 tablespoons oil, plum sauce, mustard, sugar, and seasonings. Add to the salad, tossing gently. Garnish with sesame seeds and almonds.

Pork Chow Mein

4 cups thinly sliced lean, boneless pork
3 cups chopped celery
2 cans of bean sprouts
1 teaspoon pepper
1/4 cup soy sauce
1 chopped yellow onion
3 cups water
2 teaspoons salt
1/3 cup corn starch
2 tablespoons brown sauce

Spray wok or skillet with cooking spray, and fry pork and onion together until tender. Add celery, salt, pepper, and water. Cook for 20 minutes. Drain. Add bean sprouts, and bring to boil. Make a paste of the corn starch, soy sauce, and brown sauce, and pour it over the mixture, cooking only until thickened. Serve over chow mein noodles.

Chinese Cabbage

2 heads cabbage, shredded
1/2 pound butter

Boil cabbage for five minutes. Serve topped with melted butter.

Mexican fiesta dishes

Taco Salad

2 pounds ground beef
1/2 teaspoon salt
1/2 teaspoon garlic powder
2 large tomatoes, cubed
4 scallions, sliced
2 cups crushed tortilla chips
2 pounds canned red kidney beans
1/2 teaspoon pepper
1 head lettuce, torn into small pieces
3 large avocados, cubed
1 cup grated cheddar cheese
2 cups salsa

Brown beef, and drain well. Add drained beans and seasonings, and cook at low heat for five minutes. Toss together with the lettuce, tomato, avocado, scallions, cheese, and tortilla chips. Top with salsa and serve. Makes 12 to 14 servings.

Chili Salsa Salad

1 large bottle medium-hot salsa
1 medium can of diced green chilies
1 tablespoon chili powder
2 small cans of corn, noncreamed
2 tablespoons lime juice
Crumbled tortilla chips

Mix first five ingredients together, and chill. Sprinkle with crumbled tortilla chips just before serving.

Taco Picante Casserole

2 boxes Spanish-flavored or Mexican-style rice
2 pounds extra-lean hamburger
2 7 1/2-ounce cans of nonfat refried beans
2 small onions, chopped
2 4-ounce cans of sliced black olives
2 teaspoons ground cumin
Scallions
4 corn tortillas
1 24-ounce jar of medium-hot picante sauce
6 cloves of garlic, chopped
4 4-ounce cans of diced green chilies
2 large packages of low-fat sharp cheddar cheese
2 7-ounce cans of corn, drained

Prepare the rice according to directions on box. Brown hamburger, garlic, onions, and cumin in a heavy skillet sprayed first with fat-free oil. Drain well on a paper towel, and combine with the rice mixture. Prepare two round glass casserole dishes with fat-free spray. Cut six tortillas into eight triangles each. Arrange eight triangles in a pie shape on the bottom of each dish, followed by a layer of the beef mix, beans, whole green chilies, picante sauce, corn, and cheese. Repeat the process, ending with a topping of grated cheese and eight more tortilla triangles. Finally, garnish with sliced black olives and chopped scallions.

Bake at 375° for about 40 minutes, until melted together. Let set for 10 minutes before serving. Makes 12 to 14 servings.

Tijuana Tamale Pie

1 1/2 pounds ground beef
5 cups milk
4 beaten eggs
2 7-ounce cans of whole kernel corn
2 teaspoons chili powder
2 14 1/2-ounce cans whole peeled tomatoes, undrained and chopped
2 packages Lawry's Spices and Seasonings for Chili or Lawry's Taco Spices and Seasonings
2 small cans of sliced black olives
2 1/4 cups yellow cornmeal
1 pound grated cheddar cheese
2 teaspoons garlic salt
1 large jar medium hot salsa

Brown ground beef until crumbly, and drain well. In a large bowl combine milk, 2 cups cornmeal, and eggs. Add beef and remaining ingredients, except for the cheese and 1/4 cup of cornmeal. Stir together, and pour into two lightly greased 12" x 8" x 2" baking dishes. Bake uncovered in 350° oven for 40 to 45 minutes. Sprinkle with the cheese and remaining cornmeal, continue baking until cheese melts and cornmeal is browned. Let stand for 10 minutes before serving. Serve with salsa. Makes 16 servings.

Mexican Nachos
Combine shredded jack cheese and shredded cheddar cheese three parts jack to one part cheddar, and microwave on high for two minutes, stirring halfway through. Serve with large tortilla chips.

Note: See Chapter 111 for a special Mexican dessert—Mexican Sopaipillas.

Italian pasta feast cuisine

There are two easy ways to host an Italian pasta feast. The first is to make it a potluck, asking each guest to bring one hot pasta dish, such as spaghetti, fettuccine, ravioli, cannelloni, lasagna, or stuffed manicotti. All you'll need to provide are an antipasto tray, a green salad, and toasted garlic bread.

Or you can host your own pasta bar that features spaghetti and fettuccine noodles, plus ready-made sauces in specialty flavors, such as:

+ Tomato and basil.
+ Mushrooms and ripe olives.
+ Sun-dried tomato.
+ Alfredo with mushrooms.
+ Garlic and herb.
+ Vegetable primavera.
+ Italian sausage and fennel.
+ Roasted peppers and onions.
+ Creamy mushroom.
+ Tomato alfredo.
+ Tomato, spinach, and cheese.
+ Florentine spinach and cheese.

Serve each sauce in its own bowl. Write the names of the sauces with black felt-tip pen on six-inch lengths of uncooked lasagna noodles, and prop them in front of each corresponding bowl of sauce. Your guests will never know you purchased these ready-made sauces at your supermarket—unless you tell them, of course!

Be sure to serve several flavors of grated cheeses as well, such as Parmesan, Romano, garlic herb, and zesty red pepper.

You'll also need to add a salad and garlic bread.

Serve Italian ice for dessert.

Irish cuisine

Corned Beef & Cabbage

6 pounds well-trimmed corned beef brisket
1 large head green cabbage, cut into wedges
3 cloves garlic, minced
2 small onions, quartered
6 red potatoes, peeled and quartered

Place brisket in large kettle, and cover with cold water. Add garlic and onions. Heat to boiling. Reduce heat, cover tightly, and simmer for four hours, or until tender. About 30 minutes before meat is tender, add potatoes to the pot. Remove the meat when it is tender, place on a hot platter, and cover it with foil to keep it warm while you cook the cabbage. Add cabbage to the kettle, and boil until cabbage and potatoes are tender, about 15 minutes. To serve, surround the brisket with the drained cabbage and potatoes. Important note: Brisket must be sliced thinly across the grain.

Irish Stew

6-pound lamb roast, cut into cubes
8 cups cubed potatoes
2 teaspoons salt
2 bay leaves
1 teaspoon thyme

2 cups each of chopped carrots,
turnips, celery, and yellow onions
1 teaspoon pepper
1/4 cup minced parsley
Mint leaves

Roll meat in flour, and brown in hot olive oil. Cover with boiling water, and simmer for two hours. Add vegetables and seasonings, and simmer 45 minutes, or until vegetables are tender. Thicken liquid for gravy. Garnish with mint leaves.

Irish Potatoes

The Irish like their potatoes straight up, just boiled in their skins, drained, and served. Small new potatoes are their favorites.

Note: See Chapter 111 for a special Irish dessert—Irish Appleberry Crunch.

Tips – Food stations may be used to serve any of the international menus in this chapter, except the Scandinavian smorgasbord, which should always be served from one long table.

– Top each dish with a miniature flag representing its origin.

– Also, see Hawaiian Luau menu and recipes in Chapter 77.

111

FESTIVE PARTY DESSERTS

Many of the parties described in this book call for a decorated cake, while others cry out for something special, such as your famous homemade apple crisp or lemon meringue pies. A rule of thumb is to serve a light dessert after a heavy meal and vice versa. In any case, if you're looking for a unique, new dessert recipe—something to dazzle your guests— you'll find it in this chapter.

Blueberry Surprise

It's hard to believe that a serving of something this delicious only has 135 calories and 2 grams of fat—but it's true!

1/2 gallon nonfat vanilla ice cream or frozen yogurt

3 cups fresh or frozen blueberries, raspberries, or strawberries

2/3 cup sugar

3 small cantaloupes, thinly sliced and peeled

2 1/2 cups orange juice

2 1/4 tablespoons cornstarch

In a small saucepan stir together the sugar and cornstarch. Add the orange juice and berries. Cook and stir until beginning to thicken, then cook for two more minutes. Cool in refrigerator for 20 minutes. Scoop 1/3 cup ice cream or yogurt into each dessert dish. Arrange cantaloupe slices on one side of the dish. Pour berry sauce over top of ice cream or yogurt. Serve immediately. Makes 20 servings.

Decadent Brownies

These definitely have more than 135 calories and 2 grams of fat! But—what the heck!

2 19.8-ounce boxes fudge brownie mix

2 12-ounce containers of whipped topping

1 cup Kahlua

16 Heath candy bars

Bake the brownies according to directions and cool. Punch holes in brownies with a fork, and pour the Kahlua over the top. Tap the Heath candy bars with a hammer right in the wrapper, and crumble the pieces over the top of the soaked brownies. Top with whipped topping.

Don't worry—you'll probably only gain three or four pounds!

Magic Mountain Sundaes

Serve bowls filled with scoops of various flavors of ice cream. Then let the guests make their own sundaes by adding:

Sauces

Chocolate sauce	Hot fudge sauce
Butterscotch sauce	Caramel sauce

Kiwi sauce (three peeled kiwi, blended with 3 tablespoons honey, 2 teaspoons lemon juice, and 1 teaspoon vanilla)

Fruits

Strawberries	Raspberries
Boysenberries	Sliced bananas
Sliced mango	Sliced kiwi
Sliced peaches	

Nuts

Chopped walnuts	Chopped almonds
Chopped pecans	Chopped peanuts

Crumbled Candy Bars

Heath candy bars	Hershey candy bars
Butterfinger candy bars	

Whipped Topping

Cool Whip whipped topping	Fresh-whipped whipping cream

Swedish Macaroon Tea Cakes

4 cups sifted flour	1 cup sugar
2 cups softened butter	2 eggs
1 tablespoon vanilla	

Cream sugar and butter together, then beat in the eggs and vanilla. Stir in the flour, and mix well. Drop a rounded teaspoonful of batter into each greased tiny muffin cup, pressing batter over the bottom and up around the sides—a coating of about ¼-inch thick.

Chill, and then fill each hollow with:

Almond Macaroon Filling

4 eggs	1 cup sugar
1 teaspoon almond extract	3 cups finely chopped almonds

Beat eggs until foamy. Add sugar, and mix until blended. Add almonds and almond extract. Bake at 325° for about 25 minutes, until browned and set. Makes four dozen tea cakes.

Raspberry Lemon Trifle

Now, here's a nice surprise—something that looks spectacular, but takes very little work!

1 large boxes of ladyfingers	Brandy or fruit liqueur
1 large package frozen raspberries	1 jar of apricot preserves
1 large package lemon pudding mix	Whipping cream
A clear glass bowl with high sides	

Alternate layers of ladyfingers, drizzled with the brandy or liqueur, and layers of the preserves, thawed raspberries, and prepared pudding. Top with a layer of fruit piled with freshly whipped cream. Refrigerate for at least one hour. Makes 20 servings.

Mexican Sopaipillas

4 cups flour	2 teaspoons salt
4 level teaspoons baking powder	Water
1/4 cup shortening	Shortening for deep frying

Sift dry ingredients together. Cut in the shortening. Add a little water, just enough to hold the dough together. Roll thin, and cut into two-inch squares or triangles. Fry to a golden brown in deep, very hot shortening. They will puff up. Serve hot with butter and honey, or sprinkle with powdered sugar.
Note: These are tricky because unless you fry them in very hot oil or shortening, they will fall flat. Try out a batch ahead of time just to be sure you've got the hang of it. Makes 12 to 15 servings.

Irish Appleberry Crunch

1 1/2 pounds apples	1 1/2 pounds blackberries
1/4 cup water	1 1/2 cups sugar
2 sticks butter	2 cups flour
1 1/3 cup oatmeal	1/2 cup dark brown sugar

Peel, core, and slice the apples. Add to washed blackberries, and place in a large shallow baking pan. Dribble the water and sugar over the top.
Combine softened butter, flour, oatmeal, and brown sugar in a bowl, and mix together until all the ingredients stick together and become crumbly. Spread these crumbly pieces over the top of the fruit, packing down lightly. Bake in preheated 400° oven for 15 minutes. Then reduce heat to 375°, and cook for another 15 to 20 minutes, or until cooked thoroughly and crunchy on top. Serve warm with whipped cream or vanilla ice cream. Makes 16 servings.

Melon Ball Compotes

1/2 gallon raspberry sherbet	10 cups melon balls
3 cups chilled ginger ale	

For each serving, surround one scoop of sherbet with six or eight small melon balls. Pour 1/4 cup ginger ale over the top. Makes 12 servings.

Baked Alaska Cake

Bake a one-layer cake colored pink by adding red food coloring. When cool, cover with a six-inch high mountain of strawberry ripple ice cream and leave in freezer for 30 minutes.

Preheat the oven to 450°. Make meringue by beating four egg whites until stiff, and continue beating as you add superfine sugar a little at a time. Take the ice cream mountain out of the freezer, and cover with the meringue as quickly as you can, or the ice cream will start to melt. Bake in 450° oven for five minutes, or until the peaks of meringue are beginning to brown. Serve immediately.

Cappuccino Cookie Float

Pour 3 or 4 tablespoons of chocolate syrup in the bottom of a tall clear glass. Add one crumbled cookie (use Pepperidge Farm Chocolate Laced Pirouettes Cookies, delicate rolled cookies that look similar to tiny stovepipes) and one scoop chocolate ice cream. Pour iced cappuccino (use any instant cappuccino mix) over the ice cream, to within an inch of the top of the glass. Add a small scoop of praline ice cream, a squirt of whipped cream, and another cookie that should be stuck into the side of the praline ice cream.

Tip – For a dramatic flare, turn the lights down low, and enter the room carrying the dessert topped with lighted sparklers or sugar cubes!

112

Festive Party Drinks

This chapter contains recipes for many popular new party drinks, including smoothies, specialty fruit drinks, punch recipes, and specialty coffee drinks. Try them out ahead of time before adding them to your party menu. I'm sure you'll find that an interesting new party drink will be a welcome addition to the standard fare of wine, soft drinks, plain coffee, and tea.

California smoothies

Smoothies are a frosty-cold blend of fruits, juices, yogurt, or sorbet that are prepared in a blender. In addition to the basics just listed, smoothie experts customize their recipes with almost anything you can think of, from brownies to tofu.

A smoothie is considered to be more healthful than a milkshake and more substantial than a lemonade—the trendy new drink of the decade. *Newsweek* magazine, in fact, has declared it to be the new cool brew and predicts it will become as popular as specialty coffees.

The ingredients listed in the following smoothie recipes should be blended together to make one large smoothie.

The Inner Child Smoothie

1 cup frozen vanilla yogurt	1/2 cup peanut butter
1/2 cup apple juice	1/2 cup honey

Strawberry Refresher

1 cup frozen strawberry yogurt	1 banana
1/2 cup fresh strawberries	1 cup orange juice

Malibu Tango

8 apricots, pitted and chopped	1/2 cup frozen vanilla yogurt
3 small peeled, sliced tangerines	1 tablespoon sugar

Mint Zinger

1 cucumber, peeled, seeded, and chopped
1 cup apple cider
1/2 cup crushed ice
2 tablespoons finely chopped mint leaves
1 cup lemon sorbet

Papaya Pleasure

1 cup peeled, seeded, and chopped canteloupe
1/2 cup frozen vanilla yogurt
1 cup freshly squeezed orange juice
1 papaya, peeled, seeded, and chopped

Goes-Down-Easy Mango

1 chilled mango, peeled and chopped
1 cup chilled fresh pineapple chunks
1/2 cup crushed ice
1 1/2 cup frozen vanilla yogurt
1 teaspoon ground cardamom

Too-Good-to-Believe Berry

1 cup frozen vanilla yogurt
1 cup blackberries
1 cup raspberries
1/2 cup apple juice

Tip – Garnish your smoothies with a wedge of orange or lime, or a slice of pineapple, peach, or mango.

Festive fruit drinks

Peachy Pleasure

3/4 cup peach nectar
1 tablespoon lime juice
3 tablespoons grenadine syrup
1 Alberta peach, pitted and sliced (do not peel)
1 1/2 cups ice

Process the ice, nectar, peace slices, and lime juice in a juicer. Pour grenadine into bottom of each glass. Pour blended mixture on top. (Syrup will send brilliant streaks to the top of the glass, creating a peachy sunset.)

Slushie Slurpie

2 large apples, cut into wedges
1 1/2 cups blueberries
2 1/2 cups blackberries
Whipped cream

Process the three fruits in a juicer, and top with a dollop of whipped cream.

Wee Bit o' Shamrock

1 1/2 cups Thompson seedless green grapes
2 pears, cut into wedges
3 plums, pitted and cut into wedges

Process the fruits in a juicer. Garnish with a slice of lime.

Polynesian Breeze

3 mangoes, peeled, pitted, and cut into wedges
1 cup chopped, fresh pineapple
1 cup raspberries

Process fruits together in a juicer.

Southwestern Adventure

4 large tomatoes, cut into wedges
3 jalapeño peppers, stemmed
2 teaspoons horseradish
1 teaspoon celery salt
1 medium cucumber, peeled and cut into wedges
2 teaspoons Worcestershire sauce

Process all the ingredients together in a juicer.

Strawberry Blast

12 large strawberries
1 small apple, cut into wedges
Whipped cream
1/2 small cantaloupe, peeled and chopped

Process the strawberries, cantaloupe, and apple together in a juicer. Serve topped with whipped cream.

Cow Jumped Over the Moonbeam

1/2 honeydew melon, peeled, seeded, and chopped
1 cup ginger ale
1 apricot, pitted and chopped
2 peaches, pitted and chopped

Blend the fruits together until smooth. Add the ginger ale, and mix very gently.

Kiwi Silk

2 kiwi, peeled and cut into wedges
1 cup freshly squeezed grapefruit juice
1 large peach, pitted, and cut into wedges
1/4 cup freshly squeezed lime juice

Process the kiwi and peach in a juicer. Add grapefruit and lime juice, and mix well.

Tip – Garnish your fruit drinks with a sprig of mint, a wedge of orange or lime, or a slice of pineapple, peach, or mango.

"Pleased as punch" recipes

Here are a few popular new punch recipes to consider:

Mocha Punch

1 cup instant coffee granules
4 cups hot water
3 cups sugar
1 quart whipped cream
2 gallons whole milk
1 gallon vanilla ice cream
1 gallon chocolate ice cream

Combine the coffee, water, and sugar, and set it in the refrigerator for one hour. About 15 minutes before serving time, set the two gallons of ice cream out to soften. Combine one half of the cooled coffee mixture, ice cream, and milk. Spread half the whipped cream evenly over the top of the punch, and serve. (Return the rest of the ingredients to the refrigerator or freezer to use as needed to refill the punch bowl).

Sangria Punch

1 gallon red wine	4 oranges, sliced and quartered
4 apples, peeled, cored, and sliced	1/2 lemon, sliced
1 1/2 cups sugar	2 tablespoons cinnamon
1 cup light rum	

Mix ingredients together in a large crock, glass, or plastic container, and store overnight in a cool place. Do not refrigerate. Just before serving, add a block of ice.

Comforting Christmas Nog

12 egg yolks	1 pound powdered sugar
1 quart dark rum or brandy	2 1/2 quarts whipping cream
1 quart whole milk	6 egg whites
1/2 teaspoon salt	Freshly grated nutmeg

Beat egg yolks until light in color. Beat in powdered sugar, liquor, cream, and milk. Cover and refrigerate for at least four hours. Beat egg whites until stiff, and fold lightly with the salt, and combine with the chilled mixture. Top each serving with freshly grated nutmeg.

Wonderful Wassail

5 medium baking apples	1 cup sugar
1/4 cup water	3 cups ale
3 1/2 cups apple cider	1 teaspoon allspice

Core apples, and sprinkle with 1/2 cup sugar. Add water, and bake at 375 degrees for 30 minutes, or until tender. Combine ale, cider, remaining sugar, and allspice in saucepan, and place over low heat. Stir until sugar is dissolved, but do not boil. Place roasted apples in punch bowl, and pour ale mixture over them.

Spicy Cranberry Punch

5 tea bags	5 cups boiling water
1/2 teaspoon allspice	1/2 teaspoon cinnamon
1/2 teaspoon nutmeg	1 cup sugar
1 quart cranberry juice cocktail	3 cups water
1 cup orange juice	3/4 cup lemon juice

Pour boiling water over tea bags and the spices, and steep for five minutes. Strain, add sugar, and let cool. Add cranberry juice cocktail, water, orange, and lemon juice, and mix. Pour into punch bowl with ice cubes made from lemon juice. Float thin lemon slices on top of the punch.

Mimosa Punch

2 bottles chilled Champagne	2 quarts chilled orange juice
12 sliced strawberries	Frozen orange juice cubes
Fresh mint garnish	

Combine all ingredients except mint garnish in six quart punch bowl. As punch is served, garnish each cup with a sprig of mint.

Hawaiian Volcano

1 gallon cold Hawaiian fruit punch 2 cups guava juice
2 bottles cold ginger ale or 1/2 gallon rainbow sherbet
  lemon-lime soda

Mix the fruit punch and guava juice together, then add the sherbet. Pour the ginger ale or lemon-lime directly on top of the sherbet, which will make the punch foam like a volcano.

Tip – Don't add plain ice to your punch because it will water it down. Add frozen juice instead. (Freeze ahead in circular gelatin molds or in ice cube trays).

Specialty Coffee Drinks

Cafe au Rhum

Add 1 ounce rum and a twist of lemon peel per cup.

Cafe Cacao

Add 1 ounce creme de cacao per cup.

Cafe a L'Orange

Add 1 ounce Orange Curacao per cup with a cinnamon stick to stir.

Cafe Mocha

Equal amounts of coffee and hot chocolate topped with whipped cream.

Irish Coffee

Add 1 ounce Irish whiskey and 3 teaspoons of sugar. Top with whipped cream.

Cafe Cappuccino

Equal amounts of espresso (brewed from pulverized Italian dark-roast coffee) and hot milk. Add 2 teaspoons sugar and sprinkles of cinnamon and nutmeg. (Or use instant cappuccino mix—see Cappuccino Float below).

Caffe Borgia

Equal amounts of espresso and hot chocolate, served in a demitasse cup, topped with whipped cream and grated orange peel.

Coffee a la Mode

Add a couple tablespoons vanilla or coffee ice cream to the coffee just before you serve it.

Tip – It has become popular to serve alcohol-free party drinks. In fact, several organizations have published no-booze drink recipe books, including a booklet called *Cheers!*, created through a partnership between the Hard Rock Café and RADD (Recording Artists, Actors, and Athletes Against Drunk Driving). To obtain a free copy of this great little booklet, visit your nearest AAA office.

113

CHILDREN'S PARTY MENUS

Children's parties require gimmicky menus. This chapter includes good ideas for:

+ Salads.
+ Mini-meals.
+ Special desserts.
+ Cakes.
+ Snacks.
+ Party drinks.

Salads

Poison Spider Salad
Spread each plate with large lettuce leaves. Place a large canned pear half upside down on top of the lettuce. Press red-hot candies into the tops of the pear halves. Add licorice or black pipe cleaner legs.

Jell-O gelatin "jigglers"
Pour Jell-O gelatin into a shallow pan. When gelled, cut into squares or shapes, using a knife or cookie cutters. Or pour Jell-O gelatin into small paper cups, drop a gummy bear into each one, and refrigerate. When ready to serve, place the cups in lukewarm water for a few seconds, then unmold onto a serving plate.

Make-Your-Own Fruit Kabobs
Provide one wooden skewer per child, along with bowls of bite-sized fresh fruits, such as pineapple chunks, grapes, melon balls, orange sections, strawberries, and cherries. Decorate the end of each skewer with crinkle ribbon. Let each child create his or her own kabob by sliding pieces of fruit onto his or her skewer, then eating one piece at a time.

Pineapple Boat Kebobs
Hollow out half of a fresh pineapple cut lengthwise, fill with pineapple chunks, maraschino cherries, grapes, banana slices, cheese and ham chunks, all skewered with cocktail picks or ruffled toothpicks.

Watermelon Boat
Cut a watermelon in half. Scoop the watermelon out in balls, using a melon-baller. Place the watermelon balls back into the shell, along with mini-scoops of raspberry sherbet.

Mini-meals

Hot Dogs and Beans
Let the children roast their own hot dogs over a campfire or the flames in your fireplace. Tuck them into buns, add mustard, and serve alongside a mound of baked beans.

Bean Boats
Split hamburger buns, and place them with flat surface up on cookie sheets. Butter the buns, and top with layers of canned pork and beans, grated cheddar cheese, and real bacon bits. Place under broiler until bubbling and browned.

Waffle Surprise
Toast two frozen waffles. Spread one with pineapple cream cheese and raspberry jam, the other with chunky peanut butter and chopped peanuts. Put the two halves together, and serve.

Do-It-Yourself Shish Kabobs
Provide the children with metal barbecue skewers, plus bowls of bite-sized pineapple, brown-and-serve sausage links, sour dough French bread, baked ham, bananas, apples, and tomatoes. Let the children skewer their own kabobs, cover with buttered-flavored cooking spray, and cook over a barbecue or campfire. The meats have been precooked so there is no fear of undercooked foods.

Peanut Butter Banana Dogs
Fill a foot-long hot dog bun with sliced bananas, gobs of peanut butter, chopped nuts, and M&M's candy.

Hamburgers and Potato Chips or French Fries
Serve small-sized hamburgers with all the trimmings, plus chips or fries.

Personal Potato Toppers
Provide one baked potato per child, along with toppings: hot chili, sour cream, crumbled bacon, cooked hamburger with taco seasoning, grated cheeses, crumbled tortilla chips, and sliced black olives. Let each child create his or her own potato meal.

Hero Sandwiches
Slice a whole loaf of French bread in half lengthwise. Let the children help you fill the bottom layer with mustard, relish, pickle slices, pepperoni, lunchmeats, sliced cheeses, sliced tomatoes, lettuce, etc. Then, place the lid on the sandwich, and cut into child-sized portions.

Giant Pancake with Fruit Topping
Cook giant pancakes in a round cast-iron skillet. Serve in the skillet, topped with fresh berries and piles of whipped cream.

Animal Sandwiches
Cut sandwiches into animal shapes, using a cookie cutter.

Macaroni and Cheese
Canned or homemade, kids love this stuff!

Personalized Pizzas
Prepare individual eight-inch pizzas using refrigerated pizza dough, canned pizza sauce, shredded mozzarella, and cheddar cheeses. Make faces with cherry tomato noses, sliced green pepper lips, and black olive eyes. Bake according to the directions on the pizza dough package.

Muffin-Pizzas
Provide the children with English muffins, along with grated cheeses, pizza sauce, black olive slices, pepperoni pieces, etc. Let the children design their own custom mini-pizzas.

Do-It-Yourself Taco Bar
Lay out large heated taco shells and all the ingredients: cooked ground beef, chopped tomatoes, shredded lettuce, diced green chilies, chopped olives, shredded cheeses, salsa, and sour cream.

Pigs-in-a-Blanket
Wrap biscuit dough around canned cocktail wieners, and bake them in the oven until the dough has browned on top.

Corn Dogs Dipped in Mustard

Special Desserts

S'mores
Let the children roast large marshmallows over a fire, using sticks or straightened coat hangers. As soon as they begin to brown, help the children smash the marshmallows and half a flat chocolate bar between two graham crackers.

Snowballs
Roll scoops of firm vanilla ice cream in flaky coconut.

Rice Krispies Cereal Squares
Follow the recipe on the back of the Rice Krispies cereal box.

Marshmallow Fondue Dip

This is really messy, so you might want to take this project to the patio! Provide fondue forks, large marshmallows, and a fondue pot full of warm chocolate sauce. Let the children skewer the marshmallows, dip them into the chocolate, and eat them.

Frozen Fruit Balls

Cut the top off a large orange. Scoop out the fruit and its juice. Decorate the oranges with happy faces, using black felt-tip permanent markers. Fill the empty orange shells with scoops of orange sherbet, and freeze until ready to serve.

Edible Headbands

Sew wrapped candies together using long strands of dental floss cut into headband lengths, with three or four inches left over for tying. Tie a piece of curled crinkle ribbon at each juncture of candy, hiding the dental floss and decorating the headband. The children may want to make their own headbands. They make excellent party favors.

Rocky Road Sandwiches

Slice chocolate cupcakes in half to make a top and bottom for each sandwich. Place a small scoop of rocky road ice cream between the halves, press together, and serve.

Do-It-Yourself Sundaes

Provide bowls, several types of ice cream, ice cream scoops, chocolate, caramel and strawberry sauces, maraschino cherries, crushed pineapple, sliced bananas and strawberries, nuts, and whipped cream.

Popsicles

Purchase them, or make your own version by hollowing out orange halves, filling with fruit juice, and freezing.

Snow Cones

Fill paper cups with real snow or crushed ice from the blender with red fruit juice.

Tasty Party Necklaces

Provide long, thin strands of licorice, and bowls of donut-shaped dry cereals, such as Cheerios cereal and Trix cereal. Let the children make their own party necklaces by threading the licorice through the cereal pieces and tying the ends together with a double knot.

Decorate-Your-Own Cupcakes

Place a plastic tablecloth over your table. Set out cupcakes, frostings, frosting tubes, candy sprinkles, novelty cake decorations. Provide the children with plastic knives, let them decorate their own cupcakes.

Sugar Cookies

1 cup melted butter	1 1/2 cups sifted confectioner's sugar
1 egg	1 1/2 teaspoon vanilla
2 1/2 cups all-purpose flour, sifted	1 teaspoon baking soda
1 teaspoon cream of tartar	Canned white frosting
Food colorings	

Mix the first four ingredients together thoroughly. Sift the flour, soda, and cream of tartar together, and add this mixture to the first four ingredients. Cover and chill for three hours.

Heat oven to 375°. Roll the dough on a lightly floured cloth-covered board until it is approximately ¼-inch thick. Cut into desired shapes, and bake on lightly greased baking sheet for seven or eight minutes until lightly brown on the edges. Let cool and frost (see Butter Cream Frosting recipe later in this chapter).

Ice Cream Babies

2 gallons strawberry ice cream	Shredded coconut
1 tiny plastic baby per guest	Red food coloring
(Six for $1.99 at party supply stores)	White doilies

Tint the shredded coconut with a few drops of red food coloring, which will turn the coconut pink. Use a large tea cup to scoop solid balls of strawberry ice cream onto a cookie sheet, forming wide flat skirts. Pack each skirt with the pink-tinted coconut. Insert one baby doll into the center of each skirt, cover with waxed paper, and freeze until ready to serve. Serve on white doilies.

Doll Buggy Eclairs

1 eclair per guest (purchase eclairs from your favorite bakery)	Round red and white peppermint candies
White pipe cleaners	Tiny plastic babies
White paper doilies	

Press the peppermint candies against each eclair, creating four wheels. Bend a single pipe cleaner to form a handle. Cut a small slit at one end of the top of the eclair. Insert a plastic doll into the eclair at the slit, its head sticking out over the blanket. Set each eclair on a paper doily.

Dirt Pie

1 small clay flower pot per guest	1 large plastic drinking straw
Rocky road ice cream	Oreo cookies
Single-stemmed fresh flowers, preferably daisies, tulips, or daffodils	

Wash flower pots well, and let them dry thoroughly. Place one Oreo cookie over the hole at the bottom of each pot. Fill each pot with rocky road ice cream to within one inch from the top. Insert a straw in the center of the ice cream, and cover the rest with crushed Oreo cookies. Freeze until time to serve. Insert the stem of one fresh flower into each straw before serving.

Gummy Worm Cake

Bake any kind of cake or cupcakes. Press gummy worms down inside the cake after it has baked. Frost the cake, and add more gummy worms on top.

Cupcake Spiders

Remove the cupcake paper from a chocolate cupcake. Frost the top and sides of the cupcake with thick white icing. Add eight black licorice legs (four on each side), chocolate sprinkles, and red hot candies for the eyes.

Cakes

Bake your own cake

If you decide to make the cake yourself, you have two options:

✦ Bake the cake in a standard-sized rectangular, square, or round cake pan, and decorate the top of the cake, using theme-related decorations available at a party supply store.

✦ Bake the cake in a cake pan that's already in the shape of your theme-related animal, character, or object. These cake pans are made by Wilton and are available at party supply stores. What I love about these pans is that they come with a sized picture that shows exactly what the finished cake should look like after it has been frosted and decorated.

Butter Cream Frosting (can be used to frost and decorate)

Measure into a large mixing bowl:

1 1/4 cups shortening	1 teaspoon salt
2 teaspoons clear vanilla, lemon, or almond flavoring	

Beat at medium speed for three minutes. Add, all at once, two small boxes sifted powdered sugar and 9 tablespoons milk or fruit juice. Beat at medium speed until you achieve the consistency of whipped cream.

Character Bundt Cake

1 bundt cake	1 can of frosting

1 small plastic character, or animal, appropriate to the party's theme, such as a plastic dinosaur for a Brontosaurus Party or a lion for a Safari Party, etc.

Frost the cake. Insert the character into the hole in the center of the cake.

Barbie Doll Cake

1 angel food cake	1 can of frosting
Food coloring	1 Barbie doll
1 glass jar or pint-sized milk carton	

Place the Barbie doll's legs into the jar or milk carton, and insert in the center hole of the cake. Ice the cake with frosting to resemble a skirt. Fold the Barbie doll's real skirt over the top of the frosting skirt.

Snacks

Popcorn Balls

Roll six cups of popped corn in eight ounces of melted vanilla caramel candies mixed with one tablespoon butter (microwave for one minute on high to melt the caramel.) Shape the coated popcorn into small balls. Wrap each in plastic wrap, and tie with a bow.

Popcorn Roasted Over the Fire

Let the children pop their own popcorn over the fire using a campfire popcorn popper.

Painted Toast

Let the children paint pieces of bread using food coloring and paint brushes, then toast.

Celery Stuffed with Peanut Butter

Wash celery stalks and pat dry. Fill with peanut butter. Cut into three-inch pieces, and serve.

One Box of Animal Crackers Per Child

Bowls of Sugared Cereal

Children love to snack on sugared cereal served dry in bowls.

Fortune Cookies

Party drinks

Serve any of the following:

+ Milk shakes.
+ Root beer floats.
+ Hot chocolate with marshmallows and whipped cream.
+ Nonalcoholic smoothies (see Chapter 112).
+ Hot cider served in mugs with cinnamon sticks.
+ Bug punch (any kind of fruit punch served in a punch bowl with ice cubes frozen with raisins inside).

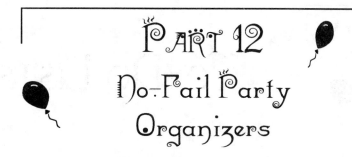

Part 12
No-Fail Party Organizers

"Being organized is the key to enjoying your own party."

The worksheets that follow have been created to help you:
+ Know what to do to plan your party, and when to do it.
+ Stay organized.
+ Establish your party budget.

These worksheets won't do you a bit of good, however, unless you use them. The biggest mistake you can make is to try to keep track of everything in your head. Take it from me: If you want the planning to be easy and successful, don't trust your memory. Although a brain isn't a computer, it is known to become overloaded and drop data from time to time—especially when it is under stress. So get in the habit of using these worksheets as you plan.

By the way, feel free to make enlarged photocopies of these worksheets, three-hole-punch them, and place them in a three-ring notebook. This handy tool will keep you on track and make your party the easiest and most successful one you've ever hosted.

114

TO-DO LISTS

Here are lists that will help you with your planning. Use the right-hand column to record the date each task has been completed.

To be done weeks in advance	Date done
Enlist a co-host and/or volunteers to help with the party.	
Confer with your guest(s) of honor, if applicable, regarding a convenient date and time for the party.	
Choose a location for the party.	
Choose a party theme.	
Handcraft or purchase invitations.	
Assemble a guest list with addresses.	
Address and mail invitations.	
Plan a menu, with detailed recipes, a shopping list, and a list of foods to prepare or purchase in advance and freeze.	
Place order with your delicatessen or caterer, if applicable.	
Place order with your bakery (rolls, cake, etc.).	
Plan the entertainment, including games, activities, door prizes, music, and toasts.	
Make or purchase favors.	
Purchase prizes.	
Make or purchase name tags.	
Make or purchase place cards.	
Make, purchase, borrow, or rent decorations.	
Purchase film or single-use cameras.	
Assemble and clean all crystal, china, silver, linens, etc.	
Decide what you're going to wear to the party, and get it ready, including hose, shoes, and accessories.	
Other.	

To be done one week before the party	Date done
Call any guests who have not responded to your RSVP.	
Start filling out the name tags, and place cards.	
Place order with florist.	

To be done one or two days before the party	Date done
Shop for perishable food items, and prepare them as far as you can ahead of time (dicing, marinating, rinsing lettuce, etc.).	
Pick up rented or borrowed decorations, and start decorating.	
Confirm floral and bakery orders and delivery or pick up time.	
Call to confirm deli or catering arrangements, if applicable.	
Call to confirm arrangements with musicians, entertainers, etc.	
Call your guest(s) of honor and anyone who has volunteered to help you with the party to confirm their time of arrival.	
If the guests will be wearing coats or jackets, clear out your coat closet and fill it with quality hangers.	

To be done the day of the party	Date Done
Last minute cooking and baking.	
Pick up your bakery, deli, and floral orders.	
Last minute decorating, including fresh flowers and any exterior decorating (balloons tied to gate, etc.).	
For a sit-down meal creatively arrange place cards so each guest is seated next to someone he doesn't know.	
If you will be serving food from a buffet table, scatter TV trays around the room, or provide lap trays for the guests.	
If you plan to serve snacks or appetizers, set them out before your guests are scheduled to arrive.	
Other:	

115

FILL-IN-THE-BLANKS PLANNING SHEETS

These easy-to-use planning sheets are self-explanatory and guaranteed to keep you organized.

Master Planning Sheet

Name(s) of guest(s) of honor

_____

Name of co-host(s), if applicable

_____

Date of party

_____

Time of party

_____

Location of party

_____

Party's theme

_____

Date invitations mailed

_____

Type of food to be served

_____

Games, activities & entertainment

_____

_____

_____

Guest List

Name	Address	Telephone	Reply?

Total number of guests who will be attending: _____

Volunteers

Name	Telephone	Duty?

Rental of Party Site

Name and location of site

Name of contact person

Telephone number

Site rental fee

Date and amount of deposit

Date and amount still due

Other fees (custodial? parking? coat attendant?)

Equipment available: (Tables, chairs, utensils, cooking ware, coffeepot, table linens, dishes, glasses, etc.)

Equipment you will need to provide

Restrictions, if any

Parking facilities

Total Cost Of Party Site: $ _____
(Transfer this amount to the Master Party Budget in Chapter 116.)

Party Decorations

Item	Source	Cost
Flowers		
Balloons		
Candles		
Crepe paper		
Banners		
Ribbon and bows		
Tiny white lights		
Table centerpiece		
Tablecloth		
Napkins		
Napkin rings		
Candles		
Paper cups, plates, utensils		
Place cards		
Favors		
Novelty props		
Other		

Total cost of party decorations: $_____
(Transfer this amount to the Master Party Budget in Chapter 116.)

Party Menu

Snacks and appetizers:

Item	Source	Cost

Soups:

Item	Source	Cost

Salads:

Item	Source	Cost

Sandwiches:

Item	Source	Cost

Meat dishes:

Item	Source	Cost

Party Menu

Side dishes:

Item	Source	Cost

Breads:

Item	Source	Cost

Condiments (butter, jellies, relishes, pickles, olives, etc.):

Item	Source	Cost

Desserts:

Item	Source	Cost

Drinks:

Item	Source	Cost

Total cost of party menu: $ _____

(Transfer this amount to the Master Party Budget in Chapter 116.)

Game Supplies

Game	Item	Source	Cost

Total cost of game supplies: $ _____
(Transfer this amount to the Master Party Budget in Chapter 116.)

Prizes (Including Door Prizes)

Item	Source	Cost

Total cost of door prizes: $ _____
(Transfer this amount to the Master Party Budget in Chapter 116.)

Party Entertainment

Type	Provided by	Cost

Total cost of party entertainment: $ _____
(Transfer this amount to the Master Party Budget in Chapter 125)

Party Rentals

Item	Source	Cost

Total cost of party rentals: $ _____
(Transfer this amount to the Master Party Budget in Chapter 116.)

My personalized toast to the guest of honor

_____

_____

_____

_____

_____

_____

_____

_____

Wording for the invitations

_____

_____

_____

_____

_____

_____

_____

_____

_____

116

PARTY
BUDGET PLANNER

If you're high on party spirit, but low on party funds, here are a few helpful suggestions:

+ Hold the party in your home or any other gratis location.
+ Don't invite more guests than you can afford to entertain. The bigger the party, the bigger the expense.
+ Ask a friend to co-host the party with you, which will cut the costs in half.
+ Serve punch or soft drinks instead of alcoholic beverages.
+ Decorate with things you already have around the house, items that can be borrowed, or big bangs for the buck, such as balloons and crepe-paper streamers.
+ Buy balloons in bulk from a party supply store and rent or purchase a helium tank for blowing them up.
+ Send handmade invitations or invite guests by telephone or in person.
+ Choose a theme with an affordable menu, such as a Dessert Party or a Progressive Dinner.
+ Purchase food in bulk from a wholesale food supplier.

Remember, the more you spend on a party doesn't necessarily mean the more fun it will be. You need to decide how much money you have available for hosting the party and then stay within that budget.

Transfer the total costs for each category from the Planning Sheets in Chapter 115 to the Master Budget on the following page.

Master Budget

Category	Amount Budgeted	Final Cost
Party site	$	$
Party decorations	$	$
Game supplies	$	$
Door prizes	$	$
Party menu	$	$
Entertainment	$	$
Party rentals	$	$
Other:	$	$
Other:	$	$
Other:	$	$

Total final cost of the party: _____

Notes

EPILOGUE

As you launch into your party plans, here are my final words of advice:
+ Once the party begins, keep it moving. Don't give it a chance to fizzle out.
+ Relax and enjoy your party, and don't forget to smile.
+ Be a loving, caring host, and your guests will leave feeling cherished.

Good luck,

Diane Warner

P.S. I will be updating this book from time to time and would love to hear about any interesting parties you have planned or attended. Please write to me in care of my publisher:

Diane Warner
c/o Career Press, Inc.
P.O. Box 687
Franklin Lakes, NJ 07417

RESOURCES

Books

Anderson, David A. *Kwanzaa*, Gumbs & Thomas Publishers, 1992.

Brenner, Leslie. *The Art of the Cocktail Party*, Penguin Books, 1994.

Dlugosch, Sharon and Nelson, Florence. *Games for Wedding Shower Fun*, Brighton Publications, Inc., 1985.

Drucker, M. *The Family Treasury of Jewish holidays*. Boston, Mass.: Little, Brown, 1994.

Ehrlick, A. *The story of Hanukkah*, Penguin Books, 1989.

Ernstein, Don. *The Complete Party Book*, Viking Studio Books, 1994.

General Mills, Inc. *Betty Crocker's Buffets*, Random House, Inc., 1984.

Hazen, Janet. *Janet's Juice Book*, Chronicle Books, 1993.

Home Decorating Institute. *Decorating for Dining & Entertaining*, Cy DeCosse, Inc., 1994.

Hubbard-Holmes, Janice. *Terrific Parties for Kids*, Horizon Publishers, 1992.

Ickis, Marguerite. *The Book of Religious Holidays and Celebrations*, Dodd, Mead and Company, 1966.

Keao, Lee and Mae. *The Hawaiian Luau Book*, The Bess Press, Inc., 1989.

Kemp, Jim. *Stylish Settings, The Art of Tabletop Design*, Gallery Books, 1990.

Kimmelman, L. *Hanukkah Lights, Hanukkah Nights*, Lothrop, Lee and Shepard Books, 1992.

Kirkham, Jenni. *The Wedding Craft Book*, Kangaroo Press, 1994.

Koch, Karl-Heinz. *Pencil & Paper Games*, Sterling Publishing Co., Inc. 1991.

Lansky, Bruce. *The Best Birthday Party Game Book*, Meadowbrook Press, 1996.

Lazar, W. *The Jewish Holiday Book*, Doubleday, 1977.

LeFanu, J. Sheridan. *Best Ghost Stories*, Dover Publications, 1986.

Levie, Eleanor. *Halloween Fun*, Berkley Publishing Group, 1993.

Maguire, Jack. *The Halloween Book*, Berkley Publishing Group, 1992.

McClester, Cedric. *Kwanzaa: Everything You Wanted to Know But Didn't Know Where to Ask*, Gumbs & Thomas, 1985.

The Mother Connection, Inc. *Homespun Fun*, St. Martin's Griffin, 1993.

Muller, Marianne and Mikolasek, Ola. *Great Napkin Folding and Table Setting*, Sterling Publishing Co. Inc., 1990.

Newton, Deborah M. *Kwanzaa*, Children's Press, 1990.

Post, Peggy. *Emily Post's Etiquette, 16th Edition*, HarperCollins Publishers, 1997.

Renberg, D. *The Complete Family Guide to Jewish Holidays*, Adama Books, 1985.

Reynolds, Renny. *The Art of the Party*, Penguin Books, 1992.

Riddell, Mrs. J. H. *The Collected Ghost Stories of Mrs. J. H. Riddell*, Dover Publications, 1974.

Salcedo, Michele. *Quinceañera; The Essential Guide to Planning the Perfect Sweet Fifteen Celebration*, Henry Holt and Company, Inc., 1997.

Simmons, Marie and Lagowiski, Barbara. *The Bartender's Guide to Alcohol-Free Drinks*, New American Library, 1990.

Skinner, Gwen. *The Cuisine of the South Pacific*, Hodder and Stoughton, 1983.

Smith, Susy and Lansdown, Karen. *The Creative Art of Table Decorations*, Longmeadow Press, 1987.

Thompson, Helen Davis. *Let's Celebrate Kwanzaa*, Gumbs & Thomas Publishers, 1990.

Watts, Irene N. *Great Theme Parties for Children*, Sterling Publishing Co., Inc., 1992.

Williams, Judy. *How to Give Children's Parties*, Smithmark Publishers, Inc., 1992.

Wills, Maralys. *Fun Games for Great Parties*, Price Stern Sloan, Inc. 1988.

Wisdom, Emma J. *A Practical Guide to Planning a Family Reunion*, Post Oak Publications, 1988.

Wiswell, Phil. *Great Party Games for Grown-ups*, Sterling Publishing Co., 1988.

Party supplies

Advanced Graphics, (925) 432-2262. This company provides life-size stand-up cutouts of celebrities for your party. Pose your guests beside one of these "celebrities" and you'll have a great photo opp for your instant camera. Call for their brochure.

Anderson's Prom and Party Supplies, 800-328-9640. Call to order their catalog, which features special theme decorations and favors.

Benco Party Favors, 800-874-7970. Call for their catalog.

Craft King Discount Craft Supply, P. O. Box 90637, Lakeland, Florida 33804. Send them your address, along with $2 and they will furnish you with their crafts catalog that features creative, festive party decor, gifts and craft supplies.

Creative Cookie, Inc., 800-451-4005 (creates personalized messages for fortune cookies; however there is a 500 cookie minimum.)

Idea Art Catalog, 800-433-2278. Great source of specialty papers suitable for laser printing.

Lighter Side Catalog, (941) 747-2356. Includes "Host Your Own Murder Mystery Party Game."

Oriental Trading Company, Inc. 800-228-2269. Call for their catalog, which features party favors, decorations, name tags, invitations, place cards and affordable gifts.

Paper Direct, 800-272-9640. Request their catalog, which includes high-quality paper products for your party invitations, etc.

Petals, 800-920-6000. Call for their catalog, which features natural-looking floral arrangements and other party decorations.

Sally Distributors, 800-472-5597. Catalogs feature party decorations, favors and costumes.

Sherman Party Theme Novelties Catalog, 800-645-6513, ext. 3025. Their catalog features party favors, hats and other theme novelty items, including karaoke party props.

Stumps Party Supplies and Decorations, 800-348-5084. This is a great source for theme party props and decorations.

Supergrams, 800-3BANNER. If you need a customized, laminated banner, this company is for you.

Viking Office Products and Paper Sale Catalogs, 800-421-1222. Their catalogs include specialty papers for invitations, name tags, menus, etc.

Wilton Yearbook of Cake Decorating. If you plan to bake and decorate a cake for your party, you'll find creative ideas in this yearbook, which is available at all party supply stores.

Tapes

"Sing Along Birthday Songs," a musical tape with 19 favorite sing-along party and game songs for children's birthday parties, available for under $10.00 from Practical Parenting by calling 800-255-3379

"Sing-Alongs," 47892 Oasis Court, Palm Desert, CA 92260—sing-along tapes and matching song sheets for theme parties.

Web sites

American Rental Association -http://www.njara.org/ proud_members_of_the_american_re.htm —names of rental companies near you.

Michaels Stores—www.michaels.com. Craft instructions for your party.

Recipe encyclopedia—www.epicurious.com. Recipe suggestions.

60s stuff—http://artitude.com.

Smart Wine Magazine—http://smartwine.com. Wine news and info.

Song lyrics—http://archive.uwp.edu/pub/music/lyrics. Provides words to thousands of songs.

Wilton Enterprises—www.wilton.com. Great ideas for cake decorating.

INDEX